Studies in Diplomacy

General Editor: **G. R. Berridge**, Professor of International Politics, University of Leicester

The series was launched in 1994. Its chief purpose is to encourage original scholarship on the theory and practice of international diplomacy, including its legal regulation. The interests of the series thus embrace such diplomatic functions as signalling, negotiation and consular work, and methods such as summitry and the multilateral conference. Whilst it has a sharp focus on diplomacy at the expense of foreign policy, therefore, the series has no prejudice as to historical period or approach. It also aims to include manuals on protocol and other aspects of diplomatic practice which will be of immediate, day-to-day relevance to professional diplomats. A final ambition is to reprint inaccessible classic works on diplomacy.

Titles include:

G. R. Berridge
DIPLOMACY: THEORY AND PRACTICE
2nd Edition

G. R. Berridge, Maurice Keens-Soper and T. G. Otte
DIPLOMATIC THEORY FROM MACHIAVELLI TO KISSINGER

Herman J. Cohen
INTERVENING IN AFRICA
Superpower Peacemaking in a Troubled Continent

Andrew F. Cooper (*editor*)
NICHE DIPLOMACY
Middle Powers after the Cold War

David H. Dunn (*editor*)
DIPLOMACY AT THE HIGHEST LEVEL
The Evolution of International Summitry

Brian Hocking (*editor*)
FOREIGN MINISTRIES
Change and Adaptation

Michael Hughes
DIPLOMACY BEFORE THE RUSSIAN REVOLUTION
Britain, Russia and the Old Diplomacy, 1894–1917

Gaynor Johnson
THE BERLIN EMBASSY OF LORD D'ABERNON, 1920–1926

Donna Lee
MIDDLE POWERS AND COMMERCIAL DIPLOMACY
British Influence at the Kennedy Trade Round

Mario Liverani
INTERNATIONAL RELATIONS IN THE ANCIENT NEAR EAST, 1600–1100 BC

Jan Melissen (*editor*)
INNOVATION IN DIPLOMATIC PRACTICE

Peter Neville
APPEASING HITLER
The Diplomacy of Sir Nevile Henderson, 1937–39

M. J. Peterson
RECOGNITION OF GOVERNMENTS
Legal Doctrine and State Practice, 1815–1995

Gary D. Rawnsley
RADIO DIPLOMACY AND PROPAGANDA
The BBC and VOA in International Politics, 1956–64

TAIWAN'S INFORMAL DIPLOMACY AND PROPAGANDA

Studies in Diplomacy
Series Standing Order ISBN 0–333–71495–4
(*outside North America only*)

You can receive future titles in this series as they are published by placing a standing order. Please contact your bookseller or, in case of difficulty, write to us at the address below with your name and address, the title of the series and the ISBN quoted above.

Customer Services Department, Macmillan Distribution Ltd, Houndmills, Basingstoke, Hampshire RG21 6XS, England

The Berlin Embassy of Lord D'Abernon, 1920–1926

Gaynor Johnson
Lecturer in History
Bolton Institute

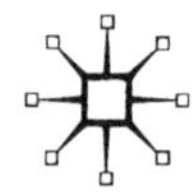

First published 2002 by
PALGRAVE MACMILLAN
Houndmills, Basingstoke, Hampshire RG21 6XS and
175 Fifth Avenue, New York, N.Y. 10010
Companies and representatives throughout the world

PALGRAVE MACMILLAN is the global academic imprint of the Palgrave Macmillan division of St. Martin's Press, LLC and of Palgrave Macmillan Ltd. Macmillan® is a registered trademark in the United States, United Kingdom and other countries. Palgrave is a registered trademark in the European Union and other countries.

ISBN 0–333–94549–2

This book is printed on paper suitable for recycling and made from fully managed and sustained forest sources.

A catalogue record for this book is available from the British Library.

Library of Congress Cataloging-in-Publication Data

Johnson, Gaynor, 1963–
The Berlin embassy of Lord D'Abernon, 1920–1926/Gaynor Johnson
p. cm. – (Studies in diplomacy)
Includes bibliographical references and index.
ISBN 0–333–94549–2
1. Great Britain – Foreign relations – Germany. 2. D'Abernon, Edgar Vincent, Viscount, 1857–1941. 3. Great Britain – Foreign relations – 1910–1936. 4. British – Germany – History – 20th century. 5. Germany – Foreign relations – Great Britain. 6. Germany – Foreign relations – 1918–1933. I. Title. II. Studies in diplomacy (Palgrave (Firm))

DA47.2.J64 2002
327.41043–dc21 2002022013

10 9 8 7 6 5 4 3 2 1
11 10 09 08 07 06 05 04 03 02

Printed and bound in Great Britain by
Antony Rowe Ltd, Chippenham and Eastbourne

In memory of Peter Wyn Williams

Contents

Preface

While writing this book, I had the pleasure of reading Peter Neville's study of Nevile Henderson's embassy in Berlin.[1] In it, he discusses the almost unrelenting criticism his subject has received at the hands of historians. When reading material relating to the embassy of Lord D'Abernon, one of Henderson's predecessors, one is faced with the opposite problem. The published diary of his embassy has been used by historians for the last seventy years as an apparently unimpeachable source of information on German foreign policy in the early 1920s. The work of scholars, particularly Angela Kaiser, continues to confirm D'Abernon's status as one of the heroes of interwar diplomacy – the man who, almost singlehandedly, helped to prevent war for a decade by persuading Stresemann to meet Briand and Chamberlain to conclude the Treaty of Locarno.[2]

The present book contends that this view of D'Abernon is flawed. D'Abernon was not the architect of German security policy, nor did he have a particularly close relationship with the German government. He was never popular with the British government and had a noticeably strained relationship with Austen Chamberlain. His ideas were idiosyncratic and inconsistent. An early disciple of Keynes, D'Abernon nevertheless believed that it was possible for the German budget to be balanced at the height of the run on the mark in 1922–23. He discouraged German desires to seek financial assistance from the United States during the early years of his embassy, believing instead that assistance should come from Britain which, in practice, lacked the necessary resources. In foreign affairs, D'Abernon was never privy to major discussions about strategy and policy. The conclusion of a security agreement between Germany and the Allies, similar to that signed at Locarno in October 1925, for which D'Abernon has so often been given credit, had long been part of the strategy of the German government. D'Abernon was also unaware of the enthusiasm with which Rathenau and Stresemann sought to develop diplomatic relations with the Soviet Union and was surprised and dismayed by the conclusion of the treaties of Rapallo and Berlin.

D'Abernon's political views and attitudes were rooted in the conservatism of his youth and belied a personality that bordered on the eccentric. Herein lies one explanation for the contradictions endemic in his actions as ambassador to Berlin. He appears to have been liked by all who met him but many thought his behaviour bizarre on occasions. Edgar Stern-Rubarth, former press secretary to Gustav Stresemann, the German Minister for Foreign Affairs after 1923, noted that D'Abernon wrote the notes for their meetings 'on his shirt-cuff with a broken blunt pencil'.[3] He went on to describe D'Abernon as having a

> bulky, gigantic frame, topped by a small but fine head, with thick white hair and a somewhat rough, equally white beard, his astonishing neglect of all the conventions of Savile Row, his gaping collars. His almost incredible frankness, was unforgettable. He simply asked you point-blank the question he had on his mind without trace of that diplomatic finesse which one expected in an Ambassador.[4]

D'Abernon's wife, Helen, whom he married in 1890, seems to have had an equally eccentric approach to her role in Berlin. Not famed for her tact, she liked to remind the Germans that 'Britain had *won the war*!' on the rare occasions that she visited the German capital from her villa in Italy.[5]

D'Abernon's name is most usually associated with the study of Locarno diplomacy, and yet his activities have hitherto never been scrutinised by those who have sought to debunk the 'myth' of Locarno. This is partly because the only evidence we have of D'Abernon's thoughts on German militarism and Germany's status as a world power date from his embassy, between July 1920 and October 1926. A crippling stroke, seven years before he died in 1941, left him without the ability to speak or to write at length. We therefore have no evidence of what he thought of the rise of Hitler and the re-occupation of the Rhineland in 1936. Unlike Austen Chamberlain, who had much to say on both these matters, D'Abernon never left us a memoir or other note to provide us with an insight into his views about the subsequent failure of the agreement. Thus D'Abernon's embassy stands as one of the last remaining areas of Locarno diplomacy that has yet to be reappraised. The pages which follow seek to fill this historiographical void.

Acknowledgements

I am grateful to a large number of people for their assistance in the preparation of this book. Professor Geoff Berridge, my series editor, provided generous and good-humoured support for this project, as indeed did Alison Howson, commissioning editor for Palgrave Macmillan's *Studies in Diplomacy Series*. This project also benefited considerably from conversations with Dr Peter Neville and Dr Elspeth O'Riordan about ambassadorial diplomacy and British foreign policy in the interwar period. I owe a particularly large debt to Dr David Dutton and to my colleague, Professor Bill Luckin, who provided invaluable comments on the manuscript during its preparation. Most of all, I would also like to thank my family for their willingness to tolerate me during my long association with Lord D'Abernon in all his incarnations – thesis, article and now book form.

The work of the historian is made even more pleasurable because of the enthusiasm of archivists and librarians for the subject. This project on Lord D'Abernon's embassy in Berlin has been no exception. I am indebted to the staff of the following repositories for their help and for granting me permission to quote from papers in their care: the Public Record Office in Kew (Foreign Office General Correspondence files, Private Collections and xeroxed files from the German Ministry for Foreign Affairs); the British Library Western Manuscript Department (the D'Abernon and Cecil papers); the Oriental and India Office Library (the Curzon papers); Cambridge University Library's Manuscript Department (the Hardinge and Crewe papers); the University of Birmingham (the Austen Chamberlain papers); the House of Lords Record Office (the Lloyd George papers); Churchill College Archive Centre (the Hankey and Aubrey Kennedy papers) and to the Liverpool Record Office for permission to quote material from the papers of the seventeenth Earl of Derby. Considerable care has been taken to contact copyright holders, but if I have inadvertently overlooked any, the publisher will be pleased to make the appropriate acknowledgement at the first opportunity. As ever, however, the author willingly takes full responsibility for any errors that remain.

Introduction

Hitherto, Britain's relationship with Germany in the 1920s has proved less appealing to scholars than the more momentous events of the 1930s. In some ways, it is easy to see why this is the case. The 1930s were dominated by disarmament debates and the appeasement of a larger-than-life fascist dictator pursuing an eccentric, dangerous nationalist foreign policy culminating in the outbreak of the Second World War. The preceding decade, at least at first glance, seems to lack drama on this scale. It was an era dominated by national introspection, of reconstruction and reflection, after the horror of what was known until 1939 as the Great War. During the 1920s, the forms of nationalism that were most likely to result in war were on the horizon but largely remained there. Why then should Anglo-German relations in the 1920s be studied? The most obvious answer is as a background or introduction to the events of the 1930s. Yet such an approach fails to do the period full justice. Throughout the 1920s, Anglo-German diplomacy had its own dynamics. It was an era of hope. Many felt that war as a means of solving international problems could be banished forever. Some believed that the Germans would one day be re-integrated into European diplomatic affairs, and both Britain and Germany experienced a period of economic and social stability for at least part of the decade. The 1930s, on the other hand, saw many crises and diplomatic failures as Europe slipped once again towards war. Anglo-German relations during the 1920s were motivated by two opposing forces. The first, most closely identifiable with Germany in the early years of peace, was a belief that the First World War was potentially a vehicle for fundamental political, economic and social change. Some of these changes were more palatable than others, but their existence was for the most part recognised. The second was a conservative, largely British response to the war in which its importance was seen in terms of its immediate aftermath – reconstruction, rehabilitation and finance. There was a reluctance to accept that Britain was no longer the most influential and wealthy country in the world and therefore the most obvious country that Germany would turn to for assistance. The conflict that arose between these two approaches makes the study of Anglo-German relations interesting and frequently complex.

A further reason for this difficulty is that Britain's relations with Germany at this time cannot be understood in isolation. The relationship that both countries had with France, the United States and the Soviet Union, for example, were of great importance. The historiography of Anglo-German relations in the 1920s is small and disparate and reflects this point. The earliest studies focused on the attempts made by Britain and France to find a solution to the 'German Question', that is, the enforcement of the Treaty of Versailles, the establishment of a reparations total and an incorporation of Germany in a system of European security.[1] After the Second World War, a number of ground-breaking surveys of twentieth-century German foreign policy were published which emphasised the importance of the Weimar period to the study of the rise of nationalism in Germany in particular.[2] They view Britain as an imperial power and, more specifically, as a defuser of diplomatic tension in Europe, acting in a more reasonable manner towards Germany than France.[3] Diplomatic studies have been supplemented in recent years by surveys of British military strategy in the early years of peace and the bearing that it had on the conduct of foreign policy.[4]

Some historical attention has been paid to Britain's diplomatic strategy towards Germany in the 1920s.[5] What is most apparent is the level of indecision that existed in London about how Germany should be treated.[6] It has been claimed that the British government was reluctantly prepared to act independently of France concerning Germany if French policy appeared to be too harsh and intransigent.[7] But this argument has been overstated. It is usual to suggest that the vocal pro-German lobby in the British government at the end of the First World War was silenced by Lloyd George's determination not to offend the French. This study of Lord D'Abernon's embassy in Berlin suggests that these points can be extended well beyond the collapse of the coalition government in 1922 to include the activities of the Foreign Office under Ramsay MacDonald and Austen Chamberlain. An examination of D'Abernon's relationship with the British government throughout his period in Berlin therefore reveals almost as much about the Anglo-French partnership as it does about British relations with Germany.

Considering that he was the first British ambassador to Berlin after the First World War, Lord D'Abernon has attracted a surprisingly small amount of historical attention. His embassy has never been examined in its entirety by a historian of British foreign policy. The few assessments that exist focus mainly on a very small part of his dealings with the German government within the six years that he occupied the post. Despite this, D'Abernon has enjoyed a positive historical reputation, primarily because he is viewed as the driving force behind the German security initiative in January 1925 that resulted in the signature of the Treaty of Locarno. He is seen, as he himself wanted to be seen, as 'an ambassador of peace', a man who achieved the daunting task of persuading the German government to conclude a security agreement with the Allies.

The earliest discussions of D'Abernon's ambassadorial activities date from the late 1920s and are little more than exercises in investigative journalism.[8] Those who first championed him saw D'Abernon as a heroic figure who had helped deliver Germany from the grasping clutches of the French.[9] It is not difficult to understand why he was viewed in this way. It was rumoured that, during the early years of his embassy, he had given the German governments advice on how to balance the budget and gauge reparation payments. When he resigned, in October 1926, Germany's financial problems appeared to be almost resolved. In the last years of his embassy, D'Abernon had been associated with Germany's major successes in international diplomacy – the signature of the Treaty of Locarno and the subsequent admission of Germany into the League of Nations. They appeared to herald the start of a new, more cordial chapter in European history.

It is not surprising that D'Abernon was anxious to maintain this popular image of his embassy. This is reflected in the title and contents of the published diary – *An Ambassador of Peace* – which appeared in three volumes, published between 1929 and 1931. In it, D'Abernon placed himself at the heart of the government decision-making process in Berlin, frequently claiming that the German government would not take action without first consulting him. In contrast, comments on his relations with the British government are often confined to the character portraits at the beginning of each volume. This eccentric set of comments on contemporary British and German politicians is interesting only because of the insight they give into D'Abernon's prejudices. Those seeking a conventional brief outline of the careers of such figures as Lloyd George, Curzon, Stresemann and von Schubert, should look elsewhere. The diary itself also has shortcomings. D'Abernon used a certain amount of licence in dating entries and events, tending to write up his diary several days after the events described. His memory was clearly not always reliable. There are also texts in the published version that do not appear in the original diary manuscript, and which are simply transcripts of his dispatches to the Foreign Office.

In the 1950s a greater range of sources about his embassy became available. His private papers were bequeathed to the British Library under the terms of Lady D'Abernon's will. The papers, which included the original manuscripts of *An Ambassador of Peace* edited in D'Abernon's own hand, became available for inspection in 1955. The papers cover his life from 1880 to 1929. The files that relate to his embassy in Berlin are dominated by copies of extracts from his diary that he sent to the Foreign Secretary, Lord Curzon, and to the Cabinet Secretary, Sir Maurice Hankey, for communication to the Prime Minister. D'Abernon abandoned this practice after the collapse of the Lloyd George government in 1922. There is little that could be described as genuinely private correspondence. D'Abernon appears to have had little time for social or informal letter writing, although there is a small file of letters to his wife. These, however, are of limited use because most were written in a private code. The remainder of the collection for this period consists of copies of his official dispatches, the originals of which are in the Foreign Office General Correspondence series (FO371) in the Public Record Office at Kew.[10] He was blessed with reasonably legible handwriting but preferred the use of the typewriter to the pen.

German sources are primarily from the records of the Foreign Ministry in Bonn and Coblenz and in collections of private papers in these repositories, although the documents cited here are copies now held in the Public Record Office in Kew. Some of the papers relating to Weimar foreign policy have been published in the many volumes of the *Akten zur Deutschen Auswärtigen Politik*.[11] They naturally present a different perspective on D'Abernon's activities than British sources. Von Schubert's records of the discussions he had with D'Abernon about European security between the autumn of 1924 and the summer of 1925, for example, provide a good illustration of what it must have been like to work in close proximity to him for quite a long period – a level of intimacy which was naturally denied to British Foreign Office officials.

The first scholarly assessment of D'Abernon's embassy to use his private papers was produced in the late 1960s and focused on D'Abernon's conversations with the *Staatssekretär* at the *Auswärtiges Amt*, Carl von Schubert, about international security between November 1924 and February 1925.[12] D'Abernon is seen as the architect of the German security note presented to the British government in January 1925, which eventually formed the basis of the Treaty of Locarno. The argument also confirms earlier views that D'Abernon had a close and amicable relationship with the German government. Von Schubert is viewed as an astute politician who, while mindful of the advantages to Germany of concluding a security agreement with Britain and France, nevertheless required guidance about how and when to make the necessary diplomatic approaches. It is assumed that resolving this issue with the western European powers was the German government's sole preoccupation. No mention is made of the parallel negotiations in which the German government was engaged with the Soviet Union that resulted in the Treaty of Berlin in April 1926. Thus we are only presented with half the picture.

Despite important work by Jon Jacobson and others in debunking the 'myth' of Locarno, historians have continued to perpetuate the idea that D'Abernon played a central role in formulating German security policy.[13] Later work, published in the 1980s, which includes a book about D'Abernon's entire embassy, has continued to uphold this view.[14] It is based overwhelmingly on German archive sources and makes no reference to private papers and diaries, therefore making it unclear whether the private thoughts and statements of the officials of the German government with which D'Abernon came into contact were the same thing. Hitherto, it has been argued that there was a pattern of contact between D'Abernon and von Schubert between November 1924 and the spring of 1925 that typified the intimacy of his relationship with the German government throughout his embassy. Consequently, D'Abernon's involvement in the formulation of the German security note of January 1925 should not be singled out but seen as one example of his many important and influential interventions with the German government.

This book asks whether D'Abernon deserves such a positive historical reputation. It will be claimed that D'Abernon underestimated the ability and willingness of the German government to formulate policies independently of his advice, especially on the key issues of reparations and security. He found it difficult to maintain a consistent line of argument and frequently adopted an eccentric point of view. He also grossly overestimated the degree of influence he had with the German government. Some of his comments about the centrality of his role emerge as little more than wishful thinking. D'Abernon's relationship with the British government, which is not discussed before, is considered at length. He had a chequered relationship with Curzon and the Foreign Office.

He shared many of Lloyd George's preferences for diplomacy by conference and for the use of experts to advise on government policy, but nevertheless failed to penetrate the Prime Minister's intimate circle. In the later years of his embassy, D'Abernon's relationship with Austen Chamberlain, Foreign Secretary in Baldwin's second administration, was marred by major differences over the security needs of France and Germany. This had a significant and largely negative impact on the development of British security policy in the mid-1920s. The discrepancy between D'Abernon's real and imagined influence in Berlin led to a series of misjudgements which frequently undermined his relations with the German government and brought criticism and condemnation from British and French sources.

The first two chapters place D'Abernon within the operation of the 'new' conference diplomacy that was so prevalent after the First World War. Both in terms of his selection as ambassador to Berlin and in his early dealings with the German government, he was viewed very much as an 'expert' diplomat – one who justified his appointment because of his specialist knowledge of international finance. The next three chapters set his activities within a wider context. They evaluate D'Abernon's ability to influence the thinking of the British and German governments on issues relating to European diplomacy as a whole as well as on specifically commercial affairs. The final two chapters develop these themes and question the extent to which he influenced British and German security policy and the admission of Germany to the League of Nations. They also provide an insight into the operation of a more traditional form of diplomacy, which relied more on direct, personal, private negotiation than on the use of conferences to resolve differences between nations. It is not the purpose of this study to conclude which of these forms of diplomatic negotiation was the most effective. But this survey does show the problems caused to the operation of European diplomacy at a time when they were first required to coexist. D'Abernon, himself, frequently found it difficult to keep abreast of developments. This, combined with personal idiosyncrasy, lack of experience and a fundamental misreading of the objectives of German foreign policy, account for many of the errors of judgement that he made.

1
The Making of an Ambassador

Lord D'Abernon was born Edgar Vincent in Slinford, Surrey on 19 August 1857, the seventh and youngest son of the Reverend Sir Frederick Vincent, eleventh baronet, rector of Slinford and prebendary of Chichester Cathedral.[1] His childhood home was The Manor House, in the village of Stoke D'Abernon, Surrey. A house had stood in this location by the River Mole since the land had been given to one Roger D'Abernon in 1086 for services rendered to William the Conqueror.[2] Ownership passed to the Vincent family in 1620, but the house that D'Abernon knew as a boy dated primarily from the eighteenth century. It contained a large Robert Adam drawing room and a fine mahogany staircase and was widely regarded as one of the finest houses dating from this period in the county.[3]

In the surviving record of his life, D'Abernon's parents and siblings are entirely absent. They are never mentioned and no correspondence with them has survived. This unconventional situation in an era renowned for letter writing provides an explanation for D'Abernon's unusual personal and intellectual self-containment. Nevertheless, his childhood seems to have followed the pattern typical of a nineteenth-century aristocrat and there is no indication that it was anything less than happy. He was educated at home until the age of seven and was then dispatched to a prep school on Manfolkin Terrace in Brighton. Here he must have showed some academic ability as he was taught with boys older than himself. D'Abernon later reflected that he 'did the work well enough and without effort'.[4] During these years, he excelled at sport, particularly football and cricket – aptitudes which, he was later to claim, demonstrated that he was one of life's 'team players'. At the age of twelve, D'Abernon went up to Eton, where he enjoyed an unexceptional career, being described by his house master, the Reverend C.C. James, as 'lazy and impertinent'.[5] In 1882, in his only attempt to write an autobiography, D'Abernon explained away his boyhood indolence as 'boredom due to lack of crisis', claiming that his mind was only spurred into action when faced with a major intellectual challenge. He clearly found recounting the events of his life too tedious because he abandoned the endeavour after this account of his school days, instructing his readers to 'ask other people' about his life thereafter.[6] This is no easy task because he seldom merits more than a passing mention in the memoirs of his contemporaries.

At the age of twenty, D'Abernon was commissioned into the Coldstream Guards, but his disposition was unsuited to the discipline of military life and he spent the following three years developing his skills as a linguist. Throughout his career in public life D'Abernon was to demonstrate a talent for languages. His first published work was a *Handbook to Modern Greek*, produced in collaboration with T.G. Dickinson in 1879, which became a standard primer, widely and favourably reviewed in the national press.[7] D'Abernon spoke French fluently, could converse in Spanish and Italian and had some knowledge of Mandarin, Arabic and Russian. Despite such proficiency, when he was appointed ambassador to Berlin, he confessed that his knowledge of German was confined to an ability to read the language rather than to speak it. When this fact was pointed out to Lloyd George, D'Abernon claimed that the Prime Minister did not think an inability to speak German would undermine his effectiveness in Berlin.[8] This curious statement provides a further indication of the eccentric approach of both men towards D'Abernon's appointment and towards Britain's relations with Germany.

A career in the Diplomatic Service would have provided an obvious and natural outlet for his talents, but D'Abernon lacked a clear idea about where his future lay. It is likely that in his youth he would have found the prospect of conforming to diplomatic etiquette even more disagreeable than he was to find it forty years later in Berlin. In 1880, he chose instead to accept the post of private secretary to Lord Edmond Petty-Fitzmaurice, the Commissioner for Eastern Roumelia. D'Abernon demonstrated that he was an able administrator. In September 1880, he wrote a critique of a memorandum by Sir Francis Bertie, then acting senior clerk at the Foreign Office, on the importation of arms and ammunition into Bulgaria, that was highly regarded.[9] The following year, he became British commissioner for the evacuation of Turkish territory ceded to Greece under the terms of the Treaty of Berlin. In this post, he impressed George Goschen, the British ambassador to Constantinople, with his concise and dispassionate reports about troop movements in the region and about the size and development of the Bulgarian army.[10] Goschen frequently asked D'Abernon for advice about the conduct of diplomacy and it was to be D'Abernon's views on finance that were to make the greatest impression on him when he became Chancellor of the Exchequer four years later.[11] In recognition of his talents, D'Abernon was appointed British, Belgian and Dutch representative on the council of the Ottoman public debt in Constantinople.

At the same time, D'Abernon's insights into the crisis in Sudan, which stemmed partly from his travels in the region in his late teens, led to a two-year appointment as Financial Adviser to the Khedive of Egypt. It was while in this post that the first indications of D'Abernon's attitude to the British government's treatment of him become apparent. He relished the freedom associated with administrative authority but believed that his masters in London did not respect this in their dealings with him. It was in a fit of pique over this issue that he declined the award of Companion of the Order of the Bath on his departure from office. In explaining his reasons for doing so, he wrote:

> The position which I held in Egypt was one of great difficulty. I have been refused all legal powers, I have no regular administrative authority, and under the circumstances I am held responsible for the finances of a country, which the best financial opinion considers insolvent. Everything therefore depends on personal authority and influence and personal authority and influence depends in a great measure upon the manner in which I am treated by H.M.G. It is perfectly obvious that if I am made a Member of the Council of Ministers and then treated as an inferior to the Ministers, my advice will not carry much weight with my colleagues.[12]

The impact of personal influence on the conduct of commercial relations was to be a theme to which he returned in accounts of his activities in the 1880s and 1890s. It is ironic that a point conveyed with such force and cynicism at the end of his period in Egypt was to be made in a very different way between June 1920 and October 1926 during his period in Berlin.

Egypt and Constantinople

In 1889, D'Abernon began to write a book – *Egypt in 1887* – in which he attempted to give fuller voice to his complaints about the way he had been treated by the British government, but after three years' work and the completion of five of the projected six chapters, D'Abernon abandoned the manuscript.[13] He was to demonstrate considerably more tenacity in producing his memoirs of his period as ambassador to Berlin. While in Egypt, D'Abernon was not without his critics. Evelyn Baring, later Lord Cromer, and future President of the Unionist Free Trade Club, was sceptical whether D'Abernon's proposals to make the Egyptian economy solvent would work. He thought them too complicated, inconsistent and lacking in clarity.[14] D'Abernon worked closely with Baring examining ways in which Egyptian government expenditure could be reduced. He believed that the administrative costs were too high and that the government should produce a breakdown of departmental expenditure that would be used to calculate the annual budget. He did not rule out taking draconian measures to ensure the stability of the Egyptian economy. If necessary, government departments should be disbanded if they failed to meet their revised, lower targets for expenditure. Baring favoured the abolition of the Sinking Fund; D'Abernon favoured its retention.[15] In January 1884, D'Abernon persuaded Sir Evelyn Wood, first British *sidar* in the Egyptian army and charged with improving lines of communication with Khartoum, to make substantial reductions in the army budget.[16]

It was while he was in Egypt that D'Abernon developed a scepticism about the French, believing them to be 'too judgemental and difficult'.[17] His eccentric approach to diplomacy at this time is evident in a diary entry written when he was in Egypt. In discussing ways of persuading the government of the Khedive to cooperate with him, he noted: 'The more I see of foreigners the more convinced I am that the way to get on with them is to pay great attention to trivial details of formality: calling on them, leaving cards, dancing with their wives and sending them in to dinner in the proper order.'[18] He was to adopt similar tactics in his dealings with the German government but, as was also the case in Egypt, demonstrations of respect and tolerance were appreciated more than strict adherence to the niceties of diplomatic etiquette. His views towards foreign nationals of any race – be they Africans or Europeans – were typical of the paternalism and condescension of many of his generation. But D'Abernon was quick to condemn such an attitude in others. He accused the British government of 'bigotry' for failing to bring stable government to Egypt.[19] By August 1884, when he felt that his patience had been tried to the limit, his views on the conduct of diplomacy had undergone something of a change. He noted that it was now 'hopeless to get an Englishman, who has not been brought up to it… to conceal his contempt for the little formalities to which they attach so much importance'.[20]

D'Abernon was appointed Governor of the Imperial Ottoman Bank in 1889 and remained in this post until 1897, when he was forced to resign because of his association with a financial scandal, in which many of the bank's customers lost their life savings. The debacle, which today might have left him open to charges of insider dealing, inevitably did serious damage to his reputation. Matters were made worse by his unceremonious exit from Constantinople – through a rear window of the bank – because he believed that facing the consequences of his actions would be 'too onerous'.[21] For the rest of his career in public life, the French government, which underwrote the Imperial Ottoman Bank, took every possible opportunity to expose the duplicity of '*Le Voleur* Sir Edgar Vincent'.[22] Such statements did little to improve relations between the British and French governments during the diplomatically sensitive years immediately after the First World War or to enhance D'Abernon's reputation in Berlin.

Yet before the scandal, D'Abernon used his period as Governor to develop his views on international finance and it was to be these ideas that were to have a direct bearing on his attitude towards Anglo-German relations during his embassy in Berlin. He told Goschen that all measures possible had to be taken to ensure that London remained the financial centre of Europe.

> Dealing with the London market from the outside, I see how important it is, in view of the rivalry of Paris and Berlin, to reduce the charge of both financial and commercial transactions in London to a minimum. Direct telegraphic communications gives London an immense advantage for finance, sea communication with all parts of the world gives England an advantage for commerce. But everything should be done to increase these national facilities so that London may become more and more the centre of the trade of the world. Commissions and brokerage are so much lower in Paris and Berlin that they (and Berlin especially) are serious competitors.[23]

This was particularly important, he believed, given the rapid industrial expansion of Germany. D'Abernon was thus one of an increasing number who believed that Germany posed a threat to British economic hegemony in Europe but not to European peace. Even in the years immediately before the First World War, D'Abernon continued to regard Anglo-German rivalry as nothing more than the natural expression of free market economics.

On his return to Britain from Constantinople, D'Abernon decided to abandon his career in international finance. He embarked on what was to be a brief parliamentary career, being elected Conservative MP for Exeter in 1899, before surrendering his seat in 1906 to join the Liberal party because he disagreed with Unionist policy on tariff reform.[24] He stood for Parliament again, unsuccessfully, as the Liberal candidate for Colchester in the first of the two general elections held in 1910. As a report in *The Times* put it, D'Abernon's parliamentary career was 'distinguished by the ability and firmness with which he opposed Mr [Joseph] Chamberlain's policy'.[25] D'Abernon became a close associate of the Liberal leader, Herbert Asquith, and began a lifelong friendship with Asquith's children, particularly Raymond and Violet (later Bonham Carter) and Asquith's second wife, Margot Tennant.[26] Although not always the shrewdest judge of character, the latter told D'Abernon in 1909 that her husband valued his views on tariff reform more than those of anyone else.[27]

At Asquith's instigation, D'Abernon was appointed a member of the Royal Commission on Imperial Trade established in April 1912 in response to Resolution 20 of the Imperial Conference held the previous year. The Commission was chaired by Lord Inchcape and included Sir Charles Owens and Sir Rider Haggard, as well as representatives from Canada, Australia, New Zealand and South Africa.[28] D'Abernon was appointed because of his passionate belief in free trade. In November of that year, he took over the chairmanship of the commission and embarked on a tour of Australia and Polynesia in the spring of 1913.[29] This led to a subsequent tour of South Africa and later of Canada to assess the impact of free trade policies on the Empire.[30] The Commission's report, published in the autumn of 1914, concluded that the principal countries in the Empire were suffering from a severe shortage of educated and skilled workers to make their economies sufficiently competitive in the world market. Consequently, it was suggested that special efforts should be made to induce women to emigrate to help expand the population and to encourage soldiers returning from the war to start a new life in the colonies.[31]

Central Liquor Traffic Control Board

In May 1915, Asquith appointed D'Abernon Chairman of the Central Liquor Traffic Control Board to assess the effect that workers' consumption of alcohol during working hours was having on the production of munitions.[32] Other members of the Board included Neville Chamberlain,

Waldorf Astor and Philip Snowden. The effects of the Board's rulings on shortened licensing hours and on the dilution of spirits sold in public houses influenced Lloyd George's decision as Chancellor of the Exchequer to double the duty on spirits, quadruple it on wine and sextuple it on sparkling wine.[33] These proposed measures were, however, abandoned because of strong Conservative opposition, notably from Bonar Law and Austen Chamberlain, who argued that only the areas where the munitions factories were located should be subject to such measures.[34] Consequently, the measures imposed by the Central Liquor Traffic Control Board were applied to all munitions factories, ports and shipbuilding in Britain and to the whole of London after September 1915.[35]

D'Abernon was surprised at the speed at which this legislation improved the war effort. Almost immediately after the measures had been put in place, statistics revealed that in Liverpool, for example, the number of prosecutions for drunkenness at work fell from 240 per week, before the establishment of the Board, to 164. In Cardiff, the improvement was even greater, with prosecutions falling from thirteen per week to five. At a conference of chief constables of the areas under the jurisdiction of the Board, D'Abernon stated: 'I confess that these results exceed my most sanguine expectations. If they can be maintained, a notable triumph would have been won, but the habits of a lifetime are not modified in a month and you must be prepared for a counter-attack.'[36] It is doubtful, however, whether D'Abernon anticipated the form that the 'counter-attack' would take. In November 1915, he received a number of deputations from dockers' unions asking for improvements in canteen facilities to help diminish the lure of the public house. During the winter of 1915, D'Abernon was invited to open dockers' canteens in Liverpool, Newcastle and Edinburgh.[37] By the summer of the following year, the Board had embarked on a review of the state of public houses, taking steps to close dilapidated establishments and to open larger, more attractive premises. These measures, it was hoped, somewhat optimistically, would encourage the consumption of more non-alcoholic drinks. The first of its kind was the so-called 'model pub', the Gretna Tavern, at whose opening D'Abernon was present, in July 1916.[38] D'Abernon advocated a drastic reduction in the number of public houses because he believed that in its present form the brewery business was not cost effective. In an interview with an American journalist in April 1916, D'Abernon set out his case. In an industry worth £186 million per annum, he argued, £64 million was absorbed by taxation, with the cost of materials being approximately £40 million, leaving a balance of £82 million for retail expenditure and profit. Therefore, he claimed, between 30 and 40 per cent of public houses should be closed.[39]

By May 1917, the work of the Central Liquor Traffic Control Board had broadened, with the establishment of a subcommittee, chaired by D'Abernon, that examined the effect of drunkenness on workers' health.[40] He also used his position to praise the role of women in the war effort. In December of that year, he presented a paper entitled *Public Health and Alcoholism among Women* in which he argued that the war had demonstrated the value of women as an economic asset to the country.[41] He recommended that measures restricting the consumption of alcohol in the work place should remain in operation after the war to ensure the efficient running of the economy.[42] At a meeting with the Central Liquor Traffic Control Board at Caxton Hall in October 1918, D'Abernon went further, putting forward an eight-point plan that included the avoidance of long opening hours for public houses, the dilution of spirits, the brewing of beers with a lower alcohol content and a national programme for the establishment of workers' canteens.[43] His proposals came under severe criticism in an open letter from the trade union leader, Ben Tillett. Discussing D'Abernon's uncompromising approach to his role as chairman of the Central Liquor Traffic Control Board, Tillett wrote:

> Summing up the value of your committee, I very much regret to say that you have made profiteers of both distillers and brewers, together with public-house owners, and the consumer of the ordinary healthy beverages has been mulcted in exorbitant costs. If you think that a reward for your services you are welcome to do so, but so far as the nation is concerned, the Army and the workers in particular, they have suffered materially by your mischievous administration, and while there may be some results of usefulness in your committee, on the whole I think it has been an egregious failure, and a very unwarrantable cost to the community. We regard it as the most Hun-like Department that ever the war has produced.[44]

Despite such criticism, by the end of the war, D'Abernon had established a reputation as an authority on industrial relations, giving a paper on *Rival Theories of the Causes of Drunkenness* to the Society of Arts on 27 November 1918.[45] It was his ability to combine economic ideas and sociological analysis that led him to become interested in defusing the tension between the government and the trade unions over the operation of the railways and the coal industry in the spring of 1919. In a letter to *The Times* in April 1919, D'Abernon predicted a long and continuous cycle of strikes and unrest. The solution to the problem, he concluded, lay in a redefinition of the relationship between the government and the trade unions. He wrote:

> The result must be that a fresh alteration to a fresh basis will have to be sought. If we continue on the old lines, a cycle of strikes and lock-outs is inevitable before agreement is once more reached, an agreement no more stable than the present one. It is possible that in this country the innate reasonableness and love of compromise in the English character will result in these disputes being again settled without any revolutionary upheaval; but if the view is correct that the disputes are avoidable and are due to a remediable cause, it is surely unwise to expose our national life to so severe a strain and to so grave a danger.[46]

These views led him to recommend to the Sankey Commission – established to investigate the possible nationalisation of the coal industry – that miners' wages should be fixed at a level that did not leave them subject to fluctuations in the price of coal.[47] It is only possible to view such an idea, which clearly had little grounding in sound economics, as an attempt to appeal to the commissioners' hearts rather than to their heads. Such words also suggest that D'Abernon was not always a reliable source of sensible advice on economic policy.

While Lloyd George and Balfour were at the Paris Peace Conference, D'Abernon visited the French capital to address what the *Ligue Nationale contre l'Alcolisme* termed 'a peace conference on alcohol'. In a paper entitled *The Effects of War-Time Control of the Liquor Traffic in England*, D'Abernon gave a detailed economic analysis of the impact of convictions for drunkenness, deaths from alcoholism, cases of delirium tremens and suicides prompted by drunkenness.[48] D'Abernon socialised extensively with members of the British delegation to the peace conference, especially Balfour, and became known as something of an authority on some of the most politically sensitive and controversial issues of the time. He was also readily accepted into the company of senior government ministers. His ignominious departure from Constantinople had long been forgotten by all except the French. He may not have been an obvious choice as ambassador to Berlin, but his ability to cope with difficult briefs combined with his insight into the operation of contemporary economics may have brought him to the notice of Lloyd George and of Curzon, when the latter assumed Balfour's mantle as Foreign Secretary in October 1919.

At the end of the First World War, therefore, D'Abernon enjoyed a relatively high profile among senior politicians. He had the respect of both Asquith and Lloyd George – a feat that not many were able to accomplish – and had established his credentials as an expert on the connection between economic policy and the successful prosecution of the war. He was thus more qualified than most to make an examination of the connection between economic policy and the successful prosecution of the peace. But as the post-war world in which he was required to operate turned so many old certainties on their heads, D'Abernon can be seen as a sound choice for the post of ambassador in so far as anyone with some knowledge of international finance would have been appropriate. Other factors also need to be taken into consideration, most notably the operation and opinions of the Diplomatic Service, of which D'Abernon was not a member. The decision to appoint D'Abernon as ambassador to Berlin indicated an obsession within British government circles with the 'new' *expert* diplomacy and showed that Britain's relations with Germany were viewed primarily in terms of economics – the payment of reparations and the cost of the army of occupation, rather than political considerations.

Resumption of diplomatic relations with Germany

After the Armistice, a long debate took place between the Allies about when and how to resume diplomatic relations with Germany. The First World War had two important consequences for Britain that had a direct bearing on these issues. The first was the effect on the diplomatic priorities of Britain and France. The 'German Question' was the central issue of Anglo-French diplomacy during the first years of peace. The Cabinet believed that the timing of the reinstatement of diplomatic relations with Germany must be linked, like so many other matters, to maintaining a modus vivendi with France. In many respects, the timetable for sending diplomatic representation to Berlin formed a logical focus for the debate between the British and French governments about how Germany should be treated.[49] In addition, domestic remnants of wartime Germanophobia were mixed with uncertainties about the political and economic climate in the immediate aftermath of the Paris Peace Conference. As a result, Allied attempts to establish a joint policy regarding the resumption of diplomatic relations with Germany were made more difficult.[50] All major powers that had fought the war had a clear need to seek some form of permanent security. But most British politicians were sceptical about becoming too involved in preserving and guaranteeing European peace and stability.[51] There was another point of view to which Curzon subscribed, namely that it was in Britain's interest to conclude a peace settlement as soon as possible, to expedite German recovery and so obtain reparation payments that could be used to repay British war loans to the United States.[52] At the same time, the British government was inclined to distance itself from the uncompromising policy of France towards Germany over the implementation of the Treaty of Versailles.[53] Brokering a relationship between France and France's principal former enemy formed the foundation of British involvement in western European diplomacy throughout the 1920s.[54]

In the early years of peace, British policy towards Germany consisted primarily of short-term responses to the current political, military and economic situation, and Curzon and Lloyd George contributed equally to the formulation of such policy.[55] The uncertainty that made the devising of a long-term policy difficult was partly due to the volatility of domestic affairs in Germany, but also stemmed from differences within the British government about the way in which foreign policy should be conducted. 'Old' diplomatic practices were linked to the pre-war era and widely regarded as an important cause of the war. Such practices were also widely viewed as élitist in that they tended to be practised by those upper echelons of society traditionally employed by the Foreign Office partly as a means of maintaining social predominance. 'New' diplomacy was intended to dispel the secrecy and suspicion that had surrounded pre-war diplomatic practices and help promote international security through the open discussion of problems. But it is dangerous to view these different approaches to the conduct of relations between states as incompatible opposites, creating unbridgeable divisions within the Foreign Office and between Curzon and Lloyd George.[56] When the events surrounding the decision to appoint an ambassador are analysed, it becomes clear that Curzon and Lloyd George played equal parts in guiding Allied policy on the matter.

Liberal and Labour politicians believed that the war was potentially a vehicle for fundamental political, economic and social change. The era of mass politics and the enfranchisement of women in the years after 1918 have been well chronicled, but within the government, this process of change had started during the early years of the war. The Foreign Office had begun to contemplate reform in its recruitment patterns as early as 1914. In that year, the MacDonnell Commission had concluded that Britain possessed the most expensive and 'snobbish' Foreign Service in the world and that it had also failed to develop the commercial aspect of its role.[57] In future, diplomats were to be moved about as often as possible to gain broader experience, and the commission recommended that an integral part of the process of peacemaking should be the need to involve economic and financial experts in the conduct of diplomacy. Thus the origins of the expert diplomacy that was to become so synonymous with Lloyd George in the early 1920s were not as radical as many contemporaries and historians have thought. Its foundation in interdepartmental politics also explains why Curzon was never entirely repelled by it and was even willing to use it to enhance his position as Foreign Secretary rather than denouncing it in its entirety. D'Abernon's appointment as ambassador to Berlin represented one such opportunity.

The recommendations of the MacDonnell Commission influenced British policy towards Germany in the period leading up to the resumption of diplomatic relations between the two countries in January 1920. As early as July 1919, the governments of Britain, France, Italy, Japan and the United States sent a note requesting that the German government resume diplomatic relations with them after the shortest possible delay.[58] This request came as members of the Allied delegations at the Paris Peace Conference considered the establishment of committees to coordinate the operation of the Treaty of Versailles. The records of the conversations kept by Eustace Percy, Secretary to the then Foreign Secretary, Arthur Balfour, reveal that the Allies intended to appoint chargés d'affaires in Berlin as soon as the treaty was ratified.[59] The matter was discussed again in October when Sir Eyre Crowe, acting as replacement for Lloyd George as head of the British delegation during the closing weeks of the peace conference, suggested that the Allies should agree the conditions under which diplomatic relations with Germany would be resumed. The head of the Italian delegation, Tittoni, believed that before such discussions could take place, a decision should be taken about whether the Allied governments would be represented by ambassadors or chargés d'affaires.[60] This preceded the production of a letter by the British delegation, for submission to the Allied Supreme Council, which stated that the five Great Powers had 'agreed on a uniform course of action as regards the resumption of diplomatic relations with Germany' and proposed to be represented in Berlin by chargés d'affaires until a suitable date for the dispatch of an ambassador could be agreed.[61] The British government then asked how the names would be chosen and when the appointees would proceed to their posts.[62]

In response, the Allied Supreme Council set up a Special Committee to investigate the matter. Its report, which was published in November 1919, concluded that 'there would be no objection to immediately sending to Berlin agents whose mission would be of an economic character, such as commercial attachés'.[63] The presence of military and naval attachés was deemed provocative and therefore undesirable. Its final conclusion, that the proliferation of commissions of control were such as to 'diminish the importance of the task of these offices', was to provide useful Foreign Office ammunition against the War Office in the coming months as both departments sought to direct British policy towards Germany.

The discussions about the resumption of diplomatic relations with Germany that took place in the following months illustrate the different attitudes of the British and French governments towards Germany that were to be such a feature of European diplomacy throughout the 1920s. Curzon wanted the Allied powers to act together on the matter. In January 1920, Lord Kilmarnock, a career diplomat who had held a number of junior consular posts in Germany before the war, was appointed British chargé d'affaires in Berlin.[64] Curzon was anxious to appoint an ambassador within three months of Kilmarnock's arrival. But progress was hampered when it became apparent that the French government wished to see how far the German government was prepared to comply with the reparation and disarmament clauses of the Treaty of Versailles before committing itself to the appointment of an ambassador. What was more, the French insisted on special consideration because France had borne the brunt of the physical devastation during the war and was the most vulnerable to any future German invasion. Lloyd George argued that it was precisely because there could be problems with German compliance with the terms of the Treaty of Versailles that the Allied powers should be represented by ambassadors in Berlin.[65] Nor was he surprised at the French reaction since he had anticipated that there would be 'difficulties for the next fifteen years'. Anyone who thought that all the controversies surrounding the treaty could be resolved within six months 'could not have read it'.[66] The French position nevertheless remained intractable. Curzon argued that the attitude of the French government was dangerous because if France did not agree to appoint an ambassador at the same time as Britain and Italy, it would demonstrate an embarrassing lack of unity among the Allies.[67] Nevertheless, the minutes of this meeting suggest that the French representatives accepted Curzon's argument as they reveal that the British, French and Italian governments intended to dispatch ambassadors to Berlin within three months of the ratification of the Treaty of Versailles, that is from 10 April 1920.[68]

At the inter-Allied conference at Lympne in June 1920, Lloyd George and Millerand, the French Prime Minister, announced that the British and French governments intended to replace their chargés d'affaires in Berlin with ambassadors.[69] Central to the decision was the Allied need to discuss the reparation clauses of the Treaty of Versailles with the German government in detail, in particular the establishment of a final total and the means of payment. At a meeting of the Allied Supreme Council the following day in Boulogne, Millerand, Curzon and the Italian Minister for Foreign Affairs, Count Sforza, proposed 1 July as the date when the ambassadors' appointments would take effect.[70] As economic affairs lay at the heart of the decision to dispatch Allied ambassadors to Berlin, it was logical to appoint candidates who had a detailed knowledge of such issues, especially given the complexity of the reparation clauses of the peace treaty.

As indicated earlier, Foreign Office enthusiasm for the establishment of permanent diplomatic representation in Berlin was also fuelled by the activities of the War Office. Officials attached to the British army of occupation had a greater grasp of the social, economic and political mood in Germany than most members of the government in London. Through the War Office, they sent suggestions about the future conduct of Anglo-German relations to London. This was viewed as a threat to the right of the Foreign Office to be the principal architect of British policy towards Germany. Curzon responded by stepping up the search to find a suitable candidate for the post of ambassador to Berlin. It is difficult to overstate the impact that strained relations with the War Office had on Foreign Office morale on this matter. Sir Charles Hardinge, Permanent Under-Secretary at the Foreign Office, summed up the feeling of resentment, commenting: 'It is really very difficult to work with the War Office who seem to barge in on every occasion on matters abroad whether military or political.'[71] However, others saw the appointment of an ambassador to Berlin as an opportunity to enhance the prestige of the Foreign Office. On the day that D'Abernon's selection was announced, Sydney Waterlow of the Central European Department, wrote:

> Our Berlin Embassy is very much in the limelight and is likely to be more so in the early future. If it does not shew up well – if the Prime Minister continues to feel that it cannot be depended upon for intelligent information, he is likely to turn more and more to the soldiers.

The position and prestige of the Foreign Office itself are closely involved in the success of the British Embassy.[72]

Containing the influence of the War Office, which was headed by one of his sternest critics, Winston Churchill, was as important to Lloyd George as it was to the Foreign Office. In March 1920, Lloyd George told Cambon, the French ambassador to London, that it was important for an ambassador to be appointed. He believed that 'great danger lay in the military members of the various missions each expressing their own views, whilst the chargés d'affaires did not possess sufficient authority to keep them in order'. As a result each of the Allied powers should be represented by an ambassador who 'represented the political conscience of the people'.[73] It is doubtful whether D'Abernon ever did that, but he did provide an effective tool in the power struggle between the War Office and the Foreign Office. Lloyd George came under considerable pressure from Churchill to send a 'great man to Berlin'.[74] The Prime Minister stood accused by Churchill of pursuing a tentative policy towards Germany while disregarding the possibility of communist infiltration. When D'Abernon's appointment was announced, he was almost as well known for his hostility to Bolshevism as he was for his financial expertise. Commenting on these events years later, Sir Robert Vansittart, a man not known for his pro-German views, described D'Abernon as 'handsome, brilliantly intelligent, financier, scholar, as good a judge of a horse as of a picture, white-bearded as an acute Father Christmas with something more than an eye for a pretty girl, excellent company, one of those Britons who contrive to be cosmopolitan in culture and insular in outlook; he was in fact almost everything but great'.[75]

D'Abernon's selection as ambassador

Nevertheless, Curzon's decision to appoint D'Abernon as ambassador to Berlin on 30 June 1920 indicates a sound grasp of the realities of contemporary diplomacy and the fact that it was not always desirable to adhere to traditional means of selection based on experience and seniority.[76] Nor was D'Abernon's appointment unique in this respect. Curzon had adopted a similar rationale when appointing Sir Auckland Geddes, a businessman, as ambassador to Washington in April 1920, a post where once again financial affairs dominated the role of the diplomat. On his appointment, Curzon described Geddes as a 'new type of ambassador'.[77] It was conventional for all senior diplomatic appointments to be discussed with the Permanent Under-Secretary, but in the case of D'Abernon, Curzon did not do so because he knew that Hardinge was likely to be hostile.[78] Curzon also realised that D'Abernon's experience of international diplomacy was limited, in the distant past and was not based on a knowledge of European affairs. As this was also an almost perfect description of his own credentials as Foreign Secretary – a post that he felt that he had been born to fill – he saw little reason why D'Abernon's relative lack of experience of European diplomacy should act as a bar to his appointment to Berlin.[79]

Nevertheless, Curzon was reluctant to admit openly to his hand in D'Abernon's appointment. The only indication of Curzon's role lies in the diary of the British ambassador to Paris, the Earl of Derby, in March 1920, and it was widely believed inside Foreign Office circles and in the press that it was Lloyd George who had forced the appointment on Curzon.[80] This was not a myth that Curzon was anxious to debunk. After all, if it was believed that Lloyd George had been responsible for D'Abernon's appointment, should his embassy prove to be a failure, the blame would not be laid at Curzon's door.[81] As it was, in D'Abernon, Curzon and the Foreign Office had access to an individual who was more able than they were to interpret and explain the complexities of the economic clauses of the Treaty of Versailles and the subsequent plans to establish a reparations total.[82]

Lloyd George himself approved of the appointment of a financial expert as ambassador to Berlin, but had reservations about D'Abernon's suitability given his association with the share scandal at the Imperial Ottoman Bank in 1897.[83] Curzon persuaded him that there were no other candidates with D'Abernon's knowledge of financial affairs.[84] The ease with which Curzon convinced the Prime Minister suggests that any reservations that Lloyd George had about D'Abernon's suitability were not great. He seemed little concerned that, even if the Germans welcomed the appointment of someone who could advise them on meeting their financial obligations under the peace treaty, the French were likely to be much less impressed. Both he and Curzon must have realised that the appointment of a man who had almost brought about the collapse of the bank would be unpopular in Paris and cause friction between the British and French governments.[85]

When the official announcement of D'Abernon's appointment was made, his experience in international finance was cited as the principal reason for his selection.[86] Opposition came from two quarters: *The Times*, and through the less public channels of the Foreign Office. Both believed that D'Abernon's appointment represented further evidence of

Lloyd George's desire to dominate the conduct of foreign policy and to marginalise members of the Diplomatic Service with greater experience. *The Times*, under the editorship of Wickham Steed, had been critical of Lloyd George's conduct of foreign affairs since the Paris Peace Conference.[87] It seized on the news of D'Abernon's appointment as an opportunity to launch another attack upon the Prime Minister, accusing him of breaking a number of diplomatic conventions relating to the way in which ambassadors were selected and of trying to undermine the role of the Foreign Office.[88] A series of barbed articles appeared implying that D'Abernon was unsuitable for the post and expressing outrage at the government's decision to resume full diplomatic relations so soon after the war. The strongest indictment came in the leader column on 30 June 1920, which expressed dismay at the decision to send an ambassador to Germany at all, let alone such an eccentric choice. It concluded that,

> we should have preferred the choice of the Prime Minister to have fallen upon a public man whose career had been free from any connection with international finance; and we hold that the Prime Minister would have been well-advised had he paid heed to the representations upon the appointment of D'Abernon which we believe to have been made to him by Curzon, and other responsible members.[89]

The debate rumbled on for several days. On 2 July 1920, in the House of Commons, the Lord Privy Seal, Andrew Bonar Law, was asked to explain what 'qualifications' D'Abernon possessed that were 'superior' to those of experienced diplomats. Bonar Law replied somewhat lamely that D'Abernon was deemed to be the most suitable candidate.[90] Recognising Foreign Office fears about his selection, *The Times* then focused attention on German reactions to the news of D'Abernon's appointment. Quoting an extract from the *Berliner Tageblatt* that linked D'Abernon's reputation as a financial expert with Allied desires to 'complete the diplomatic activities of the Reparation Commission', *The Times* accused the British government of unnecessarily abandoning pre-war diplomatic procedures.[91] This comment played on German fears that, because the Reparation Commission was based in Paris, it was little more than an extension of the French government.

Curzon's role in D'Abernon's appointment also offers a valuable insight into his relationship with the Foreign Office, and illustrates the difficulties that it experienced in reconciling pre-war diplomatic practices with the realities of post-war diplomacy. Curzon must have anticipated Foreign Office hostility to D'Abernon's appointment. Hardinge was the most strenuous critic – his main objection being that D'Abernon lacked diplomatic experience and that more suitable candidates had been passed over.[92] In April 1920, he had warned that 'it would be hardly fair to appoint an outsider' when there were members of the Diplomatic Service with greater and more relevant experience.[93] He made specific reference to Sir Horace Rumbold, who had held the rank of counsellor at the British Embassy in Berlin before the war and was currently Minister to Poland.[94] While Curzon saw fit to ignore this advice, Hardinge automatically assumed that it had been Lloyd George who had forced D'Abernon's appointment on the Foreign Secretary. By mid-July 1920, Hardinge's opposition had intensified. In a letter of commiseration to Rumbold, he wrote: 'I am afraid you, like many other people, were disgusted at the appointment to the Embassy in Berlin. There is nothing to be done as far as I can see, for the prospects for the Service are very poor.'[95] In reply, Rumbold complained that D'Abernon's selection represented 'clear proof that the regular diplomats cannot aspire to become ambassadors'. Rumbold was in no doubt that Lloyd George was 'at the bottom of it all'. He feared for the future of the Diplomatic Service, noting that the 'present system [was] bound to take the heart out of the Service'. His contempt for Lloyd George was such that he felt sure that the abandonment of the traditional way of selecting diplomats that D'Abernon's appointment represented was a 'matter of indifference to the higher power'.[96]

Inter-Allied mission to Poland

Foreign Office resentment came to a head at the beginning of July 1920 when Lloyd George decided to dispatch D'Abernon as head of an inter-Allied mission to offer advice to the Polish government during the Russo-Polish war.[97] It is not clear why D'Abernon was chosen for this task. One consideration would undoubtedly have been his hatred of Bolshevism, but it could also have been a means of mollifying French opposition to his selection as ambassador to Berlin by dispatching him to offer advice to the government of France's foremost ally in eastern Europe.[98] Lloyd George made the appointment without consulting Curzon. The strength of the latter's response indicates his confident attitude both towards his position as Foreign Secretary and towards his relationship with Lloyd George. Curzon wrote:

> While it is true that we are living in days of sudden decision, the precedent is rather a dangerous one if the Foreign Secretary may

> wake up any day to find that one of his principal subordinates is about to be sent off elsewhere. Hence my gentle protest, which I am sure you will not think unreasonable.[99]

D'Abernon's dispatch to Poland further inflamed Foreign Office and Diplomatic Service hostility towards Lloyd George. When the ambassador arrived in Warsaw, Rumbold commented that he knew 'quite well' that neither Hardinge nor anyone else at the Foreign Office had been responsible for D'Abernon's appointment either as ambassador to Berlin or as head of the mission to Poland.[100] Rumbold expressed relief when D'Abernon left the Polish capital to survey the Polish military situation, but noted that, 'If D'Abernon comes back again the situation will become impossible. If I am practically superseded, the result must inevitably be to discourage me and to impair my authority with the Poles.'[101]

Hardinge asked Curzon to curtail D'Abernon's visit to Poland, arguing that if D'Abernon returned to Warsaw, Rumbold's position would be 'rather a false one', but Curzon refused, insisting that it was Lloyd George who was responsible for the mission. Curzon's letter of protest was therefore more concerned with the potential threat to his own position than with disagreement with the decision to dispatch D'Abernon to Poland. Hardinge attempted to reassure Rumbold that he had the full support of Lloyd George – which, under the circumstances, can have been of little consolation. He described Lloyd George's enthusiasm for D'Abernon as a temporary aberration – that the Prime Minister was 'going through a phase of a sort of blind admiration and hero worship of D'Abernon and thinks that nobody can do anything except D'Abernon: all this will pass and you needn't be a bit afraid as to your future prospects'.[102]

The news of D'Abernon's dispatch to Poland also prompted attacks against Lloyd George in *The Times*. Aubrey Kennedy, who had been sent to report on the activities of the inter-Allied mission, thought that Lloyd George had been unwise to send D'Abernon to Poland to take precedence over the existing diplomatic staff.[103] This gave Lloyd George a bad press at a time when he was anxious to maintain the reputation of an international statesman that he had enjoyed at the Paris Peace Conference and when Curzon was trying to secure the role of the Foreign Office in the conduct of foreign policy and enhance his position in the Cabinet.[104]

Relations with the British government

More junior officials at the Foreign Office hoped that D'Abernon would only occupy the embassy in Berlin for a short period and that eventually he would be replaced by a career diplomat. Opposition to his appointment had led to the creation of a small group of Foreign Office officials who took every opportunity to criticise D'Abernon's activities and to complain about Lloyd George's role in the conduct of foreign affairs. This group, led by Sir Miles Lampson and Ralph Wigram in the Central European Department, sought ways of finding alternative uses for D'Abernon's knowledge of financial affairs. Lampson and Wigram wished to reinstate traditional procedures for the selection of diplomats but, by the time that the Lloyd George administration fell in October 1922, they were forced to concede that D'Abernon had proved a useful interpreter of financial issues.[105] In November 1922, it seemed as though a compromise might be possible when it was rumoured that Sir John Bradbury, the head of the British delegation to the Reparation Commission, was retiring.[106] Lampson was in the vanguard of those who recommended that D'Abernon be appointed in his stead. Curzon, however, refused to agree because by then D'Abernon's strong pro-German sympathies were well known and were likely to arouse hostility at the meetings of a commission that was based in France.[107] This decision serves as a reminder of the sensitivity of Britain's relationship with France at this time – an era when the friction between Curzon and Poincaré, the French Prime Minister, brought relations between the two countries to their lowest ebb since the war.[108]

Throughout his embassy, D'Abernon was convinced that Lloyd George had been responsible for his appointment.[109] Even when he was contemplating retirement in 1926, almost four years after the fall of the Lloyd George government, he wrote that he had 'always recognised' that it had been through the former Prime Minister that he had become 'connected' with the Berlin embassy.[110] More significantly, D'Abernon believed that the early years of his embassy had been under Lloyd George's 'auspices and guidance', while feeling that Curzon was 'out of touch with the modern world'.[111] Sir Maurice Hankey, Secretary to the Cabinet, was later to tell Lloyd George that D'Abernon attached 'more importance to your *personal* confidence than to anything else'.[112] D'Abernon clearly thought that he was a favourite of Lloyd George and that this gave his position as ambassador to Berlin a particularly high status. It was from this perceived position that D'Abernon criticised Curzon and the operation of the Foreign Office. He believed that the Foreign Office's conduct of diplomacy was antiquated and excessively bureaucratic. He also thought that the Diplomatic Service possessed 'insufficient acquaintance with commerce [and] finance', and lived in an insular world in which 'contact with men of affairs [was] too rare'.[113]

He recommended that, at the very least, a scheme should be introduced that would strictly limit the duration of diplomatic appointments. Junior diplomatic staff should be interchanged on a regular basis, with experience of commercial affairs being made compulsory. While these comments were confined to his diary, they were not confidential or private. D'Abernon, like Lord Derby and other diplomats of his generation, was in the habit of sending copies of substantial parts of his diary to Lloyd George, Curzon and Hankey as 'supplements' to his official dispatches.[114] It was not merely D'Abernon's views on what kinds of individuals should be employed as diplomats that was a source of friction, but the similarity of his views with those of the Prime Minister concerning the conduct of diplomacy. In particular, D'Abernon and Lloyd George had similar views about Britain's role in European affairs.[115] They both believed that the Treaty of Versailles would be most effectively enforced by treating Germany on the same terms as the Allied powers.[116]

The relationship between Curzon and D'Abernon was never close. 'More than once Curzon let [D'Abernon] down', wrote a reviewer of the first volume of *An Ambassador of Peace*, 'but, fortunately, such desertions were never serious enough to destroy his credit in Berlin.'[117] The first part of the statement is true; the second much less so. Apart from coming from a similar social background, the two men had little in common. Their views on the nature of diplomacy and on Germany were different.[118] Curzon had little interest in German affairs and viewed the French as the most dangerous rivals to Britain in international affairs.[119] D'Abernon, by contrast, was, with the exception of Sir Nevile Henderson in the 1930s, the most pro-German British diplomat of the interwar period.

Curzon's attitude towards D'Abernon's appointment and the way in which he encouraged Foreign Office opposition to Lloyd George's approach to diplomacy suggests a man confident of his own position as Foreign Secretary. The reinstatement of diplomatic relations with Germany after the First World War represented one of the most important steps in British foreign policy during the interwar period. It was the culmination of a process of negotiation that demonstrated the fragility of the relationship between Britain and France. It also proved to be controversial as the process of selecting an ambassador became part of the debate between traditional and newer methods of conducting diplomacy. It was particularly significant that Curzon, as head of the Foreign Office, was willing to break with convention and appoint a man to a key diplomatic post whose views about the conduct of diplomacy were closer to those of Lloyd George than to his own. The impact of such internal rivalries within the Cabinet on D'Abernon's activities in Berlin were to be considerable. His first and principal task was to offer financial advice to the German government. On this subject, he received incomplete information from London, which immediately placed him at a disadvantage in his dealings with the German experts.

2
The Debate about Reparations, 1920–22

The Treaty of Versailles created a preliminary structure for the payment of reparations through the Reparation Commission, but did not define a final total. The multitude of reparations conferences in the early 1920s attempted to calculate a final total of German indemnity. The resolution of this issue was considered by politicians and economic experts to be of fundamental importance to the peaceful development of all aspects of European diplomacy. One of the great challenges to writers of twentieth-century European history has been interpreting and understanding Germany's economic problems in the early 1920s. Much ink has been spilled by scholars in analysing two key issues: the payment of reparations and the hyper-inflation and subsequent collapse of the German economy in 1922–23 – issues with which D'Abernon was greatly concerned. These subjects cannot be wholly understood within a political or economic context. In fact when the state of Germany's finances and the efficiency of the economy in this period are examined, the studies of politics and economics merge. This was the main point of the prickly exchange between David Felix and Sally Marks in the early 1970s.[1] It is also reasonable to identify a direct connection between German domestic and foreign policy. To make such claims about the link between politics, economics and foreign policy is not new. What is interesting about the study of the German economy during the Weimar period is the extent to which the problems were deliberately created by the Germans and the Allies to gain diplomatic advantage.

When considering the prolonged negotiations about the payment of reparations, questions about the peacemaking process at the end of the First World War need to be asked. What were the Allies trying to achieve through the Treaty of Versailles? How much did they understand Germany's economic position and how reliable was the information they received about it? How far did differences between British and French policy towards Germany affect the economic recovery of these countries? D'Abernon was perfectly placed to analyse the German position and to influence the way the answers to the above questions could be framed. But it will be suggested that the absence of a coherent policy concerning the implementation of the peace treaty weakened the Allies' ability to collect reparations. The situation was made worse because D'Abernon's views on reparations and financial affairs lacked consistency and because he misjudged the amount of influence that he had with German financial experts. His dispatches led the British government to believe that the Germans were susceptible to British influence. However, German sources suggest that the most influential German officials were not afraid to act independently of D'Abernon's advice and were shrewd negotiators who did not always trust him. The discussion below is not intended to provide a detailed technical assessment of the reparations proposals and counter-proposals that were put forward during the early years of peace. Instead attention will be focused on D'Abernon's role in the origins of these proposals and his ability to influence the negotiators at these conferences. It is through an exploration of the latter that most is revealed about D'Abernon's relationship with German financial experts.

The need for reparations payments

At the end of the First World War, Britain, along with all of the major industrialised nations in Europe, suffered an economic slump. Lloyd George had come under increasing pressure from City analysts to adopt a dear-money policy that would bring down the cost of living and make Britain competitive in world markets. The Treasury had brought about substantial price deflation and had managed to consolidate much of Britain's floating debt. British policy on reparations did not always appear politically clear sighted, but it was consistent. In Paris in 1919, Lloyd George had put forward a recovery scheme that would have ensured the flow of American resources to Europe through the guarantee of German reparations payments to the Allies. Shortly afterwards, the British government realised that there were strict limits to the amount of reparations that could profitably be collected without reducing Germany's purchasing power.[2] British policy on reparations therefore followed an often difficult course between extracting realistic sums from Germany while trying to minimise the effect of growing American insistence on the repayment of war debts.

In France, the idea that Germany should pay reparations had a wider significance. There were purely practical considerations. Reparations payments were to serve as a means of reducing the budget deficit and to enable an appreciation in the value of the franc to take place. Inflation in France was never as severe as in Germany but was enough of a problem to create greater unemployment and produce only limited industrial expansion in the 1920s. Government policy, however, did not aim at this result. Deflationary measures were taken even when there were substantial budget deficits as many French financial experts hoped to restore France's pre-war trading status.[3] At the same time, German reparations payments were also symbolic to the French. Since 1870, France had been invaded twice by Germany – something that Britain had not had to endure. There was therefore a strong desire not only to make sure future invasion was impossible but to make sure that France's chief enemy in the past century was conspicuously punished for her acts of aggression. This desire to avenge the humiliation of occupation and conquest was the chief psychological difference between British and French policy towards Germany, particularly regarding the reparations question.

The complex diplomacy of establishing a reparations total and defining methods of payment dominated the first two years of D'Abernon's embassy. It was in the realm of international finance that it would be reasonable to expect his contribution to European diplomacy to be greatest. But curiously, it is debatable whether this was so. Indeed, even D'Abernon's staunchest admirers would maintain that when his embassy is viewed as a whole, he was more at home discussing security policy than he was analysing financial and commercial issues.[4] There are a number of reasons for this. Some centre on D'Abernon's personality, especially his tendency towards over-optimism regarding predictions about the actions of individuals and the exaggerated degree of importance the German government placed on his advice. Other issues concern the complex nature of D'Abernon's relationship with the Foreign Office, which, throughout the early years of his embassy, tolerated rather than trusted him. Matters were made worse as D'Abernon's strongly pro-German sympathies brought him into conflict with Curzon, who was anxious to preserve a close relationship with France. Like the celebrated economist, J.M. Keynes, D'Abernon believed that the Treaty of Versailles had been too harsh and that Allied demands on Germany were excessive.[5] He saw Germany as the victim of French greed and desire for revenge and was sympathetic to German protests about the enormous size of reparations totals that were discussed before a final figure was arrived at in May 1921.[6] D'Abernon was perfectly placed to analyse the German capacity to pay reparations and to influence the way in which Allied policy was developed. For the British government, the situation was made worse because of wrangling between the Treasury and the Foreign Office over who should control this important area of commercial policy. The Foreign Office contention that it fell within its remit because reparations concerned Britain's relationship with a foreign power was vitiated by an inability to understand the technicalities of the economics concerned.

D'Abernon's position in Berlin was also undermined by the British government's insistence on presenting a united front with France regarding the reparations question. British support for the French position was interpreted by the Germans as condoning the hard-line attitude of Clemenceau and Poincaré towards German compliance with the terms of the Treaty of Versailles. During the early days of D'Abernon's embassy, Lloyd George, although sympathetic to the German position, nevertheless gave greater priority to reinforcing Britain's shaky alliance with France. By the beginning of 1920, British and French differences over the Treaty of Versailles had brought relations between the two countries to a low ebb. At a conference in San Remo in April 1920, Lloyd George had met his French opposite number, Millerand, to try and reconcile their differences.[7] Lloyd George believed that it would benefit Allied reparations discussions if the British and French governments could speak with one voice on the subject. He sensed that Millerand could be persuaded to move away from the uncompromising stance that his predecessors had taken since the Armistice and that he would agree to a scheme that allowed the Germans to pay reparations in lump sums instead of in instalments. At the Boulogne conference two months later, Lloyd George and Millerand fixed an amount for Germany's lump sum indemnity.[8] Progress was also made concerning payments in kind. A month after the Boulogne Agreement had been concluded, the German government met the Allies at the Belgian resort of Spa to consider coal deliveries as a form of reparation payment. D'Abernon, who was not directly involved in the discussions, learnt a great deal about the determined approach which the Germans took to the negotiations through reports he received from Curzon, who was convinced that all German politicians were loud, arrogant and opinionated.[9] At the subsequent reparations conferences at Brussels, Paris and London, Curzon was content to allow D'Abernon to represent British interests.

Brussels conference, 1920–21

When he was appointed, D'Abernon told Curzon that he would encourage the German government to reject establishing a final reparations total in favour of a more fluid settlement. He hoped that the Allies would use the forthcoming conference at Brussels to create 'an elastic scheme' to assist German financial recovery and to reappraise Germany's ability to pay reparations.[10] D'Abernon believed that such a cautious approach was appropriate because it represented the 'best chance of [an] enduring result and of avoiding a crisis later which might easily occur if any cut and dried solution was offered or imposed prematurely'.[11] The strategy also met with approval in Paris. Sir Charles Hardinge, now ambassador to Paris, received an assurance from Leygues, the French Prime Minister, stating that the French delegation at Brussels would treat its German counterpart 'with the utmost frankness' in order to find a solution to the reparations question.[12]

Matters therefore augured well for the rapid conclusion of a satisfactory reparations agreement. But by the second day of the Brussels conference, which was convened in December 1920, that atmosphere had all but disappeared because D'Abernon suddenly changed his mind about the best way to resolve the reparations question. He announced that hitherto British policy had taken insufficient account of the volatility of German public opinion. As a result, British interests were unlikely to be accorded the prominent position they deserved by the German delegation at the conference. It has been suggested that D'Abernon changed his mind as a result of pressure being brought to bear on him by Lloyd George to abandon the idea.[13] This is unlikely. Such a level of interference was not characteristic of Lloyd George's relationship with D'Abernon. There is nothing to suggest that the latter's views underwent any forced metamorphosis. Indeed, it is difficult to explain this volte-face as anything other than intellectual inconsistency. There were sound reasons why an abandonment of his original argument would have been appropriate, but they were not mentioned or discussed by him. These included a fear that if the German government was allowed to adopt a fluid framework for the payment of reparations, the Allies would lose control over the implementation of a key area of the Treaty of Versailles. Given Germany's acute economic situation, it was more sensible to agree a temporary total of indemnity until the German economy could withstand the payment of more fluid sums under a long-term plan.

Bergmann

Despite his statements to the contrary, D'Abernon's relationship with German financial experts during the first years of his embassy proved to be less intimate than he had hoped. He assumed that they had little idea how to rebuild the German economy and he underestimated their intellectual tenacity.[14] At the Brussels conference, the German delegation was led by Carl Bergmann, an able and highly respected State Secretary at the German Treasury.[15] When he met D'Abernon, Bergmann wished to reach a satisfactory agreement on reparations as soon as possible and required little encouragement in that respect. Bergmann also had a clear view about what would be acceptable to his political masters in Berlin. At the outset of their negotiations, D'Abernon and Bergmann believed that the Boulogne Agreement offered the best framework for a solution of the reparations question.[16] D'Abernon enthusiastically noted that Bergmann was 'anxious to make a great effort' to ensure that the German economy was strong enough to meet the terms of the agreement.[17] Yet privately, Bergmann was sceptical about the Boulogne Agreement.[18] Soon his concerns about the practicability of the scheme extended to doubts about D'Abernon's agenda at the conference. Such doubts were placed in his mind by the Belgian Prime Minister, Delacroix, who warned that 'one of the British delegates was quietly planning a material extension of the scope of the conference'.[19] Bemused by D'Abernon's change of heart, Bergmann accused him of failing to understand the link between the size of the reparations total and German ability to meet it. Bergmann argued that 'immeasurable damage' would be caused 'if a theoretical amount were to be demanded without regard to actual possibilities'. He feared that if D'Abernon continued to overlook these considerations, the resulting economic crisis would 'drive Germany into despair'.[20] Bergmann suspected that D'Abernon had an ulterior motive, believing that he took a 'far too optimistic view of the possibility of an agreement' and felt betrayed by the ambassador's 'ambitious desire privately to rush a speedy solution'.[21] D'Abernon feared that if the German delegation continued to attach such little importance to British advice, the Brussels conference would end in stalemate.[22] He pressed for the conclusion of an immediate agreement that would act as a basis for negotiation at the forthcoming conference at Paris.

Meanwhile, the remainder of the German delegation, with the exception of Bergmann, that had attended the Brussels conference, began to have misgivings about the practicability of the Boulogne Agreement.

They believed that the levels of German indemnity were too high and that Germany would be unable to make cash reparations payments without jeopardising the value of the mark. D'Abernon was not entirely unsympathetic. He told Bergmann that an understanding could be reached between the British and German delegations to the effect that reparations payments that had already been made would be deducted from the final total.[23] He remained confident that the Brussels conference would produce a positive outcome. With greater optimism than the circumstances merited, D'Abernon informed Curzon that he had persuaded Bergmann to accept his arguments about the Boulogne Agreement. After a further interview with the chief German negotiator on 21 December, he reported that Bergmann's attitude was now 'much more satisfactory and hopeful'. Curiously, D'Abernon believed that Bergmann was willing to reappraise the entire German position at the conference. In an extraordinary further assessment of their relationship at this time, D'Abernon even noted that Bergmann regarded him as his 'mentor'.[24]

D'Abernon had misinterpreted Bergmann's mood. His up-beat accounts of their meetings contrasted sharply with those sent by Bergmann to Berlin, which expressed concern that the German position at the conference was being undermined by D'Abernon's desire to establish a final reparations total. Bergmann was also worried by the Allies' apparent unwillingness to pay sufficient attention to objections made by the German delegation. He reported that, 'the car has now attained a high speed thanks to the pressure of some Allied representatives, and it cannot be stopped without injury; it only remains to guide it cautiously down its dangerous course'.[25] Thus when the Brussels conference ended, D'Abernon had made little progress with Bergmann.[26] At a time when British politicians wished the Germans to view Britain as the more reasonable and approachable of the European Allied powers, the Germans clearly saw British and French policies on reparations as one and the same thing.

The differences between Bergmann and D'Abernon extended beyond the establishment of a reparations total. The two men held widely differing views on how German payments should be financed. Bergmann favoured opening German negotiations with the United States as soon as possible. He wanted German development to be based on the realities of the present rather than determined by the British who possessed smaller financial resources and justified their position in the post-war world through reference to the past. At a meeting with D'Abernon, Bradbury and Delacroix, Bergmann outlined a plan to raise an American loan to stabilise the German mark. Bergmann told D'Abernon that 'the future of German finance depends upon equilibrium of the Budget – equilibrium of the Budget depends upon the level of exchange – the level of exchange depends upon the existence of the above mentioned fund – [100 million gold dollars] and the above mentioned fund can preferably be derived from American loans'.[27] D'Abernon disagreed, believing that American aid should only be sought when all attempts to find a solution to the reparations question financed by the European powers had failed. He believed that if the German government made overtures to the United States, this would represent an insult to Britain.[28] A principle that underpinned all of D'Abernon's actions in Berlin was the belief that Britain had a right to a dominant role in German affairs. This stemmed from Britain's status as a Great Power and the long history of commercial relations between Britain and Germany.

Despite Bergmann's misgivings, D'Abernon continued to argue that Allied attention should focus on creating a European scheme to enable the German government to meet the terms of the Boulogne Agreement. At a meeting between them on 28 December 1920 to discuss how to present the German position at the forthcoming conference in Paris, D'Abernon spoke at length and later recorded that he had succeeded in 'very considerably' modifying Bergmann's views.[29] But once again D'Abernon misinterpreted Bergmann's mood, failing to realise that he and his political masters in Berlin continued to question the ambassador's motives. The Fehrenbach government believed that D'Abernon was trying to bully Germany and on New Year's Day 1921, Bergmann was instructed to oppose his plans. Von Simons, the German Minister for Foreign Affairs, feared that 'the wagon under Lord D'Abernon's whip [was] moving too fast and [was] going down the wrong road'. Von Simons was determined not to be swayed by D'Abernon's attempts to force him to agree to short-term proposals that would have to be revised at a later date and that could have resulted in a high total of reparations indemnity. Bergmann was instructed to do his utmost to 'put off a final understanding on the size and nature of [Germany's] payments' until American economic assistance could be guaranteed. Von Simons accused the British government of seeking a rapid denouement of the reparations question to 'feather its nest' and as a ploy to postpone the arrival of American economic aid.[30] This resulted in von Simons' unprecedented and controversial decision to seek French advice on how to present a proposal for the payment of reparations that would be acceptable to the Allies.[31] After consultation with Bergmann, Seydoux, the chief reparations expert at the Quai d'Orsay, was approached, primarily because he had a reputation for being sympathetic to Germany's economic plight.[32] Nevertheless, he was the servant of a government which had been consistently more hostile to Germany than had Britain since the end of the war.

Paris conference, January 1921

When, therefore, the Paris conference began during the second week of January 1921, it was with Seydoux rather than D'Abernon that Bergmann preferred to negotiate. The day before the conference opened, Bergmann discussed Germany's capacity to pay reparations with Seydoux, who recommended the establishment of a fixed total until American economic assistance could be secured. The Frenchman suggested that German payments would be fixed at two milliard gold marks for the first two years, of which three-quarters would be made up of payments in kind, and the remainder in cash. In the final three years the German government would guarantee payments of three milliard gold marks per annum. At the end of the five-year period, the Allies would be expected to present the German government with a final total of reparations and to be able to outline a payment scheme.[33] It was with this suggestion – not a proposal formulated by D'Abernon or Bradbury – that Bergmann returned to Berlin.[34] Von Simons agreed with Seydoux but preferred to keep the options for negotiations open by not announcing a final rejection of the five-year scheme. He wished to leave the decision about whether the German government should adopt the scheme until the outcome of the plebiscite in Upper Silesia was known. This gave the German government a stake in the diplomacy of the reparations debates between the Allies that D'Abernon seemed surprised that they wished to have. Bergmann asked D'Abernon to persuade the British government to support the German case in the plebiscite.[35] Publicly he refused, stating that Britain would not offer support of that kind under any circumstances. Yet privately he recognised that the situation would have to be reviewed when the result of the plebiscite was known.

Relations between Bergmann and D'Abernon during the Paris conference remained strained. D'Abernon complained of Bergmann's intransigence and unhelpfulness. He also expressed dismay at the absence in Bergmann's brief of any formal German acceptance of the Boulogne Agreement as a basis for negotiation. D'Abernon's disillusionment grew as Bergmann's remarks became increasingly cautious. The figure of three milliard gold marks per annum was deemed to be 'far beyond

Germany's capacity to pay'. Consequently the German government would only be able to make reparations payments in kind. D'Abernon was dismayed and convinced that Bergmann had not gone 'to the full length of his instructions'.[36] Nevertheless, he failed to change his mind. At subsequent reparations conferences, Bergmann and other German financial experts continued to express reservations about the soundness of D'Abernon's advice, viewing it as ambiguous and idiosyncratic. This led to wider confusion. After the Paris conference, the German government was unsure how to proceed at the forthcoming conference in London. The *Berliner Tageblatt*, a newspaper often critical of D'Abernon's activities, increased the confusion by claiming that 'authoritative English circles' in Berlin had recommended that the German delegation at the London conference should present 'concrete proposals' to the Allies.[37]

By the beginning of 1921 the diplomatic climate had begun to change. The threat of sanctions against Germany for failing to make adequate reparations payments was introduced and then withdrawn because of tension between London and Paris. But the possibility of the use of sanctions in the future remained. It became clear to the German government that creating deliberate distance between German and Allied advisers was likely to prove counter-productive. Consequently, before the first London conference, D'Abernon found his opinions being actively sought by financial experts in Berlin. But the divisions that had led to the rift with Bergmann at Brussels and Paris continued. D'Abernon clung to his views about the need to establish a final reparations total and became increasingly preoccupied with the effect that direct American involvement in German affairs would have on Britain's relationship with Germany. While the continuing American reluctance to commit financial assistance to Germany disillusioned von Simons, it was a source of relief to D'Abernon. He hoped that German feelings of resentment would rapidly translate into a complete abandonment of the United States as a potential source of revenue and investment. He believed that German enthusiasm for closer links with the American government would be short lived and reassured himself that Germany was much closer to Britain both geographically and historically.

But once again D'Abernon found that events had overtaken him as it rapidly became clear that he had misjudged von Simons' policy objectives. While D'Abernon wished to restore German financial stability, he realised that it would be impossible to balance the German budget. Before the Brussels conference had ended, Bergmann had informed the Allied delegations that the German economy would not be able to recover without international assistance. The loan that he had discussed with Seydoux could only be used to best effect if the German economy was in a stable condition. While D'Abernon acknowledged that external assistance was essential, he was anxious that such assistance should be British rather than American in origin. Yet it is difficult to understand how D'Abernon thought that the German economy would recover under a loan scheme underwritten by the British government. As a financial expert, he would have been aware that Britain was not in a strong enough position to offer large-scale assistance to Germany.

Sir John Bradbury

Despite the perceived eccentricity of D'Abernon's views, German relations with the British delegations at the numerous reparations conferences held between December 1920 and the spring of 1921 were not entirely unsatisfactory. Bergmann had a particular respect for Bradbury and recorded that their discussions about reparations in kind were always 'cordial and sensible'. The context in which this remark was made leaves the reader to decide the appropriate contrasting adjectives to describe Bergmann's relationship with D'Abernon. Such was the scale of Bradbury's success that D'Abernon was forced to concede that Germany could 'better show her good faith' by making reparations by deliveries in kind than through the payment of cash reparations.[38] Bradbury's negotiating style was flexible – an approach that was in marked contrast to D'Abernon's dealings with the German experts. Bergmann thought it important that a sum of reparations in kind should be fixed within the capacity of the German economy to expedite the economic regeneration of Germany. He favoured the Spa Agreement as a basis for determining the sum.[39] The German government also wished that future reparations schemes should take into account the amounts already paid by Germany – a point that had been firmly underlined to Bergmann by D'Abernon but largely disregarded. Annuities were to be paid over the thirty-year period specified by the Treaty of Versailles, along with German cash reparations, on the understanding that Allied assistance would be forthcoming to restore stability to the German exchange and to the budget.

Ironically, Bradbury believed that D'Abernon had been too accommodating in his dealings with Bergmann. He recommended that Britain should adopt an uncompromising attitude towards the German government and should adhere to the letter of the Boulogne Agreement. He argued that any modifications to the Agreement could only be implemented at the expense of Britain's share of any reparations payments.

Bradbury expressed concern about the effect that uncertainty about the establishment of a final reparations total would have on the German economy. He doubted whether the German government would be able to meet the annual payments of three milliard gold marks. The payment of cash sums, he concluded, should be strictly limited and their level determined by the strength of foreign exchanges. The greater part of the reparations indemnity should consist of payment in kind, particularly coal. He believed that such payments would most appropriately benefit France and Belgium – the two countries which had suffered the greatest devastation during the war.[40] Lloyd George recognised the logic of this argument but was nevertheless anxious to ensure that British interests were also preserved. Curzon, however, believed that Lloyd George was allowing the French government to dictate Allied reparations policy and that it was wrong that the British claim to payment should be seen as less important than those of the other Allied powers. This dispute reveals much about the continuing bickering that went on when Britain's policy towards France was discussed. Yet despite this, Curzon and other members of the Cabinet were reluctant to distance the British government officially from the actions of its French counterpart and ally.

The continuation of the wartime *entente* between Britain and France added a further dimension to D'Abernon's ability to influence British diplomacy on the reparations question. Differences of opinion between D'Abernon and Bradbury were not simply a matter of emphasis. Unlike D'Abernon, Bradbury did not share a Keynesian view of the German financial position and the Treaty of Versailles.[41] The usual effect of Bradbury's statements was to reinforce German fears that the Reparation Commission operated under the auspices of the French government. This unfortunate situation was compounded by Keynes's own disapproval of what he deemed to be the Treasury's excessively cautious attitude towards the reparations question.[42] D'Abernon was also sceptical about the ability of the Reparation Commission to make an objective assessment of Germany's capacity to pay. He believed that the Commission had made 'constant efforts to induce the German government to institute a radical reform of taxation and currency, but they were never prepared to give [the Germans] a long enough breathing space to enable them to carry through such a programme'.[43] Despite D'Abernon's reservations, Bradbury's views gained the support of the Treasury.

Impact of relations with France and the United States

The diplomatic exchanges between the Allies and the German government during the reparations conferences between December 1920 and the spring of 1921 also revealed much about D'Abernon's attitude towards the British position and his views on Britain's relations with France and the United States. At the Brussels conference, D'Abernon expressed doubts about a scheme proposed by Delacroix, the Belgian Prime Minister, which suggested that the German government should 'cede annuity to America against annulment of France's debt to America'.[44] D'Abernon believed that the plan would leave Britain more vulnerable than France to German refusals to make reparation payments, which he believed was contrary to the 'spirit' of the *Entente Cordiale*.[45] He anticipated that if Delacroix's scheme were to be implemented, the American government would probably refuse to recognise all German payments made thus far because diplomatic relations between the United States and Germany had yet to be reinstated.[46]

At this time, D'Abernon strongly believed that the British government should not act in isolation from France over the reparations issue. His views were to change substantially in 1923 when French and Belgian troops invaded the Ruhr, but in the years immediately following the signing of the Treaty of Versailles he feared that, if the Allies did not present a united front, the French and Belgian governments might be tempted to make independent representations to the United States. An even greater concern to him was the possible impact on Anglo-German relations if the German government made secret independent requests for American financial assistance. With this in mind, D'Abernon was anxious to cultivate an atmosphere of trust between the Allies and the German government. After the Brussels conference, he travelled to Paris to persuade the French to make a gesture of good faith that would give the German government sufficient confidence to adopt the Boulogne Agreement. To reinforce his argument, D'Abernon widened the discussion to include the disarmament question, informing Millerand that there was no reason why France should fear a military threat from Germany.[47]

By the first week of January 1921, however, the French government had become much less receptive to D'Abernon's overtures about the German position. Indicative of the new French mood was the formulation of the Seydoux Plan. At a meeting with Seydoux on 8 January 1921, D'Abernon learned that the French delegates at the forthcoming Paris conference no longer intended to propose the creation of a long-term reparations plan because they believed that the sum put forward 'would be too far removed from French expectations'.[48] Seydoux also suggested that the discussion of cash reparations should be postponed indefinitely. Despite his support for the Seydoux Plan, D'Abernon believed that failure to establish a final total for cash reparations was likely to make the French and German governments pursue American financial aid. Consequently, he felt that the French had 'rather let [Britain] down'.[49]

It was rumoured that the French change of heart resulted from instructions that Seydoux had received from Loucheur, the Minister for Liberated Regions, which stated that a reduction in the total of reparations was only possible under three conditions. These were that France would receive a guarantee that the new lower payments would in fact be made; that French claims would be given priority so that regions devastated by the war could be reconstructed; and that the process would be funded by an American loan. Joseph Addison, a counsellor at the British embassy in Berlin, warned the Foreign Office that Seydoux's motives were less than altruistic. He reported a rumour that Seydoux had presented harsh reparations proposals to the Allied and German delegations at Brussels because 'French public opinion was practically converted to the idea that disappointment was inevitable'. Addison had also heard that the French delegation believed the conference to be 'only minor' and that its conclusions did not need to be 'taken too seriously should they prove unpalatable'.[50] Sir George Grahame, the ambassador in Brussels, was also sceptical about the attitude of the French delegation. He warned D'Abernon against being lulled into a false sense of security by Seydoux and Leygues and stressed that he should remember that French views were usually hostile towards Germany.

Despite French enthusiasm for American financial assistance, D'Abernon remained convinced that any help given by the United States would be minimal and insufficient.[51] The French attitude gave D'Abernon little scope for negotiation. Hardinge reported that the Leygues government had decided to abandon the Brussels proposals until the meeting of the Allied Supreme Council so that Bergmann could be presented with a plan based on the Boulogne Agreement. The French government had announced that 'the German answer can be given without need for further discussion'. Ominously, Hardinge stated that the French offer represented Germany's 'last opportunity to secure an agreed solution of reparations instead of [the] question being determined over her head'.[52]

An ironic consequence of the new mood of French hostility towards Germany was greater French support for D'Abernon's early views on establishing a final total of indemnity.[53] On 24 January 1921, D'Abernon had a conversation with Loucheur and Doumer, the French Minister of Finance, during which the latter handed him an analysis of the German economic situation which concluded that, unless a total was established, the French economy would collapse. The result would be 'perpetual disputes' between France and Germany that would 'injure the credit of the Allies and of Germany herself'.[54] The best way to regulate payments would therefore be through delivery to the Allies of German bond securities. These would be negotiable on the international stock market at an interest rate of 5 per cent repayable in thirty years. Doumer was in no doubt that the German government could make payments of this scale. He was anxious to encourage closer Franco-German relations and was confident enough of the practicability of his proposals to claim that Germany had 'only to form the will and make the necessary effort to attain rapid economic reconstruction'.[55] D'Abernon however was dismayed to hear Doumer dismiss the Boulogne Agreement as simply 'a project', rather than as a proper basis for discussion. Having invested a great deal of mental energy in trying to persuade the German government to adopt the Agreement, he believed that he and the British government would appear ridiculous in Berlin should the idea now be abandoned simply to appease French public opinion. He told Doumer that Britain regarded the Boulogne Agreement as the only feasible basis for negotiation and that, if France were to abandon it, Doumer's present proposal would be ignored. D'Abernon was also critical of the size of the suggested bill of indemnity, judging it preposterous to expect Germany to make payments of 12 milliard gold marks per annum, which amounted to approximately three times the total German gold reserve.

On 24 January 1921, D'Abernon told Curzon of his doubts about the Doumer proposals and recommended that the British government should reject them without further consideration.[56] Of equal concern and embarrassment was the evidence of Bradbury's influence on the text and substance of the proposals, particularly in the terms relating to reparations in kind.[57] It is not clear whether Bradbury was consulted by Doumer, but as it was well known in French political circles that Bradbury thought D'Abernon too accommodating in his dealings with the German delegation at Brussels, such a scenario is not inconceivable. The French government would also not have allowed an opportunity to pass to exploit the differences between Bradbury and D'Abernon and to try to discredit the British expert most sympathetic to the German cause. Doumer and Loucheur later heard that Lloyd George still believed that a settlement should be based on the Boulogne Agreement and that he did not think the Doumer scheme practicable. In the face of such opposition, Doumer had little choice but to abandon his plan. Nevertheless, the French change of heart was brought about as a result of Lloyd George's intercession rather than through D'Abernon's influence.

D'Abernon's position in Berlin was rendered more difficult by the failure of Loucher and Doumer to convince von Simons of a French desire to resolve the reparations question quickly.[58] To simplify his discussions with the German government, D'Abernon had divided the Paris proposals into three sections: the size of the annuities payable over the first five years; the establishment of a fixed annuity from the sixth to the forty-second year of the scheme; and the creation of a 12 per cent export tax. He anticipated ready German agreement to the first and third headings with only a small amount of negotiation necessary to secure support for the second. But the German government saw the situation differently. At the end of January 1921, Wirth, the Minister of Finance, requested that the British government give consideration to a five-year scheme similar to that proposed at Brussels. He argued that unless the Allies agreed to reconsider this proposal, the German government would be unwilling to undertake responsibility for accepting five annual payments that 'already represent[ed] a great concession on [their] part'.[59] In effect, the German government would cease to recognise the proposals discussed at Brussels, based on the Boulogne Agreement, as a basis for future negotiation.

Events were further complicated when Charles Laurent, the French ambassador to Berlin, recommended that von Simons should accept the Seydoux proposals as a framework for discussion and agree not to bring further pressure to bear on the Allies to establish a final total of reparations indemnity. Von Simons felt betrayed by D'Abernon. He complained that through the 'intercession of British diplomatic representatives in this capital', the German government had agreed to the Seydoux proposals only to find them superseded by the Doumer plan in Paris. The German government was offended that the British had apparently entertained French ideas for a solution to the reparations question (even if those ideas were subsequently rejected) while not giving similar consideration to German proposals. Von Simons was also concerned that Allied calculations at Paris did not appear to take into account reparations payments already made by Germany, particularly those made in kind.[60] The fears expressed by Bradbury at Brussels on this point had proved justified.

Several days later, D'Abernon had a further interview with von Simons, who expressed dismay that the Paris conference had proceeded on the 'absolutely different lines' put forward by Loucheur and Doumer. He could not understand why the Doumer plan had been abandoned.

In defending the British position, D'Abernon said that there would be an 'air of some astonishment' in London if the Paris decisions were rejected. Feeling that von Simons did not entirely appreciate the British position, he went on to discuss Keynes's views on reparations, arguing that Keynes had been consistently sympathetic to German calls for a review of the reparations clauses of the Treaty of Versailles and that he had made a public declaration in favour of the Paris proposals.[61] Von Simons remained unconvinced. In a letter to a business associate, D'Abernon despaired of the new attitude of the German government. If the Germans could be persuaded of the merits of the Paris proposals, he anticipated that it would be a 'great step forward'.[62]

The rift between D'Abernon and the German government was reinforced by the cool response of experts in Berlin to the introduction of the 12 per cent levy on German exports proposed at the Paris conference. Gothein, a former Minister of Finance, condemned the measure as a continuation of the French attitude of '*le Boche payera tout*'.[63] D'Abernon noted the theoretical advantages of the scheme without fully comprehending the practical realities of their implementation. He was sympathetic to the German position but anticipated that the long-term benefits of the export tax would outweigh any short-term hardships. D'Abernon saw two advantages: the levy would lead to a postponement of the taxation of German exports into Allied countries, and would cause only minor fluctuations in the value of the mark. He anticipated that the tax would also allay Allied misgivings about German desires to stage an economic recovery on a scale likely to threaten European security.

On 4 February 1921, D'Abernon met Laurent to discuss German reactions to the export tax. Laurent believed that the Allied position had been undermined by the Allied Supreme Council which had refused to adopt the five-year annuities scheme. Consequently, the German government was obliged to commit itself to a plan completely different to the one it had originally accepted. Both Laurent and D'Abernon believed that the Germans found themselves in this position because of their failure to make up their minds more rapidly.[64] Laurent suspected that the long-term implications of the export levy had not been fully understood by the German government and feared that it might be used to inflate the German economy artificially. He also realised that German acceptance of the levy would assure the price of German exports but at the expense of Allied control of the German economy. D'Abernon, on the other hand, was concerned that rejection of the scheme would leave the German economy vulnerable to French interference.

The French government had published a defence of the Paris proposals based partly on reports of D'Abernon's conversations with von Simons. The ambassador concluded that 'it is, perhaps, satisfactory that the French government [has] adopted... our defence of the Paris basis'.[65] Bradbury and D'Abernon also believed that the German government should be involved equally with the Allies in drawing up a scheme to avoid charges that British involvement was motivated exclusively by self-interest.

However, D'Abernon failed to take account of the demoralising effect that the obstructive behaviour of the French government had in Berlin. Von Simons became increasingly pessimistic about the implementation of the 12 per cent levy. In a speech at Stuttgart on 13 February 1921, he claimed that it would have an adverse effect on the German economy and would result in a further decline in Germany's commercial reputation.[66] He argued that European economic reconstruction was not possible through a series of long-term schemes, but only as a result of an international loan created to rebuild devastated areas. The export of raw materials formed a vital part of Germany's contribution to the reconstruction of devastated regions in France and Belgium. Von Simons believed that this process would be severely hampered if the 12 per cent export levy was implemented.

While being concerned about the long-term implications of von Simons's statement, D'Abernon nevertheless remained confident that the German government wished Britain to have a leading role in the economic recovery of Germany, should a system of international loans be created. He endeavoured to reassure Curzon to this effect, suggesting that von Simons was overreacting to the 12 per cent levy. D'Abernon drew Curzon's attention to the activities of the *Aussenhandelstelle* (Foreign Export Control Office). This department, he argued, imposed export duties on many items well in excess of 12 per cent without any detrimental effect on the German economy. He also presented research by the commercial staff at the embassy in support of his argument. The findings suggested that German producers of iron goods, for example, agreed with his views on the levy. What was more, most believed it to be little more than a 'bureaucratic measure which bore no relation ... to the real state of the German iron trade'.[67] However, the reliability of this information can be questioned because of the reservations that Addison had previously expressed about D'Abernon's judgement.[68] The dismissive attitude of German industrialists forced D'Abernon to make representations to the German government about the activities of the *Aussenhandelstelle*.[69] Nevertheless, von Simons's views remained unchanged.

London conference, March 1921

D'Abernon was being forced to adopt an increasingly isolated position in his dealings with the French and German experts. At the international reparation conference that met in London in March 1921, he discussed the establishment of a preliminary total of German indemnity with Schroeder, Secretary to the German Treasury. The German government recognised that the Paris proposals involved payments of 2 milliard for two years and 3 milliard for three years, giving a total of 13 milliard gold marks. The new German proposal stated that a sum of one milliard should be paid for five years plus an extra 8 milliard in the form of an immediate loan, giving a total of 15 milliard. According to the Germans, the discrepancy of 2 milliard arose because this revised proposal made no provision for the 12 per cent levy. The German delegation regarded the differences between the French and German viewpoints as irreconcilable. Reaching a provisional reparations total was therefore the only solution in the short term. Schroeder suggested that the Reparation Commission should be asked to intercede and examine Germany's capacity to pay.

Financial experts in France, however, viewed Schroeder's proposals with disdain. French political hostility towards Germany had continued to intensify. Those French financial experts who had originally been sympathetic to a temporary solution, now joined their colleagues in condemning the idea. Meanwhile, in London, another war of words was taking place. The Treasury and the Foreign Office could not decide on the best way to proceed. Lloyd George was also growing exasperated at the deadlock in the reparations negotiations. He was coming under pressure from the French government to reject a German proposal for a massively reduced reparations total. Even those who were sympathetic to the German position began to wonder if Fehrenbach and von Simons had ulterior motives for prolonging the negotiations. In particular, Lloyd George believed that von Simons was adopting an unreasonable attitude towards Allied attempts to ease Germany's reparations burden. In a display of British solidarity with France and as an attempt to add fresh impetus to the negotiations, Lloyd George agreed to the use of a more drastic measure than diplomacy. He agreed to the further occupation of German territory by the Allies – a sanction which had been contemplated in the past but never used. In March 1921, British and French troops occupied Düsseldorf, Duisburg and Ruhrort and established a customs cordon dividing these cities from the rest of Germany.

D'Abernon was involved in less dramatic attempts to reach an agreement. He travelled to Chequers for a meeting with Lloyd George to try to devise a scheme under which the annuities accumulated after the first five years of the Paris plan would be replaced by a percentage of exports. The idea was 'to provide some guarantee for the later years'.[70] The French reply was initially positive, but was subsequently rejected when it became clear that the Germans continued to link the proposal to the outcome of the plebiscite in Upper Silesia. D'Abernon remained optimistic about a favourable outcome to the negotiations but continued in vain to try to persuade the German delegation to modify its proposals.[71] The German government decided to disregard his advice and presented a third basis for discussion. However, the German delegation did not receive a second opportunity to put forward its case as the conference finally became a casualty of the strained diplomatic relations that now existed between the Allies and Germany.

The French press used the collapse of the conference as an excuse to launch an attack on D'Abernon. A prominent French journalist, *Pertinax*, in an article in the *Echo de Paris*, described him as an '*advocatus diaboli*' and held him guilty of self-interest.[72] The Foreign Office dismissed these attacks as without foundation, but there was some accuracy in the picture they presented of D'Abernon's activities. It was of course his job to protect British interests in Germany, but these comments suggest that once again the French government was unconvinced about Britain's commitment to a collective policy towards Germany. It is not difficult to understand why the French were sceptical about D'Abernon's activities. He had changed his mind a number of times about major issues for reasons that were not clear. But as *Pertinax* may have realised, D'Abernon had also often been placed in a difficult situation because of mutual mistrust between Britain and Germany.

D'Abernon's very positive attitude towards the London conference was thus particularly eccentric. He had been misled by the French and German delegations, accused of having no clear ideas and been criticised by the French press. Despite this, D'Abernon recorded that the conference had been 'nearer success than people generally imagined'. He even held himself partly responsible for the breakdown of the conference, attributing it to the increasingly isolated position that he was forced to adopt because of his failure to agree with either the British or German point of view. 'If I could get others to take my view', he noted, 'negotiations might be resumed with a good chance of settlement'. D'Abernon also attributed the failure of the conference to the constraints placed on von Simons by German public opinion and to the 'imperative and narrowly restricted mandate' of the French delegation. He remained convinced that if the French and German delegations had 'enjoyed the normal latitude usually conferred on men of inferior rank' a settlement would have been reached.[73]

The diplomacy of the reparations question helped to forge a close link between economics and foreign policy in Europe in the 1920s. These conferences also illustrated the extent to which each country attending them had embraced the economic realities of the post-war world. D'Abernon believed in 'diplomacy by conference' as a method of solving the reparations question because it gave financial experts such as himself a central role in international diplomacy. In Britain he was flattered that as an 'expert diplomat' his views were likely to find favour with Lloyd George. But there is little evidence to suggest that they did. In Germany, too, a growing number of senior politicians had a strong grounding in commercial affairs. But beyond this, it is doubtful whether D'Abernon ever embraced the more fundamental changes that the First World War brought with it – a political order where the *ancien régime* no longer had the prerogative to rule. He might have felt more comfortable in his dealings with the German government had its members been from the *Junker* class rather than from the bourgeoisie. To Bergmann, D'Abernon may well have seemed like a throwback to a bygone era from which the early governments of the Weimar Republic were particularly anxious to distance themselves. D'Abernon was also by now a man in late middle age. It would have been unreasonable to expect him to change his *Weltanschauung*.

He was not the only person unwilling to embrace the political, economic and social realities of the post-war world. What is less easy to explain is the inconsistency of his views. He patronised the German financial experts with whom he came into contact and his volte-face at the Brussels conference made it likely that his subsequent actions would be viewed with suspicion. He also underestimated the ability and determination of the German experts at the reparations conferences. D'Abernon expected Germany to behave as a defeated power – downtrodden and demoralised – but he failed to recognise that this was not the way in which the German government necessarily viewed its position. In the longer term, his attitudes and actions helped to damage Britain's relations with a country that had one of the most modern and sophisticated economies in the world. Furthermore, the crisis that was soon to be prompted by the occupation of the Ruhr by French and Belgian troops in order to force the payment of reparations was to keep these problems in sharp focus.

3
From Rapallo to the Ruhr Crisis, 1922–24

The Ruhr crisis had a profound diplomatic and economic impact on Europe.[1] It brought into focus the lack of trust between Britain and France, as well as the tensions between the Allies and Germany. The occupation of the Ruhr also provided further evidence of the burden of being on the victorious side at the end of the First World War. It sealed the fate of the beleaguered mark and proved that Europe alone was incapable of solving the problem of reparations. D'Abernon, as a financial expert, had the knowledge and opportunity to play a leading role in defusing the crisis. But this did not arise, primarily because of his own approach to the situation. This assessment also suggests that British policy towards Germany continued to lack clarity and that Britain was still willing to go to considerable lengths to preserve the entente with France. The European 'experiment' with diplomacy by conference continued into 1922. Nevertheless, the numerous international gatherings that had taken place since the Paris Peace Conference to establish a final total of reparation indemnity had spectacularly failed to predict or prevent the run on the value of the German mark. They demonstrated more clearly than any of the hostile propaganda that was directed against Lloyd George, the League of Nations and other symbols of this style of diplomacy that the use of experts as a substitute for diplomats with more traditional training did not provide a better means of resolving complex diplomatic problems. Thus between the spring of 1922, when Lloyd George's last attempt at Genoa to reinvigorate his career as an international statesman was eclipsed by the signing of the Treaty of Rapallo, and the establishment of the Dawes Committee in 1923, there was a crisis in diplomacy of more than one kind. Not only was a means of resolving the reparations question established at a high price, but with it came a gradual return to more conventional, pre-war approaches to the conduct of diplomacy. This transition had almost been completed by 1925, when the European powers turned their attention towards the question of security. But the events of 1922 and 1923, particularly in relation to the conclusion of the Treaty of Rapallo and the first year of the Ruhr crisis, provide an insight into the conflict between the traditional and the newer, 'expert' diplomacy. As his embassy progressed, D'Abernon's relationship with the German government changed little. He continued to be on the margin of the foreign policy decision-making process in Berlin, while in London, his pro-German sympathies brought him increasingly into conflict with the more francophile Foreign Office.

The Treaty of Rapallo

Evidence of D'Abernon's remoteness from the decision-making process in the *Auswärtiges Amt* can be seen in his response to the news about the signature of the Treaty of Rapallo. This reinstated diplomatic relations between Germany and the Soviet Union, renounced financial claims to debts left over from the war and promised mutual economic cooperation in the future. The first D'Abernon heard of the treaty was in the German newspapers and he was astounded by the news. He was puzzled as to why the Germans had felt compelled to sign an agreement with the Soviet Union and feared that Germany was moving away from the Allies.[2] Publicly and privately, he did not attempt to hide his belief that the Germans had acted rashly and would live to regret a decision that could alienate the Allies and result in the communist infiltration of German politics.[3] Curzon was equally puzzled as to why the Germans had kept D'Abernon in ignorance of the negotiations. Nevertheless, he seemed to accept the ambassador's explanation that the German government had not informed him of the negotiations with the Soviet Union because it had been feared that he might try to persuade Walther Rathenau, the German Minister for Foreign Affairs, to abandon such a strategy.[4] Curzon also accepted D'Abernon's assurance that the German government's dalliance with the Soviet Union was merely a distraction and would not inhibit the progress of closer diplomatic relations with the Allies. What was more, D'Abernon argued, the Germans had been bullied into signing the Treaty of Rapallo by the Soviet Union and would eventually see the error of their ways.[5] He wrote:

> The Russo-German Agreement is viewed in some quarters as part of a deliberate German policy. I regard it rather as an expedient of

> despair, unwillingly adopted by men who were in a corner or who imagined themselves in a corner. To those in this frame of mind – and Germans are temperamentally prone to it – the most foolish courses are easily suggested.[6]

He felt therefore that he had defended himself against any charges of incompetence and he was not chastised by Curzon, whose sights were more closely fixed on Lloyd George. The Foreign Secretary hoped that the news of Rapallo would discredit the Prime Minister's statements about the development of a more liberal relationship between Germany and the Allies.[7]

The resulting rapid deterioration in German relations with the Allies after the signature of the Treaty of Rapallo was a subject on which D'Abernon had surprisingly little to say. A man of firm judgements, he was confident that he was right about the true nature of the German government's enthusiasm for closer links with the Soviet Union and that it would be short lived. Events and conversations tended to impact on his thought processes only when he allowed them to do so. Consequently, he ignored ideas that he did not like even if they had intrinsic merit. During the hyper-inflation crisis in Germany in 1922–23, D'Abernon did not send Curzon a stream of dispatches offering a commentary on the decline in the value of the mark and outlining his attempts to persuade the German government to reappraise its attitude to the crisis. Nor did he seek regular meetings with Fehrenbach and Wirth. Instead, he recorded the facts privately, noting with dismay the continued failure of the German government to heed his advice against balancing the budget by printing more money.[8] Germany was now suffering the consequences.[9] His Presidential Address to the Royal Statistical Society in 1927 about the operation of the German economy during his embassy provides further testimony to his bitterness.[10]

During the autumn of 1922, the German government pressed the Allies for a moratorium on reparations payments. In November a note was sent to London and Paris stating that the mark could only be stabilised if all payments were suspended for the next three or four years.[11] The request was declined and in December the Reparation Commission declared that Germany was in arrears in payments in kind, particularly in timber. A similar statement was issued on 9 January 1923 declaring that Germany had failed to make sufficient coal deliveries. Two days later, French and Belgian troops entered the Ruhr, thus prompting the most serious crisis in Europe since the Great War. D'Abernon interpreted the invasion as conclusive evidence that the French were so hostile to the Germans that they were willing to threaten European peace to extract what they wanted from them. The Germans were to be beaten into submission because it was becoming clear that the implementation of the Treaty of Versailles had become a byzantine operation.[12] Poincaré, D'Abernon argued, should be condemned as a warmonger while the British government should do all in its power to distance itself from his policies. He also accused the French of pursuing a policy of economic imperialism, arguing that the Ruhr occupation marked the beginning of a more general policy to secure commercial hegemony in Europe.

British responses to the Ruhr crisis

During the crisis, D'Abernon's position in Berlin was made increasingly difficult by the lack of clarity in British policy towards French policy in the Ruhr. While the Permanent Under-Secretary, Sir Eyre Crowe, and others at the Foreign Office were willing to describe French actions as 'sickening and revolting', memoranda dispatched to the Quay d'Orsay via the British embassy in Paris stopped well short of an open denunciation of them.[13] Even before the occupation began, it had been believed that the 'adverse effect on Anglo-French relations of French independent action' in the Ruhr should be minimised at all costs.[14] British responses to the crisis were influenced by the desire to maintain the *Entente Cordiale*. The new Prime Minister, the ailing Andrew Bonar Law, summed up the British position thus:

> His Majesty's Government are definitely of the opinion that these French proposals [to take goods from Germany in lieu of reparations payments], are likely to have grave and even disastrous result upon the economic situation in Europe, and in these circumstances they cannot take part in or accept responsibility for them. His Majesty's Government at the same time, desire to assure the Government of the Republic that while they regret extremely that there should be an irreconcilable difference of opinion on a subject so serious, the feeling of friendship not only on the part of the British government but also as I believe of the British people towards the Government and people of France remains unchanged.[15]

The Bonar Law government believed that the French would not risk alienating Britain because the Treaty of Versailles could be more effectively enforced if the Allies presented a united front regarding its implementation.[16] There also lingered the hope that ultimately the French would seek means other than the use of military force as the best way of solving Europe's problems.[17] The alternative, less than five years after the end of the First World War, was unthinkable. Whatever action the French took to recoup outstanding reparations payments, the British were determined to maintain the *Entente Cordiale*, even if this meant sacrificing a good relationship with Germany. Ferris has suggested that in the early 1920s, the British government feared that French military strength could be used against Britain should a breach in the *Entente Cordiale* occur. A particular danger existed if the British government was seen to offer too much assistance to Germany in resolving the reparations question.[18] Comments about French military strength came, ironically, from D'Abernon and other British diplomats in Germany. During the early months of the Ruhr occupation, D'Abernon sent information that suggested that France was militarily and politically the strongest nation in Europe and which demonstrated, in contrast, that Germany was 'militarily powerless'.[19] As a result, the final three years of his embassy were primarily dedicated to trying to change British attitudes towards the Ruhr occupation and German security. While the British government did not offer any practical assistance to France or Germany, there can be little doubt where British sympathies lay. Far from remaining neutral in the Ruhr crisis, some British officials condemned resistance to the forces of occupation to German diplomatic representatives in London.[20] These views were, in turn, communicated to Berlin.[21]

British policy towards the Rhineland was also coloured by a desire to protect the *Entente Cordiale*, although friction between Germany and France regarding its future meant that Allied policy in this area became increasingly fraught with controversy. The activities of French-inspired Rhenish separatist movements were seen by both Britain and Germany as a threat to international security as they challenged the terms of the Treaty of Versailles. The Ruhr crisis brought a further deterioration in Anglo-French relations and resulted in a reappraisal of the future of the British presence in the Rhineland. In January 1923, a possible withdrawal was considered, but when the French began to expel senior German officials from the Rhineland, the British Commissioner in Cologne, Julian Piggott, believed that the expulsions and arrests placed the British in an 'impossible position'. He argued that the German bureaucrats had been 'invariably loyal' and as a result, a good working relationship had evolved with the British 'on which to a great extent the safety and comfort of the Army' depended. Piggott thought that if the British were to abandon the Germans, 'it would be impossible to continue our work here'.[22] The proposed withdrawal was therefore abandoned. The instructions to the British High Commissioner in the Rhineland, Lord Kilmarnock had, however, been carefully worded:

> The policy of undiminished friendship with France will, so far as the Inter-Allied Rhineland High Commission is concerned, best be served by your continued attendance at its meetings. Should, however, any question come before the High Commission arising out of the area affected by French independent action you should declare that under the instructions of your Government you are precluded from taking any decision on that particular matter.[23]

Throughout the early months of the Ruhr occupation, Curzon was anxious to justify the decision to retain a British presence in the Rhineland, a force which would, if nothing else, protect British reparations interests.[24]

D'Abernon shared Kilmarnock's fears about the scale of French military might, yet he believed that British interests would be best served if British troops in the Rhineland were withdrawn.[25] He believed that the British presence antagonised the French and therefore made the opening of security negotiations more difficult. 'Strategically', he argued, there was 'no justification for keeping a small force isolated in the centre of an agitated Europe' as it 'constitute[d] little more than a hostage to fortune'.[26] At the same time, he wanted the British government to make a stand against France over the occupation of the Ruhr, even if that entailed a dissolution of the *Entente Cordiale*. When trying to establish in his mind whether the Ruhr and Rhineland crises were concerned with reparations or security, he concluded there was 'probably an element of truth in both interpretations'.[27]

The need for British intervention

D'Abernon was certain about one issue, and this was that the Franco-Belgian invasion of the Ruhr was an act of unwarranted aggression against Germany. What was more, it was the moral responsibility of the British government to intervene both diplomatically and, if necessary, militarily to preserve German sovereignty.[28] But his arguments were eccentrically expressed and contained fundamental contradictions and inconsistencies. In particular, he undermined his own pleas for the British government to offer assistance to Germany in repelling the invasion by implying that the German government had partly brought the crisis on itself. While portraying Germany as the victim of French aggression and greed, he condemned German commercial activity during the early weeks of the occupation. He expressed consternation that the imprisonment of a number of German mine owners by the French during the early weeks of the occupation turned them into 'national heroes'.[29] He also derided several German industrialists for taking advantage of the cessation of reparations payments in order to renovate their plants.[30] D'Abernon was more generally critical of the German government's handling of the crisis. Instead of expressing outrage on its behalf, he told Curzon that German reactions gave the impression of 'artificiality and a certain element of comic relief'.[31] Within weeks of the start of the invasion, D'Abernon claimed that the German government was equally to blame for the Ruhr crisis as the French and Belgians. He informed the King that the German government possessed sufficient economic competence to have prevented the occupation.[32] He rejected the argument that the origins of the crisis lay in the failure of the Paris conference to establish a total of reparations indemnity. The Germans, D'Abernon argued, had brought their troubles on themselves because they had rejected the *Majority Report* in November 1922.[33] He maintained that if the Report had been adopted, a solution to the reparations question would have been possible that could have strengthened the German economy, stabilised the value of the mark and enabled reparations payments to be made. However, the German government had failed to be convinced of its merits and had presented alternative proposals to the French that were promptly rejected.[34] Again, D'Abernon believed, the Germans were having to live with the consequences of having ignored his advice.

Yet while expressing reservations about the German position, D'Abernon sent a stream of dispatches arguing that the British government should take a stand against France and offer practical support to the Germans. His argument was constructed around three points. Firstly, that the Ruhr occupation would be disastrous for the German economy. Secondly, that it would have an adverse effect on Anglo-German commercial relations, and finally, that failure to act would leave the German people vulnerable to communist infiltration. He repeated a warning given to him by von Rosenberg, the German Minister for Foreign Affairs, that if the Ruhr was occupied, the German government could be forced to seek a closer relationship with the Soviet Union, which could result in 'Russian Bolshevism on the Rhine'.[35] The German government, D'Abernon reported, was 'haunted' by the spectre of communism and the Soviet government was manipulating the crisis to ensure that a permanent rift between Germany and the Allies was created.[36] D'Abernon also believed that if Britain continued inactive, it was only a matter of time before a 'declaration of war' would be issued between Germany, France and Belgium.[37]

The Foreign Office turned a deaf ear to D'Abernon's attempts to solicit British support for the German plight.[38] In February 1923, he asked the commercial staff at the embassy to produce a number of reports on the short- and long-term effects of the Ruhr occupation on Anglo-German commercial relations. A month later, he communicated the findings of one of these investigations, warning that drastic measures were required to protect British trade from 'undue or illegal interference'. Dramatically, he described the general state of Anglo-German commercial relations as one of 'great delicacy, difficulty and complication' and recommended that 'some superior official' should be sent to Germany to assess the situation.[39] D'Abernon's request did not even merit an official acknowledgement and the visit that he recommended never took place. Instead, Curzon and Bonar Law became enamoured of the idea put forward by the American Secretary of State, Charles Evans Hughes, for the establishment of an international committee to examine the reparations question.[40] The solution to such a problem was now deemed to be beyond the capability of one government, let alone that of a single expert.

It is therefore difficult to determine how D'Abernon expected the British government to react to the Ruhr crisis. He viewed the conduct of diplomacy in terms of stark choices. He argued, for example, that Germany and France were historic enemies and that therefore it was impossible for Britain to be pro-German without being anti-French. He believed that German enthusiasm for closer relations with the Soviet Union implied an acceptance of the communist regime and therefore a turning away from democracy.[41] D'Abernon's statements on the growth of communism in Germany reflected his long-held belief that it was imperative to maintain Germany within a western European sphere of influence.[42] The communist threat to the political stability of the Weimar Republic during the crisis proved to be negligible and short lived, but D'Abernon used the real or imagined prospect of Russian influence in Germany throughout his embassy as a tactic to encourage the British government to make security commitments to Germany. In D'Abernon's view, it was always the intention of the Russians to rob the Allies of their influence in Germany.[43] His hatred of communism led him to believe that the Soviet Union should be viewed indefinitely with suspicion by the international community.[44]

D'Abernon was not alone in advocating British assistance to Germany. A number of senior government officials thought that the British government should come to the assistance of Germany to combat unwarranted French aggression as a matter of principle. Sir Warren Fisher, Permanent Secretary to the Treasury, believed that Britain was under a moral obligation to maintain the peace in Europe and to protect German interests against any nation that sought to undermine them. Appealing to the traditional British sense of fair play, he argued:

> By the Treaty of Versailles, which we English helped to create and which we signed, we ... deprived the Germans of all effective means of *armed* self-defence. We thereby assumed a responsibility for securing the Germans against armed brutality – unless of course we have ceased to be Englishmen and are prepared first to tie a man's hand behind his back and then encourage or allow someone to hit below the belt. We are thus in the position of trustees, directly by reason of the Treaty and generally because of our English sense of fair play. The French have played the part of bullies whenever they had or could make the chance, and they are doing so now.[45]

At the headquarters of the Reparation Commission in Paris, Sir John Bradbury astounded Curzon by recommending that a formal condemnation of French actions should be issued and that an offer of limited support should be made to the German government. His remarks prompted a number of vitriolic Foreign Office memoranda criticising the 'excessive' powers of the Reparation Commission.[46] Bradbury saw British intervention as inevitable and he chastised his political masters in London for not persuading the Cabinet to take more decisive action. In April 1923, he told the Chancellor of the Exchequer, Stanley Baldwin:

> The plain fact remains that if the Germans make a sensible offer and the French call us in to discuss it, the whole conduct of the negotiations and the settlement ... will be substantially in our hands. In such circumstances, the French obviously cannot afford 'to agree to differ' again.[47]

D'Abernon willingly maintained a relative silence when it became apparent that the British government was not going to offer immediate assistance to Germany. On no occasion did he express his opinions about British policy to Curzon or to other senior officials, but reserved his comments for the privacy of his diary. Most references are very brief and anodyne; his strongest remarks being reserved for British reactions to a German note, about which he wrote: 'Hitherto there has been plenty of reproach and criticism [and] no words of recognition. This is unjust and unwise.'[48] Somewhat unexpectedly given his views, he often appeared to think it disloyal to criticise British policy towards Germany in public and private correspondence. It is perhaps for this reason that D'Abernon hastened the publication of his embassy diary to demonstrate that he did not always agree with the views that his official position compelled him to support.

D'Abernon sought to influence British attitudes towards the German position through more subtle means. He sent a number of dispatches containing accounts of the consequences to Germany of the Ruhr occupation and of German pleas for British help, but they had little effect on Curzon. British policy towards the Ruhr crisis was not explained to D'Abernon. It would have been difficult to present a rationale for a policy about which the British government itself appeared to have such hollow convictions and which resulted in it being subjected to consistent domestic attack.[49] It was not that officials at the Foreign Office necessarily disagreed with D'Abernon. Restricted by the desire to maintain the *Entente Cordiale*, Curzon in particular disliked having a line of argument presented to him with which he privately agreed but about which he felt unable to take action.[50] As the crisis progressed, D'Abernon's views were perceived as too subjective and likely to undermine aspects of British policy towards Europe that were diplomatically sensitive.[51] Curzon marginalised him and increasingly used Sthamer, the German ambassador to London, as his source of information on the views of the German government. Sthamer also tried to secure British help, but he lacked D'Abernon's dogged persistence and strength of personality.[52] It was therefore easier to ignore his pleas for assistance. This was not the last time that the Foreign Office was to choose to listen to Sthamer rather than to D'Abernon for this reason.

Curzon did indeed feel frustrated. His hatred of Poincaré was well known but he felt unable to condemn French action in the Ruhr directly.[53] Instead, he chastised the German government for not adopting a more 'reasonable attitude' towards the reparations question. He believed that the onus was on the Germans, not the Allies, to prove that the tactic of seizing reparations payments by force was not justified. In denying a request for British 'sympathy and moral support' in the days leading up to the Ruhr occupation, he warned Sthamer that:

> Only the ill-will or want of energy on the part of the German government and the German industrialists prevented substantial

> payments under the head of reparations. If there were a substantial foundation for the French view, the sooner the German government took action in the sense desired the better for them and the whole world.[54]

Others at the Foreign Office adopted an equally dismissive tone towards German attempts to solicit British support. At the start of the Ruhr crisis, Sir Miles Lampson of the Central European Department minuted that 'Sthamer called this afternoon. He said nothing of particular interest.'[55] Stresemann was later to complain that German interests were a constant casualty of Anglo-French diplomacy.[56] When Sthamer sought a further interview to explain German policy, Lampson's minutes of the conversation reveal the extent of his embarrassment. He wrote:

> I said that I had no intention of being drawn into a discussion of the rights or wrongs of [German] action, but ... it seemed to me that the effects of the German action might well be most unfortunate. It gave France a further pretext for strengthening her action against Germany: and though that might for the moment embarrass the French government yet in the long run it was Germany which would pay.[57]

D'Abernon was sent the minutes of Sthamer's conversations with Lampson, but despite their content, continued to give the German government the impression that British aid was imminent.[58] Attempting to maintain a positive relationship with the German government was part of his brief. But it is difficult to explain why he remained so optimistic about the arrival of assistance when it appeared highly unlikely that it would ever be forthcoming. This intellectual tenacity and indefatigability was combined with a sense of fair play. Throughout his embassy, he strongly believed that Britain had a moral obligation to protect Germany from the 'excesses' of French foreign policy.[59] As persistent as he had been during the reparations conferences, D'Abernon was so convinced that he occupied the moral high ground that he failed to understand the dilemma in which the British government found itself. Curzon certainly found him difficult to understand. It was only when D'Abernon's activities threatened the progress of Britain's relations with France that he decided to take decisive action to curb them.

Resolving the crisis

There were also fundamental differences over smaller issues of policy. After the Paris conference in January 1923, D'Abernon suggested that the best way of securing British economic assistance for Germany would be for the German budget to be balanced. British plans to establish a reparations total that had been put forward at the conference could then be adopted.[60] The British proposals had divided German reparations bonds into two groups: the First Series was to consist of 50 milliard gold marks to be issued immediately, repayable by 31 December 1954 at an interest rate of 5 per cent, the interest being suspended for four years, while the Second Series represented a total of 17.31 milliard gold marks (the amount of deferred interest from the bonds of the First Series), repayable on 1 April 1933 at an interest rate of 5 per cent.[61] As the British proposals made no reference to penalties for non-compliance, the German government decided to adopt them. Curzon, however, believed that D'Abernon was becoming too involved in private negotiations with the Germans. He had received word from the British embassy in Paris that the French government would reject any German proposal which had been accorded too much British support.[62] Curzon's instructions to D'Abernon were clear. He was to take all measures necessary to 'avoid being drawn into any form of collaboration with the German government'.[63]

A week later, the depth of the French government's hostility to the plan became apparent when D'Abernon's relationship with the German government was attacked in the French press. In general, French newspapers assumed that any diplomatic or economic initiative relating to Germany that appeared to place British interests before those of France had its origin in the British embassy in Berlin. *Le Temps* accused Cuno, the German Chancellor, of blind compliance with D'Abernon's views, of listening solely to 'His Master's Voice'.[64] D'Abernon responded by sending an angry letter to Curzon complaining that he was being placed in an impossible position as a result of the lack of clarity in British policy towards France and Germany. The choices open to him, he noted, were difficult. They amounted to: 'intervene and be responsible' or 'abstain and let things go wrong'.[65] D'Abernon had therefore not disregarded the possibility of ignoring Curzon's instructions. It was this inclination towards freedom of action that had led Bergmann, von Simons and Fehrenbach to believe that D'Abernon had his own agenda in dealing with the German government that went beyond, or even contrary to his official instructions. The dilemma cannot have been caused by his instructions from Curzon, since these had been clear. Rather, D'Abernon was concerned about the possible repercussions of going against Curzon's wishes. This could have resulted in a major and very embarrassing rift between the British and French governments that would almost certainly have led to an even greater British reluctance to support the German cause. On balance, therefore, D'Abernon decided to avoid courting controversy.

The difference of opinion between D'Abernon and the British government on passive resistance provided fertile ground for controversy inside the Foreign Office and added a further strain to Britain's relations with France. The British government saw passive resistance as an unnecessary barrier to a final solution to the Ruhr crisis. D'Abernon agreed that the German government would be better occupied devoting its attention to the 'more pressing' question of Germany's finances.[66] Nevertheless, he warned that to insist on its abandonment was tantamount to asking the German government to accept the legality of the Ruhr invasion.[67] He also described the dire political consequences for any German government that sanctioned such a policy. Once again, the Foreign Office was swayed by French reports of D'Abernon's comments. The Marquess of Crewe, British ambassador to Paris, reported that the '*whole of the Quai d'Orsay*' was convinced that D'Abernon was urging the population of the Ruhr to resist the occupying forces 'without the knowledge of the British government'.[68] Furthermore, D'Abernon's remarks were proof that the British government had wo policies on passive resistance. Crewe believed that there was some truth in these rumours. He told Curzon that the claim 'might obviously be a lie', but since it came from a reliable source, it merited further investigation. Lampson of the Central Department of the Foreign Office believed that the press reports were a psychological ploy to put the British government on to the defensive by forcing the issue of a *démenti*.[69]

Recommendations were made to send one to Paris 'discreetly' but there was little point in such discretion unless the Foreign Office believed that there was some foundation to the rumours.[70] Crewe's views were taken so seriously in London that D'Abernon felt compelled to issue a *démenti* of his own. He told Curzon that it 'betrayed a misconception of the whole position ... to suggest that a violent national revolt could have been produced at the instigation of any foreign agency'.[71] He argued that the German view of the British position bore no resemblance to French interpretations and that the Germans viewed Britain as a natural ally who was willing to offer assistance only when requested. He rejected the idea that British involvement in German affairs was clandestine, excessive or deliberately designed to promote anti-French feeling. But the rumours were never successfully scotched, thus giving a hollow ring to his assurances.

As the spring of 1923 wore on, British political opinion became increasingly divided about the Ruhr crisis. Domestic pressure was growing for the government to take decisive action. Senior politicians from the three main parties continued to disapprove of French activity in the Ruhr, while, by contrast, members of the Primrose League, led by the Earl of Pembroke, attempted to persuade Baldwin and Curzon to offer France direct British support. Public opinion urged the government to make a stand against the French. In a letter to the editor, a reader of the *Daily Mail* wrote:

> The immense preponderance of opinion is with the French and that the action – or rather, the 'gassing' of the Government is viewed with nothing short of dismay. In the street, in restaurants, and in the train one cannot help hearing bits of conversation, all to the same effect. There is a recrudescence of feeling which many people share that there is some underlying influence, in times past stigmatised as the 'hidden hand' which it is amazing has not been fully worked out. It is absolutely impossible for any reasonable person to resist the conclusion that some powerful interest – or, rather, interests – is working with potency in favour of Germany.[72]

By the summer, British political circles were beginning to draw the uncomfortable conclusion that the French and Belgians intended to continue to occupy the Ruhr with or without British approval. What was more, the consequences of the suspension of reparations payments were beginning to be felt on both Anglo-German commercial relations and Britain's relations with the United States. The inability of the British government to continue repaying war debts to the Americans brought relations between the two countries to their lowest ebb since the United States Senate refused to ratify the Treaty of Versailles in 1919. The British government had other related concerns closer to home. Fears were growing in London that the French and Belgians might be helping themselves to British reparations entitlements as well as to their own. Curzon began to consider adopting a policy that would have been unthinkable six months earlier – making a formal break with France. Such a momentous step required careful consideration. It meant deciding, as another reader of the *Daily Mail* put it, who Britain's 'friends of the future were to be – France or Germany'.[73] Curzon hoped that any split with France would be temporary and that a better relationship would be established as soon as Britain's reparations interests had been protected. But this situation could not be guaranteed.

He sounded out Crewe in Paris and Grahame in Brussels about the likely long-term impact of cooling Britain's relations with France. But Curzon did not consult D'Abernon. He was well aware what his answer would have been.

Curzon's negotiations with Crewe and Grahame culminated in the publication of a note on the effect of the Ruhr crisis on British reparations payments.[74] It stated:

> Apart from the extensive material damages suffered by Great Britain, His Majesty's Government alone among the Allies are paying interest on debts incurred abroad during the war, representing a capital sum due to the United States Government of £1,000,000,000 at the present rate of exchange. They alone have been deprived in the Allied interest, of foreign securities estimated from £700,000,000 to £800,000,000 which would otherwise substantially assist in the payment of the British debt to America. Notwithstanding these gigantic burdens, Great Britain made an offer at the Paris conference of January last to forego her rights to reimbursement of her damage, and ... to treat her share of German Reparations as if they were a repayment of her Allies of their debts due to her. It would be inequitable, and it is impossible to ask the British taxpayer ... to make further sacrifices for the benefit of France and Belgium.[75]

German responses

Cuno and Stresemann, the Minister for Foreign Affairs, were so mystified by this explanation that they wondered if Curzon had been in full possession of the facts when it had been drawn up.[76] The situation was made worse because D'Abernon's reports to Curzon did not give an accurate reflection of German reactions. D'Abernon had been so pleased that the British government had finally issued a formal condemnation of French policy that he allowed his emotions to cloud his judgement. He told Curzon that the note had been well received and had done much to forge closer Anglo-German economic links.[77] It is unclear how he came to this conclusion but, nonetheless, his enthusiasm continued to grow. Confident that the German government would now be convinced of British sympathy for the German plight, D'Abernon noted in his diary that hitherto 'there had been nothing but menace and invective. Now the tone has changed to the cooing of a dove.'[78]

Stresemann was unaware that Curzon no longer trusted D'Abernon's judgement. In the autumn of 1923, negotiations began between

German industrialists and members of the *Mission Interalliée de Contrôle des Usines et des Mines* (MICUM) representing French and Belgian interests.[79] The negotiations were acrimonious and increased tension between the French and German governments. They resulted in a series of agreements that forced the German government to pay reparations at levels that it deemed to be unacceptably high.[80] It is doubtful whether D'Abernon fully understood their practical and psychological significance. He viewed them primarily as an opportunity for an economic rapprochement between France and Germany that could reduce German enthusiasm for American financial assistance, but which, if abused, could 'deliver [Stresemann] into the enemy's hands'.[81] But it was more important to D'Abernon that such an agreement did not prejudice Britain's share of reparations payments.[82] However, the Foreign Office believed that D'Abernon was allowing just such a situation to arise. Complaints that the Germans were seeking an economic alliance 'behind [Britain's] back' were rapidly dispatched to Berlin for communication to Stresemann. Curzon recalled D'Abernon to London to check that the German government was receiving 'good advice' from Britain.[83]

MICUM agreements

Curzon's lack of faith in D'Abernon became more apparent when further details of the MICUM negotiations were released in Paris and Berlin. D'Abernon reported that the German government would 'endeavour to influence negotiations in a direction favourable to [Britain's] ideas'.[84] Curzon was unimpressed and decided to reserve judgement on the terms of the proposed agreement until he had read them himself. The reason he gave was that he wished to protect German industry from any excessive demands on the part of the French. If this was Curzon's real intention, it was a curious one given his earlier instructions to D'Abernon to avoid antagonising the French.[85] D'Abernon was aware of Curzon's scepticism, but he did not interpret it as hostility to himself. Although he disliked him, D'Abernon's character sketch of Curzon suggests that he felt sorry for him.[86] He believed that in Europe Curzon was compelled to concentrate on an area of foreign policy that did not interest him and which consequently lacked clear direction.

The situation was further complicated by the increasing hostility to the MICUM agreements in Berlin. D'Abernon rapidly changed his mind about their effectiveness. Seeing them now as an exercise in French economic imperialism, he wished Curzon to give him authority to condemn them. Curzon was reluctant. D'Abernon expressed his frustration by complaining that his instructions did not go far enough to protect British interests and that they failed to recognise the severity of the situation.[87] In November 1923, he reported that British commercial interests in Germany were being undermined by the MICUM negotiations. He decided to send an authorised communication to Stresemann requesting confirmation that any agreement between Germany and the MICUM negotiations would not prejudice British interests. Stresemann agreed. D'Abernon was convinced that if Stresemann failed to honour his promise, such an action would be 'detrimental to German interests'.[88]

As it was, D'Abernon's relief was short lived since it became apparent that, in negotiating with the MICUM representatives, the German government was gradually reducing reparations payments to Britain under the terms of the Reparation (Recovery) Act. In December 1923, the London Chamber of Commerce complained that British interests were suffering at the expense of the French. Curzon was furious and instructed D'Abernon to protest at Germany's 'intolerable' treatment of Britain.[89] However, as with the MICUM negotiations, D'Abernon had felt that his instructions concerning the Reparation (Recovery) Act issue had been insufficient. He had anticipated that making payments under the terms of the Act could pose a problem to the German government and had made independent representations to the German Chancellor, Marx, on 5 December 1923. He had also clearly not been convinced by Stresemann's earlier promise – a situation that was at odds with his earlier assurances that the latter could be relied upon to keep his word.[90]

Reparation (Recovery) Act

Curzon instructed D'Abernon to make strong protests against the 'unilateral' decision to abandon the Reparation (Recovery) Act. He demanded that an 'unequivocal declaration' be made by the German government guaranteeing that British interests would be fully recognised and accorded the same importance as those of France under the MICUM agreements. He believed that such a requirement was 'so clearly reasonable' that the Germans would agree to this request.[91] However, the German government was unimpressed by the strength of British objections. Curzon learnt through Sthamer that German treatment of British interests was to be allowed to vary according to the economic circumstances of the time.[92] In this way, the German government intended to keep its options open in its commercial dealings with Britain in a way that would have a profound impact on trade relations between the two countries for the next two years. Sthamer's reports also provide a further reason for questioning whether in Berlin British and

French policies towards Germany were viewed as significantly different from one another at this time.

By the end of 1923, D'Abernon's relations with the Foreign Office had markedly deteriorated. Curzon distrusted him. Doubts about the soundness of his judgement had eroded the limited amount of influence he possessed in London. D'Abernon had become, as he was to remain for the rest of his embassy, a casualty of the pro-French emphasis in British foreign policy during the mid-1920s. He was pro-German at a time when the Foreign Office was obsessively concerned with mollifying the French. Whoever had occupied the post of ambassador to Berlin would have been confronted by the tendency of the British government to give priority to relations with France. Yet by the end of Curzon's period as Foreign Secretary, many of the problems that D'Abernon experienced in his dealings with the British government were of his own making, especially those stemming from the inconsistency of his opinions.

D'Abernon had now been in Berlin for a year longer than had initially been intended, and he was to remain there for a further three years. He owed his survival to reasons that bore little relation to his past dealings with the German government or to his role as interpreter of the complexities of the German financial situation to the Foreign Office. In the last weeks of 1923, the Baldwin government was replaced by the fragile MacDonald administration, in which the Prime Minister also occupied the post of Foreign Secretary. Ramsay MacDonald was never at ease in the company of foreign dignitaries and found the finer nuances of diplomacy tiresome. He relied on the advice of experienced diplomats such as D'Abernon. The fall of the Baldwin government also took place when the most intense efforts so far were being made to resolve the reparations question. The establishment of the Dawes and McKenna Committees ensured that American financial assistance would be forthcoming and that the European powers could turn their attention towards other issues, notably security. The relief felt by the British government at establishing an effective framework for the payment of reparations combined with the prospect of no future wars meant that past Foreign Office hostility towards D'Abernon was overlooked.

The Ruhr crisis epitomised the major problems that had existed between the Allies and Germany since the war. It demonstrated that the reparations issue was a potent political and diplomatic weapon. It also indicated that one reason for the lack of progress in commercial relations between the victors and the vanquished was continued mutual suspicion. One of the most important features of the situation was the frailty of the relationship between the Allies themselves. The crisis suggested that if this issue were not to be addressed then the entire process of pacification and reconstruction, which every country desired, would be undermined. It is thus more difficult to see the events of the following years as a triumph for the Allies. The introduction of American financial aid suggested among other things that the European powers were incapable of resolving Europe's financial problems on their own. There were therefore broader reasons explaining Britain's diplomatic position. The British government's obsession with the maintenance of the *Entente Cordiale* made D'Abernon's task difficult and demoralising. Yet D'Abernon assumed that his opinions and recommendations carried so much weight in London that they would automatically be acted upon. He possessed an ebullient personality and this led him to express his views passionately and without reserve – an approach that was alien to the very formal and correct Curzon. Yet D'Abernon seemed surprised and even shocked when he encountered his own characteristics in others, particularly in the German politicians and financial experts with whom he came into contact. D'Abernon's complex relationship with the Germans provides additional evidence of the often contradictory opinions he expressed. As it was, the diplomatic crisis surrounding the occupation of the Ruhr and the creation of a large-scale programme of American financial assistance to Germany under the Dawes Plan in 1924 was to prove a watershed in D'Abernon's embassy.

4
The Challenge of the United States, 1922–24

The problems that D'Abernon faced as a result of the United States' involvement in European affairs have not received any historical attention. Within the wider context of American relations with Europe in the early 1920s, scholars remain divided about whether the United States government did pursue a policy of isolationism after the First World War, or whether American businessmen and financial experts seized the opportunity to find new markets in Europe.[1] D'Abernon himself believed the latter to be the case.[2] Some historians have taken a more sympathetic view of American motives, suggesting that the United States only became involved in European affairs when it became apparent that the Allies would not receive adequate reparations payments from Germany.[3] But D'Abernon's experiences in Berlin reveal little evidence of such American loyalty to the Allies. For example, France owed the American government considerable sums in war debts and it was in American interests to ensure that the French economy was strong enough to make restitution. An American businessman had told D'Abernon in the summer of 1922 that,

> the only way to bring the French to reason is to compel them to raise money. The more the USA force them to pay, the more they will realise that they have got to get credit somewhere, and in order to obtain credit they must solve reparation. Unless we press our claim there is no chance of their seeing reason.[4]

French payments to the United States, however, could only be guaranteed if France received adequate reparations from Germany. It would only be possible for the German government to make these payments if the German economy was revived and a long-term solution to the reparations problem was found. A programme of regeneration and reconstruction was to come from the American government under the terms of the Dawes Plan. Although monies were directed towards Germany, it was the French and ultimately themselves whom the Americans most intended to benefit.

British attitudes towards the United States

In the period between the Paris Peace Conference and the establishment of the Dawes Committee in 1923, the British government frequently appeared hostile towards American involvement in European affairs. As indicated earlier, this view was not shared by the German governments of the period. In Berlin, considerable energy was devoted to resuming diplomatic relations with the United States in order that American financial assistance could be secured to help rebuild the German economy. After the establishment of the Dawes Committee, the situation was almost reversed. The British government, relieved that the reparations question was now apparently resolved, welcomed American financial assistance, while in Berlin, the Germans became sceptical about the motives behind British, French and American financial and commercial proposals.[5] These changes of attitude had a significant effect on D'Abernon's position in Berlin as his hopes for a solution to the reparations question brokered by the European powers dwindled. He also found that his views on this matter became increasingly out of kilter with those of the British government after the MacDonald administration took office in January 1924. Until then, D'Abernon's views on an American role in European affairs had been similar to those of the Foreign Office. The American government was viewed with some hostility because of its uncompromising attitude towards Britain regarding the repayment of war debts. Such an attitude, it was believed, was evidence of American desires to dominate and direct European economic affairs and the diplomacy that went with them.[6] The diplomatic tension between the two countries had been further aggravated as a result of wrangles over naval superiority. These indicated many of the wider differences between British and American perceptions of the world. The British believed that their pre-war role as the dominant naval power in the world provided a mandate for Britannia still to rule the waves. The Americans argued that a basis for involvement in world affairs should be created through a more formal equality between the two powers in maritime affairs – one that recognised that the United States now occupied a position as an international power at least as important as Britain.[7]

Tension was reduced following the Washington Naval Conference of 1921–22, but the debate about Britain's role in world affairs coloured many areas of Anglo-American relations in the early 1920s.[8] MacDonald was little concerned about such issues of grand strategy. Essentially a pragmatist, he had few qualms about the creation of a more influential role for the United States in Europe. His priority was to stabilise European diplomacy by improving Britain's relations with France so that a basis could be created for a programme of large-scale American loans to break the deadlock in the reparations negotiations.

For his part, Lloyd George had been determined that any American involvement in European affairs should be on as small a scale as possible and that it should have a very specific brief. The British government resented the American government's failure to ratify the Treaty of Versailles, its refusal to join the League of Nations and its adoption of an intransigent attitude towards the repayment of British war debts. Consequently, Lloyd George advised his Cabinet colleagues not to 'cringe' under the pressure of growing American import tariffs on British goods.[9] The subsequent dispatch of the Balfour Note, and the uneasy détente of the summer of 1923 regarding the repayment of British debts to the United States left Lloyd George unrepentant. In the spring of 1923, several months after his fall from office, he told D'Abernon:

> They may criticise my Government as much as they like, but as long as we were in office, we prevented the Turks from going to Constantinople, the French from going into the Ruhr, and the American hand from coming into our till. Now they have all got there.[10]

D'Abernon's views on Anglo-German relations and towards American involvement in European affairs reflected this philosophy. Like Lloyd George, he conceded that, in the absence of a European solution to the reparations problem, American aid provided the only means of solving Germany's ever-worsening economic problems. At the same time, he was anxious that American influence in Germany should not be so great that the German government's relationship with Britain suffered. When the Committees of Experts were established in 1923, D'Abernon did not believe that the special relationship that he thought existed between the British and German governments would be affected. But once again, he overestimated the degree of influence that he had been able to wield in Berlin and misjudged the extent of German enthusiasm for American financial assistance. This misjudgement was to have a profound impact on his attitude towards an American 'presence' in Germany and towards the development of Anglo-German relations.

American involvement in German commerce

In the months leading up to the reinstatement of diplomatic relations between Germany and the United States in the spring of 1922, D'Abernon displayed misgivings about what appeared to be growing levels of American commercial activity in Berlin. In the spring of 1921, he reported that von Simons, the German Minister for Foreign Affairs, had been wilfully misled by a 'number of irresponsible [American] businessmen', who had promised many things to the German government but who had actually produced little. What was worse, the German government assumed 'that any American advice was worth listening to simply because it [was] American'.[11] His full scorn was confined to his diary, where he noted:

> The close sympathy and instinctive understanding between Americans and Germans is difficult to analyse and explain. The German accepts an American argument far more readily than that of a European. He will find the French too logical and precise, the Englishman too vague and instinctive, the Italian too subtle and ingenious, the Russian too insincere. The American he at once finds practical and convincing. His own thoroughness reconciles him to the exhaustive methods usually applied to American autobiography, and he endures without anaesthetic the tale of the corner block that was bought for five dollars by a newsboy or a druggist's assistant, and is now worth several millions of dollars.[12]

At this time, D'Abernon believed that American involvement in German affairs was unrestrained and uncontrollable because of the unofficial nature of the contact made necessary by the continued absence of formal diplomatic relations between the two countries. Nevertheless, he believed that his own attempts to secure good relations between the British and German governments had hitherto been highly successful. Consequently, he anticipated that the American experts in Berlin would provide a mere distraction from the pursuit of what he thought to be the German government's more important relationship with Britain. In the autumn of 1921, he wrote that 'the contribution on the part of America will, it is hoped, confirm and reinforce the reasonable and ... magnanimous attitude which Germany has now learnt to expect from England'.[13]

By the end of 1921, it had become clear that the German government was considering placing diplomatic relations with the United States on a more formal footing. Initially, D'Abernon predicted that such an occurrence would not damage Britain's relationship with Germany. He wrote:

> It is roughly true to say that the hope of Germany lies in the development of friendly relations with England and America. To some extent America has belied expectation, so that the centre of expectation is more than ever London ... It was appreciated that England took the broader view of the situation, and the sympathies of the people inclined more towards her.[14]

When full diplomatic relations between the United States and Germany were reinstated in February 1922, D'Abernon's views on the impact of this development on Britain's relations with Germany remained unchanged. He even went so far as to comment – for reasons that are less than clear – that the nature of the contact between the two countries would enable American ambitions in Germany to be closely monitored by Britain. He envisaged the creation of an Anglo-American partnership to oversee German recovery; a partnership in which he assumed that Britain would take the leading role. To this end, he cultivated a good relationship with his American opposite number in Berlin, Alanson Houghton, who was also a financial expert.[15] In the main, the two men enjoyed a cordial relationship.[16] Each believed that European political reconstruction and economic recovery depended upon a financially sound answer to the German reparations question and reform of the German taxation system.[17] D'Abernon was convinced that they agreed on most issues relating to the German financial position. He was in no doubt about Houghton's potential as a source of advice, later observing that Germany's financial problems 'would have remained inoperative if the USA had not been represented during the critical post-war period by men of unusual authority, and peculiarly in touch and sympathy with German life'.[18]

Houghton had a different view of their relationship. While ambassador to London in the late 1920s, he revealed that he had not shared D'Abernon's enthusiasm for creating an Anglo-American partnership to aid German economic recovery or, indeed, for any other purpose. Houghton not only believed that such an idea was impractical, he was also convinced that the consequences of such a plan being put into operation could be catastrophic. He wrote:

> To bring the English-speaking peoples into an armed and exclusive group, prepared if need be to enforce its collective will by force, would, if it were possible, tend neither to promote peace nor to assure our mutual security. Its result would be to unite all the rest of the world against us ... It would turn this earth of ours once again into an armed camp. In the end, precisely what we sought to avoid – a war – would result.[19]

On occasions, the different agendas of the British and American governments in Germany led to friction. D'Abernon appears to have been curiously unaware of this. In August 1922, he noted a strange conversation between himself and Houghton in his diary:

> Met the American Ambassador this afternoon, who said, 'I know a great many things; how much do you know?' But I could not get from him what the deuce it was. He said, 'We are almost at war'; but whether he meant America and England, or France and Germany, or some other complication, I have no idea.[20]

At this point, he abandons the subject and moves on. There are no references in his dispatches or in subsequent diary entries that clarify the meaning of the conversation, but it is noticeable that he mentioned Britain and the United States as among the possible antagonists. D'Abernon's failure to pursue the matter further may have stemmed from an unwillingness to recognise that the objectives behind British and American diplomacy in Germany were not identical. The dialogues between D'Abernon and Houghton indicated that it was the British who were reliant on significant American support to secure a future in Germany's long-term financial rehabilitation, not vice versa.

German reactions

The German government saw little practical purpose in discussing a long-term plan for German recovery with Britain. The inability of the British and French governments to solve the reparations question had fuelled German suspicions of a possible Anglo-French agenda to keep Germany economically weak. Bergmann's conversations with D'Abernon at the Brussels conference had suggested that the Allies were more concerned with furthering their own interests than finding a solution to the reparations problem. Much to his chagrin, D'Abernon noted that Wirth, the German Chancellor, continued 'inexplicably' to believe that British and French differences of opinion over the enforcement of the Treaty of Versailles were, 'usually settled at [the Germans'] expense'.[21] German scepticism was not confined to government ministers. A year after the Brussels conference, the *Vossische Zeitung* claimed that 'England carries on an exclusively English policy and is moved neither by sympathy nor antipathy to any foreign country'.[22]

German doubts about the unbiased nature of British advice had been reinforced in the spring of 1921. The British and French governments had presented the German government with an ultimatum threatening the use of military sanctions should there be any default in reparations payments. It created the impression in Berlin that the Allies intended to adopt an uncompromising attitude towards the collection of reparations and that, as a result, little sympathy would be given to German claims of hardship. Von Simons thought it a matter not only of financial expediency but also of national pride to find an alternative source of foreign revenue. He told D'Abernon that the 're-establishment of international economic life' could only be achieved through a policy of 'peaceful co-operation and agreement' with the American government.[23]

Von Simons made a series of pleas for American assistance in the spring of 1921. They received a frosty response in Washington because of the absence of formal diplomatic relations between the two countries at the time, although future assistance was not ruled out.[24] D'Abernon's reaction to the situation reinforced the German interpretation of Allied attitudes towards Germany. He later accused the American government of betraying the trust of the Germans and saw American financial advisers as a corrupting influence on the German government.[25] Yet his assessment of the situation contained contradictions and inconsistencies. In the summer of 1921, D'Abernon had told the King that the American government had adopted a 'very negative' attitude towards offering financial assistance to Germany.[26] But when writing up the comparable period for his Annual Report six months later, he reported that American financial experts had been 'favourably impressed' by the German government and had 'prophesied a rapid recovery and spoke loudly of American assistance'.[27] D'Abernon habitually presented copies of his Annual Report to the German government. Consequently, the Germans would have been well aware of the lack of clarity of D'Abernon's comments and the lack of correlation between his account and the actual course of events.

By reinstating diplomatic relations with the United States, the German government did not simply see the opportunity to gain access to apparently unlimited financial resources. It was believed in Berlin that the American government's foreign policy was based on the practical considerations of the post-war world rather than determined by the outdated, imperial *raison d'être* that underpinned British policy.[28] This was reflected in the different relationships with the German government enjoyed by Houghton and D'Abernon. The former was respected by the German government because of the directness of his approach and because his government's policy towards Germany was thought to be open and honest and lacked a hidden agenda. The United States was perceived by the Germans as a power entirely divorced from the political and economic tensions that existed in Europe.[29] By contrast, the conferences held in Brussels and elsewhere led the British government to be regarded as too bound to France to be able to develop an objective policy towards Germany. Likewise, the British were tainted by association with the diktat peace in 1919, from which the United States had made a tactical withdrawal. Memories also lingered about the liberal influence of the American government at the Paris Peace Conference in the person of Woodrow Wilson and the hoped-for peace settlement based on his unrealistically utopian ideas. However, a chance to secure American aid directly to Germany had now been created. This enabled the German government to formulate a policy towards the American government that led to a closer and more profitable relationship than that currently enjoyed with the British and French.

This point was not lost on Walther Rathenau, the German Minister for Foreign Affairs, who was responsible for a number of key diplomatic initiatives in the spring of 1922.[30] While attending the Genoa conference, Rathenau wrote that 'never before has a nation held the fate of a continent so inescapably in its hands as does America at this moment'.[31] He believed that closer economic cooperation between Germany and the United States could be secured if a German diplomat with a strong financial background was dispatched as ambassador to Washington. Rathenau's candidate was Wiedfeldt, a director of the Krupp works.[32] D'Abernon was sceptical about this choice, preferring a diplomat with no specialist knowledge of financial affairs. It is difficult to understand that he would not have recognised the advantages for the German government of being represented in Washington by an ambassador with a commercial background, especially as the reparations issue lay at the heart of American diplomatic relations with the Allies and Germany. Despite the stark economic realities of the situation, he continued to cling onto the idea that the reparations question was essentially a European problem that should be resolved with minimal involvement from the United States. Not surprisingly, the German government paid little heed to D'Abernon's views. Wiedfeldt's appointment was confirmed in March 1922 and lasted until January 1925. His embassy was to play a decisive role in establishing a strong basis for German commercial relations with the United States.[33]

The appointment of Wiedfeldt fuelled the enthusiasm of a growing number of American financial experts and politicians for greater economic involvement in Europe. The best known was the Secretary of State, Charles Evans Hughes, who had long believed that isolationism was impractical and that the poor state of Europe's economy made American financial assistance desirable and potentially lucrative. In a speech at Newhaven on 29 December 1922, he suggested that the best way to solve the reparations crisis was through the establishment of an international committee of financial experts. Hughes urged the statesmen of Europe to provide 'a financial plan by which immediate results can be obtained'. If they were unable to do so on their own, they should call upon the assistance of American experts who could 'point the way to a solution'.[34] In the autumn of 1923, two committees were established by the Reparation Commission broadly along the lines described in Hughes' speech.[35] The first, under the chairmanship of the American financier, Charles Dawes, examined the strength of the German economy and devised a reparations payment scheme; while the second, chaired by the former British Chancellor of the Exchequer, Sir Reginald McKenna, made an assessment of the size and range of Germany's foreign assets.

Resolving Allied tensions

The deliberations of the British, French and Belgian members of the Dawes Committee reflected the tensions and divisions that had hitherto undermined European attempts to find a solution to the reparations question.[36] Yet, unlike the earlier reparations conferences, the discussions did not collapse. With the safety net of American financial assistance now in place, the European Allies were able to agree a common agenda for reparations payments. The focus for discussion was no longer on what divided national interests, but how Europe as a whole could benefit from American loans.[37] One of the main advantages to the British government was the possibility of improving relations with France. The tensions in Anglo-French diplomacy created by the Ruhr crisis were now partly set to one side. The financial resources available to the American government made it expedient for national pride to be swallowed and national differences played down. The British and French were confident that the Dawes Plan provided a solution to one of the most complex and controversial problem areas in European affairs since the war. Much of the credit for the revitalisation of Anglo-French relations was due to the new British Prime Minister, Ramsay MacDonald. His strong pro-American sympathies combined with a good relationship with his French opposite number, Herriot, brought about a change of emphasis in official British attitudes towards the United States.[38] In the spring of 1924, MacDonald told Herriot:

> We must assure our well-being, but we will work also to resolve the great moral problems of the peace of the world. Lets us therefore settle first the question of the Dawes Report; then we will go on to that of inter-Allied debts, then to the problem of security, and then we will try to remove from Europe the risks of war which threaten it.[39]

MacDonald viewed the advent of American aid as a means of freeing the European Allies from the diplomatic tensions that the reparations negotiations had created and as an opportunity to establish a framework for future British foreign activity in other areas of European affairs.[40] This, he believed, would bring to an end what he termed the 'hand to mouth' diplomacy of the years since the war.[41] His talks with Herriot during the spring and summer of 1924 emphasised the need for unity between British and French foreign policy and the consequent benefits if that closeness were maintained.[42]

In the spring of 1924, D'Abernon therefore found himself in the position of being a diplomatic representative of a government that liaised very closely with the French and which was headed by a Prime Minister with diametrically opposite views to his own on American involvement in European affairs. D'Abernon liked MacDonald personally, but hoped that his government would soon be replaced by one with views on foreign policy more in tune with his own.[43] This, he believed, was likely to come about sooner rather than later since the minority MacDonald administration had a shaky grasp on power. D'Abernon nevertheless felt obliged to remain in Berlin. This was due in no small part to the new Prime Minister's flattering reliance on senior diplomats who had a greater knowledge of the finer nuances of European diplomacy than himself. For the ten months that the MacDonald administration existed, the Diplomatic Service was given a freedom of action and a degree of responsibility for conducting British foreign policy unprecedented since the war. At no point during his embassy did D'Abernon have better opportunity to develop a good relationship with the Foreign Office. Yet despite such favourable omens, he continued to find himself confronted by the pro-French bias of British foreign policy. The breakthrough that he hoped for that would then lead to more public statements in London of support for German concerns about reparations and security was not forthcoming. MacDonald may have listened to D'Abernon's advice, but he did not always heed it. There is little to suggest that D'Abernon believed that he was in a position to persuade MacDonald of the validity of his views. He noted in his character sketch of MacDonald that in the latter's performance as Foreign Secretary, 'there was no palpable or obvious break with tradition. One Minister of Foreign Affairs had succeeded another.'[44] Continuity had, unfortunately, been maintained.

The Dawes Plan

The creation of the Dawes Plan forced D'Abernon to re-evaluate his views on the future of Anglo-German relations. He refused to believe that a British financial and commercial role in German affairs had been made redundant by the injection of American loans. While he had seen Britain acting as a buffer against the excessive demands of French extremism during the early years of his embassy, from the spring of 1924 he believed that this sense of protection should be extended to include a monitoring of American policies towards Germany.[45] He prided himself on his close relationship with Stresemann and was pleased that the Germans were apparently in favour of seeking specifically British guarantees that the findings of the Dawes Report would not be imposed in a draconian manner.[46]

MacDonald did not share D'Abernon's optimism. He believed that any attempt by Britain to champion the German cause too vigorously would leave his government open to French and American accusations of promoting British interests above those of the rest of the Allies. He instructed D'Abernon not to discuss the minutiae of the Dawes Report with the German government until the Reparation Commission had considered it. He thought that the German government should be made to adopt an attitude of 'expectant reserve' – to adopt a patient and cooperative attitude towards relations with the Allies in the knowledge that a final plan to solve the reparations problem was imminent.[47] These comments by MacDonald were similar to those made by Curzon during the early months of the Ruhr crisis, when the latter had feared that Britain was in danger of upsetting the French by adopting a high profile in German affairs. It was to prove extremely difficult for D'Abernon to refrain from discussing the findings of the Dawes Committee, not least since the German government sent communications to him on an almost daily basis. He was summoned to the *Auswärtiges Amt* three times in one week alone to discuss the subject.[48] Yet, despite the strength of his personal views, he was obliged to comply with the general attitude that underpinned much of British policy towards Europe – one that appeared to be based increasingly on fear of supposed allies.

D'Abernon's concerns about the consequences to Anglo-German relations of a prominent American role in German affairs were reflected in his cool reception of the Dawes Plan. He thought it was all very well for a scheme to be devised for Germany's financial recovery, but he was amazed that 'any sane person' could expect this to occur 'while the patient [was] bleeding from so many pores'. D'Abernon began to accumulate information on German reactions to the Dawes Report. He was particularly incensed by the phrase within the report that the payment totals comprised 'all amounts for which Germany may be liable to the Allied and Associated Powers' for the payment of reparations and the costs of the armies of occupation. D'Abernon recommended that the German government should withhold acceptance of the report until this matter had been resolved. Prevented from negotiating with the German government himself, he instructed Henry Finlayson, the Financial Adviser to the British Embassy in Berlin, to prepare a memorandum on the feasibility of such a proposal.[49] D'Abernon believed that Finlayson's findings provided a damning indictment of Allied policy towards Germany and that German caution in relation to the implementation of the Dawes Report 'might be considered to justify criticism as to the attitude in the past of Germany's creditors'.[50]

Once again MacDonald did not share D'Abernon's views. He sent instructions to the effect that while Britain appreciated the problems that the Germans faced in bringing about an acceptance of the report, insistence on an immediate abandonment of French economic sanctions in Germany would further inflame France. MacDonald thought it both 'useless and unwise' for the German government to delay accepting the report because the British government intended to ensure its speedy execution. MacDonald urged D'Abernon to use 'all the authority at [his] command' to persuade the Germans of the error of their ways.[51]

German reservations

The sense of urgency and the need for immediate German action that MacDonald's dispatches often conveyed contributed to growing German reservations about Allied motives for promoting American financial aid to Germany. D'Abernon thus found himself a target of German criticism that centred on the ambiguity of his views and on doubts about whether he was sending accurate reports to London about the German government's opinions and policies. In the spring and summer of 1924, von Schubert, the head of Department III of the *Auswärtiges Amt*, wondered whether D'Abernon was doing enough to secure British protection of German interests at a time when the French seemed about to demand further reparations payments through the Reparation Commission.[52] In the past, D'Abernon had made no secret of his hostility to French policy in this regard, yet in the spring of 1924 he began to urge the German government to take a more sympathetic view of French needs. He now appeared to reject any link between the implementation of the Dawes Plan, the work of a French-dominated Reparation Commission, American loans to Germany and French desires to secure rapid and full reparations payments.[53]

A reason for this apparent contradiction is that D'Abernon was simply following instructions. His comments reflected MacDonald's emphasis on the French role in European affairs, despite D'Abernon's own mistrust of the motives of French politicians and the conduct of the Reparation Commission.[54] Yet this does not explain the activities he was also engaged in at this juncture, namely to secure closer British economic ties with Germany. The future of Anglo-German commercial relations provided the key to D'Abernon's thinking. He believed that the Germans were devoting too much time to identifying Allied plots against Germany and not enough to redefining Germany's relationship with Britain. Ironically, the lack of clarity of British policy helped fuel the very German fears that D'Abernon was attempting to dispel.

D'Abernon's relationship with von Schubert deteriorated rapidly.[55] He was quoted figures by the latter, calculated by the Reparation Commission, which suggested that, on the matter of Germany's capacity to pay reparations, the Dawes Plan was completely unworkable. Von Schubert anticipated that only when the question of German financial and economic unity had been resolved and the evacuation of the Ruhr had taken place could a complete review of Germany's capacity to pay be carried out. He insisted that, as a demonstration of Allied good faith, the French government should lift economic sanctions in the

Rhineland. For his part, D'Abernon believed that the Germans were creating too many obstacles to acceptance of the Dawes Report and that to make such conditions was 'asking too much of the French'. He advised that the report should be accepted unconditionally, stressing that the finer points of detail could be discussed at a later date. Von Schubert was not reassured. He did not think it unreasonable for the Allies to make comparable gestures, but agreed that the Dawes Report in its present form would be accepted by the German government only because 'no other basis' existed.[56]

When MacDonald and Herriot did finally agree to make concessions to Germany – in two protocols concluded in June and July 1924 – von Schubert did not revise his opinion about Allied motives. The protocols stated that the Ruhr question would not be debated so that complete attention could be given to discussion of the Dawes Report.[57] Von Schubert resented the fact that two senior Allied statesmen had discussed German affairs without German interests being represented. He saw this as evidence of an Anglo-French conspiracy to impose a settlement of the reparations question based on the Dawes Report. D'Abernon attempted to convince von Schubert that the protocols were very favourable to Germany but the latter maintained his objections. Von Schubert had hoped that the negotiations in Paris would result in a more protective Allied attitude towards Germany. He believed that the protective 'cloak' (*Mantel*) of Allied economic assistance had been exchanged for a 'straitjacket' (*Zwangsjacke*) and that the worst fears of the German government had now been realised. He was firmly of the conviction that the Dawes Report was to be imposed as a diktat on Germany in the same way as the Treaty of Versailles had been.[58] If the Dawes Report were to be implemented, Germany would be pushed to the brink of yet another serious economic crisis. Von Schubert criticised D'Abernon for not persuading the British government to take a stand in protecting German interests from the excesses of the French.

The reluctance of the MacDonald government to protect the interests of its German counterpart was not entirely due to the pro-French bias of British foreign policy. The impression received in London of German policy remained confused since D'Abernon's reports were sometimes incomplete and occasionally inaccurate. In reporting German reactions to the second Anglo-French protocol, he told MacDonald that it had been well received in Berlin and that 'no sensible person' regarded it as anything other than beneficial.[59] There are no records in the Foreign Office archives or in D'Abernon's diary of his meetings with von Schubert at the time.[60] Why D'Abernon did not communicate the full text and mood of these meetings and why he dismissed their significance is not clear. It is possible that von Schubert disagreed with him. The German records show that these differences of opinion were quite strong. D'Abernon would thus have been forced to concede that his influence over an important architect of German foreign policy was not as great as the Foreign Office hoped.

Von Schubert's views reflected those of the majority of the German government. Stresemann believed that, now that financial aid had been secured, Germany should be able to look forward to a more equal role in international affairs with the Allies as well as possible revisions of the Treaty of Versailles.[61] He believed that Germany's weak position in European diplomacy after the war could only be strengthened if the Allies were prepared to give equal weight to the German negotiating position. Stresemann believed that it would be to Germany's advantage to cultivate diplomatic relations because American financial resources were crucial to the revival of the economies of Europe.[62] What was more, American manufacturing industries faced overproduction and had a strong interest in the revival of European markets.[63] He was heartened that the MacDonald-Herriot protocols seemed to indicate that notice had been taken of German calls for a reciprocal gesture by the Allies in response to German agreement to the Dawes Report.[64] The willingness of the Allies to create a timetable for the evacuation of the Ruhr was regarded by Stresemann as a major concession. The resulting rise in his domestic standing was now combined with pressure to ensure that the timetable for withdrawal should be agreed as soon as possible. Stresemann's conversations with D'Abernon in the summer of 1924 showed confidence that he could now put forward his own agenda regarding relations with the Allies. By July 1924, Stresemann believed that his government was in a position to insist that German economic unity be restored within fifteen days of the Reichstag passing the necessary legislation for the implementation of the Dawes Report. In addition, a date for the evacuation of the Ruhr should be concluded. He told D'Abernon that, unless these conditions were met, his government would probably be forced to resign. In such an eventuality, Germany would be plunged into a political crisis that would possibly damage her diplomatic relations with the Allies.[65]

MacDonald and Herriot recognised that the German government should be put on an equal footing with the Allies in future negotiations over reparations and other issues relating to the implementation of the Treaty of Versailles. The willingness to cooperate with the Germans revealed by the Anglo-French protocols was underlined in the late summer of 1924 at the London conference, which concerned itself with the operation of the Dawes Report. A delegation of German diplomats and financial experts of the same size as that to be sent by the British and French governments should be dispatched to London. Stresemann regarded this as Allied recognition that Germany had a right to an equal role in the negotiations. Von Schubert's reaction was more guarded but was nevertheless favourable. He regarded a German presence in London as an insurance measure should the Allies attempt to adopt an unyielding attitude towards Germany.[66]

The way forward?

During the spring and summer of 1924, therefore, the potential existed for unprecedented cooperation between Germany and the Allies. The British and French governments appeared willing to detach themselves from previous prejudices concerning Germany. The most promising framework to date for a solution to the reparations question had been created and was almost in place. This was what D'Abernon had striven for for four years: it should have represented the high point of his embassy. Yet he did not feel a sense of achievement, but one of only half-hearted acceptance of the situation. He was a man still torn between his long-held beliefs concerning Britain's rightful role in the world and a reluctant acceptance of the economic realities of the post-war era. In March 1924, he had written: 'Today Europe is so Americanised that the old differences are vanishing and American opinion will more often be justified.'[67]

But it is D'Abernon's views on a German presence at the London conference that best illustrate the conflict inside his mind. He told MacDonald that it would be foolish for the British and French governments to invite a German delegation to attend since experience had shown that conferences of this type proceeded more rapidly without German interruptions.[68] Once again, he gave high priority to improving his own relationship with the German government. He hoped that if the German delegation were excluded from what was to be the most detailed consideration of German economic and commercial potential since the Paris Peace Conference, the German government would turn to him as a source of information about the proceedings. D'Abernon thought this a likely outcome because he was convinced that von Schubert attached great importance to a good relationship with him.[69] At the same time, however, D'Abernon was anxious that Germany should become fully integrated into European affairs on an equal footing with the Allies. He believed that the Dawes Plan had created a financial basis from which to resolve the reparations question and to accelerate German economic recovery. He therefore decided to tell Stresemann that the British and French governments would be mistaken in excluding a German delegation.[70] In addition, he recognised that advice to the contrary would be too controversial to be acceptable in Berlin.

A conversation on 14 July 1924 between D'Abernon and von Maltzan, State Secretary at the *Auswärtiges Amt*, confirms many of these points but suggests that the ambassador's concerns were not confined to issues relating to Britain's future role in German affairs. He now feared that the conduct of European diplomacy had become too dominated by financial experts who had little understanding of traditional methods of conducting diplomacy. Given his earlier views on the need for diplomats to have a knowledge of commercial affairs as a fundamental criterion for their deployment, D'Abernon's views in the summer of 1924 appear to reflect a change of heart. His statement in 1920 had been founded on the belief that diplomacy based on a sound knowledge of commercial affairs would be conducted in a world economy dominated by Britain and provide a means of reinforcing Britain's status as an imperial power. When Britain's supersession by the United States as the world's banker was enshrined all too finally in the Dawes Report, D'Abernon became less enamoured of this idea. Often with a tendency towards the melodramatic, he wrote of how the absence of a role for traditional diplomats meant that American infiltration of European affairs would now proceed unchecked. In order to 'guard against such an eventuality' at the London conference, D'Abernon recommended that the German delegation should be on the lookout for any bullying tactics that might be deployed by the American government. To provide an added insurance against this, he recommended that the German delegation should contain a large contingent of 'traditional' diplomats and that more effort should be made to reinforce the traditional German diplomatic lines of communication with France (through von Hoesch) and Britain (through Sthamer).[71] D'Abernon made no reference to reinforcing German diplomatic contact with the United States through Wiedfeldt. In the remaining years of his embassy, he would attempt to redefine Germany's relations with the major European powers, while, at the same time, limiting American influence as far as possible to financial and commercial affairs.

Acceptance of the Dawes Plan indicated that the British and French governments were incapable of solving Europe's economic problems unaided. The plan made Germany's economic problems a major issue of world as well as European diplomacy, while economic links between Europe and the United States also carried with them the possibility of future political ties. The British and French governments were now compelled to consider, for the first time since the Paris Peace Conference, how their relationship would be affected should the pace and direction of European diplomacy be influenced by a non-European power. Consolidating a position as a leading member of the League of Nations, an organisation of which the United States was not a member, provided an alternative means of asserting British authority in international diplomacy. Much of the original animus against American involvement in European affairs expressed by Lloyd George and others had been transformed into a desire to develop a specific and exclusively British area of activity that would exist in harmony with American interests. D'Abernon shared this wish to redefine Britain's role in international diplomacy. He nevertheless continued to believe that Britain could justify and demand a leading role in world affairs as a result of her status as an imperial power. As late as November 1924, after the London conference had ratified the Dawes Plan, D'Abernon wrote: 'I should esteem American influence here as at least equal to our own. Together we should have a decisive influence on German action.'[72] At this juncture, D'Abernon saw the future of Anglo-German relations developing in two directions. He considered the securing of a long-term commercial agreement between Britain and Germany to be of paramount importance. Once this had been achieved, the British government's attention should be focused on the second and much larger issue of Germany's future role in international affairs – security and membership of the League of Nations.

5
The Anglo-German Commercial Agreement, 1924–25

D'Abernon's response to American involvement in German affairs illustrates the complicated relationship between economics and diplomacy in Europe in the early 1920s. The shift in the economic balance of power towards the United States left many questions about Britain's role in the regeneration of Germany and the rest of Europe unanswered. Since the Dawes Plan had secured an American role in German affairs, D'Abernon was anxious to create an equally close bond between Britain and Germany. He believed that the imminent expiry of a commercial clause of the Treaty of Versailles guaranteeing most favoured nation treatment for Allied goods in Germany provided an opportunity to achieve this objective.[1] However, he encountered opposition in London as developing closer commercial relations with Germany was not a priority of the British government. In contrast, the German government pursued the negotiation of the Anglo-German Commercial Agreement with great vigour and enthusiasm. D'Abernon was disconcerted by the independence of action displayed by the German government in seeking new allies to secure Germany's future in the post-war world. He thought it necessary to persuade the Germans that there was a special bond with Britain that could exist alongside a close German relationship with the United States. Nevertheless, he continued to overestimate German enthusiasm for British advice and assistance, while the government in Berlin increasingly felt that the diplomatic agenda had moved away from commercial affairs towards the consideration of other issues, particularly security.

D'Abernon's ideas about the operation of economic principles continued to be rooted in the belief that the production of goods and services creates the demand for goods of at least an equal value. They had much in common with those of the American economist, J.W. Angell, who had criticised those who advocated the paralysis of German industry as a means of ensuring Germany's military weakness.[2] A supporter of Keynes, Angell believed that, by 1929, European peace had been sufficiently guaranteed and that 'the Germany of today is very far from being the industrial and commercial Juggernaut which her competitors have feared'.[3] D'Abernon thought that governments should remain neutral influences on the economy, ensuring that expenditure was matched by revenue.[4] Nevertheless, he did concede that by 1924 he was finding it increasingly difficult to apply such a model to the German situation. The pre-1914 international monetary mechanism was essentially an exchange system, the primary purpose of which was to preserve international financial stability even at the expense of domestic economic equilibrium. The fragility of the post-war European economies, particularly among the defeated powers, meant that economic policies became more geared towards the preservation of domestic rather than international stability. As the economies of the former Central Powers developed in the 1920s, nationalism rather than internationalism prevailed and so influenced the basis for commercial negotiations with other countries. In London, the Treasury became more sympathetic to Keynes's view than those who continued to believe that Britain was the world's foremost commercial nation.[5]

Background

In 1914, Germany had possessed one of the most rapidly expanding economies in Europe. The process of industrialisation that had taken place since 1870 had transformed the German economy out of all recognition. By the first decade of the twentieth century, German imports exceeded those of Britain, France and the United States. After the First World War, despite the problems associated with reparations payments and currency depreciation, Germany's commercial infrastructure remained largely intact.[6] This has led some historians to question the validity of claims made by the German government in the early 1920s that it was unable to afford reparation payments.[7] The preservation of the highly developed pre-war infrastructure for German commercial relations was also important because it was controlled during the Weimar era by politicians who were familiar with its operation – self-made businessmen.[8] If the massive depreciation of the currency had not taken place between 1921 and 1923, there would have been little reason why the German commercial infrastructure could not have sustained a period of rapid growth.[9] When American loans established a framework to solve the worst of Germany's economic problems, a new opportunity existed for the Germans to improve commercial relations with other countries. Thus the German negotiating position vis-à-vis Britain, as well as other countries, was one of strength rather than weakness – a position further enhanced by the willingness of politicians such as MacDonald and Herriot to regard Germany as a power which should have negotiating rights comparable to those of their own countries. This openness towards Germany had been less of a feature of Allied relations with Germany in the past and may therefore have contributed to German reluctance to pursue a more vigorous commercial policy between 1918 and 1924.

Britain's commercial relations with Germany were dictated by four pieces of legislation, and finally, in 1924, by a bilateral agreement.[10] The Trading with the Enemy Amendment Act, passed in the year of the Armistice, regulated commercial contact between Britain and the Central Powers. It imposed strict controls on the activities of German banks and insurance companies operating in Britain and was passed with the recommendation that it should remain in operation for a minimum of five years. Germans working in Britain were subject to the Non-Ferrous Metal Industry Act also passed in 1918, which prohibited the trading in non-ferrous commodities and metallic ores for a period of five years without a licence from the Board of Trade. German commercial contact with Britain suffered further under the anti-dumping provisions of Part II of the Safeguarding Act of 1921, whose operation was triggered by the rapid depreciation of the value of the mark, and which was designed to safeguard the price of imported goods.[11] In theory this Act applied to all German imports into Britain, but it was seldom used except to regulate the traffic of luxury items. All German imports were also subject to a 26 per cent duty levied under the terms of the Reparation (Recovery) Act of 1921.[12] This was intended to guarantee the protection of British commercial interests in Germany and to extract reparations. Tariffs were recoverable by German exporters directly from the German government but only in paper currency.[13] Many of these pieces of legislation were passed by the government to appease powerful industrial and commercial lobbyists but were never rigorously enforced. Thus when it seemed that the reparations question was finally near to resolution, the opportunity was created for the British government to reassess its commercial relations with Germany and to extend negotiations to matters beyond the receipt of reparations payments.

In discussions about reparations, the British government had emphasised the need for the Allies to present a united front in dealing with

Germany. A clause of the Treaty of Versailles stated that after January 1925 the onus was on individual Allied countries to negotiate bilateral trade agreements with Germany.[14] In commercial affairs, therefore, the British government was forced to consider what Britain alone, rather than the Allies collectively, required from Germany. The results were tentative – hesitance born out of a need rather than a wish to conclude an agreement with Germany and because the British government found it difficult to extract itself from the collectivist mentality of the *Entente Cordiale*. The formulation of a specifically British commercial policy towards Germany revealed that the German people as well as their government were regarded with mistrust. The economic and commercial legislation was deeply unpopular in Germany. It rapidly became a German condition for the conclusion of a commercial agreement with Britain that it should be amended or repealed. The British response was uncompromising, insisting that such changes would only be possible if 'substantial' guarantees of preferential treatment of British goods could be secured.[15] In an era when MacDonald and Herriot were endeavouring to create a sound political atmosphere for the nurturing of a common policy on security, residual post-war anti-German prejudices remained and were tolerated at the heart of the British government.

British commercial policy

British commercial policy towards Germany was not merely influenced by domestic pressure and practical expediency. Many British politicians feared that because of its forthright policy towards Germany in the Ruhr and its rigorous imposition of the MICUM agreements, the French government might be tempted to steal the British share of German reparations payments. For this reason, the MICUM negotiations between Germany, France and Belgium in 1923 and 1924 caused disquiet in London. In January 1924, D'Abernon was instructed to inform the Germans that

> if separate discussions between France and Germany are to be helpful towards a general settlement, it is essential that HMG should be consulted from the outset, and in particular that no assumptions should be made as to the attitude that they are prepared to take in regard to inter-allied indebtedness in the event of certain arrangements being made, until their views in regard to the projected arrangements have been ascertained.[16]

In the spring and early summer of 1924, memoranda were exchanged between the Treasury and the Board of Trade considering ways of protecting Britain's share of the reparations total should the French try to compromise the British position.[17] The presence of this perceived threat from France forced the strongly pro-French MacDonald and Baldwin administrations into a series of negotiations with Germany that they often found unpalatable, frustrating and irritating.[18]

Similar considerations influenced the decision to select D'Abernon as the British chief negotiator. His detailed knowledge of German affairs, particularly of financial matters, made him an obvious choice. His selection also had an additional and more subtle significance. The Board of Trade and the Treasury believed that if concerns about political French 'greed' persuaded the British government to take strong unilateral action to protect its relations with Germany, the French might construe this as a hostile act and one that could damage the development of Anglo-French relations. There was also the possibility that matters could be made worse because of D'Abernon's very public pro-German sympathies. However, D'Abernon was not easy to replace because few possessed such a detailed knowledge and understanding of German financial affairs and the question of the future regulation of Anglo-German commercial relations remained unresolved. As a result, a different approach to the situation was devised by the Board of Trade. D'Abernon's appointment to lead the negotiations with the Germans might provide a good way of protecting Anglo-French relations. The opportunity was created to explore the possibility of signing an advantageous trade agreement with Germany in the knowledge that, if British advances proved unpalatable to the French, D'Abernon could be blamed while an alternative, less controversial policy was formulated.[19]

What the Treasury and the Board of Trade had not anticipated, however, was the forthrightness with which D'Abernon expressed his pro-German views. This, in turn, led to the re-emergence of a confused and inconsistent policy towards Britain's commercial relations with Germany. D'Abernon had reported that he had been approached by representatives of British banks and insurance companies operating in Germany complaining that they were finding it increasingly difficult to function because the government in Berlin would not allow them to conduct unrestricted business. He recommended that a clause in the proposed treaty should be inserted protecting the interests of such institutions.[20] The Board of Trade was reluctant to put forward such a measure, feeling it to be too bold a step. Although it was recognised that British insurance companies and banks were in need of protection, the Treasury believed that the proposal was likely to generate bad feeling in Berlin because German banking activity in Britain was severely restricted under the Trading with the Enemy Act 1918. It was therefore concluded that 'there was little to be gained by making any reference to banks in the proposed treaty'.[21] But this was not the end of the matter. Despite Treasury reservations, the Board of Trade asked the Foreign Office to send instructions to D'Abernon telling him to pursue his proposal further.[22] D'Abernon willingly complied. Article 14 of the Anglo-German commercial agreement made provision for the protection of British banks operating in Germany. However, the indecision in London did much to damage German faith in the British government's commitment to the conclusion of a treaty and made the process of negotiation more arduous.[23]

Inter-departmental cooperation

D'Abernon's involvement in negotiating the Anglo-German commercial agreement had a bearing on his relations with the Foreign Office as well as with the Treasury and Board of Trade. The Foreign Office was sent copies of the correspondence between the Treasury and the Board of Trade. D'Abernon's appointment at the head of the British negotiating team created an almost unprecedented level of contact between these departments, although inter-departmental relations were not always cordial. Through John Thelwall, the Commercial Secretary at the embassy in Berlin, the German government had expressed reservations about the speed at which D'Abernon insisted on conducting the negotiations.[24] Thelwall believed that the German government would be more inclined to sign a commercial agreement if the negotiations were conducted at a sedate pace which gave opportunity for problems to be discussed. Too quick a tempo, Thelwall argued, would suggest that the British government was being high-handed and attempting to pressurise the Germans. Foreign Office officials were unsure whether D'Abernon should be instructed to slow down the pace of negotiation. The problem was exacerbated by the activities of Sir Otto Niemeyer at the Treasury and Henry Fountain at the Board of Trade who had visited Berlin at D'Abernon's request, and whose views were known to be held in high regard by von Schubert. Yet, if the Foreign Office was seen to adopt Thelwall's recommendations and instruct D'Abernon to slow down the pace of negotiation, it could lead to such a deterioration of relations with the Treasury and the Board of Trade that information about the progress of the negotiations might cease to be forthcoming. During the reparations conferences, experience had shown that strained departmental relations resulted in poor communications that in turn led to the marginalisation of Foreign Office views on key areas of policy relating to Germany. A rejection of D'Abernon's approach to the negotiations was equally not without its problems. There was the danger that if his judgement were to be severely questioned, it might prompt his resignation. This would create the problem of finding a replacement with an equally extensive knowledge of German commercial and economic policy. This dilemma, which in less diplomatically sensitive times would not have occupied the minds of those involved to the same degree, was to remain unresolved for the remainder of the negotiations of the commercial agreement. In a wider context, it did little to create an atmosphere of trust between the British and German government that D'Abernon was at such pains to cultivate, especially as he ultimately sought to move the agenda on to the discussion of security policy.

Reparation (Recovery) Act

A further indication of the attitude of the British government towards the government in Berlin was the link between the Anglo-German Commercial Agreement and the Reparation (Recovery) Act, which had placed the receipt of indemnity from Germany at the heart of British commercial policy for four years. It was also central to the often fraught diplomatic relationship between the British and American governments over the payment of war debts. At no juncture was the Anglo-German Commercial Agreement conceived as a replacement for it. However, it was hoped that, if sufficiently favourable terms were concluded, a relaxation of the Act might be possible. By 1924, the German economy was more stable than at any time since the war, and it became increasingly important to the British government that its negotiating position should be noticeably stronger than that of its German counterpart. One of the first acts of the MacDonald administration was to reduce the export levy determined by the Reparation (Recovery) Act from 26 per cent to 5 per cent. However, after the London conference in the summer of 1924, the levy was raised to its original level, indicating a strengthening of British resolve.[25] It was widely believed that as the German government was now in receipt of financial assistance under the Dawes Plan, the full amount of the export levy could be demanded. More importantly, this might ensure that the Treasury received as much revenue as possible from German trade at a time when Germany was increasingly looking beyond Europe for new trading partners. Furthermore, it was hoped that when the negotiation of the Anglo-German

Commercial Agreement got under way, psychological pressure could be brought to bear in Berlin to persuade the German government to recognise what D'Abernon and others termed Germany's 'moral debt' to Britain. Sir Adrian Baillie, of the Central European Department, suggested that the British position should emphasise to the Germans the 'fear' of losing such 'powerful support'.[26] The same belief was expressed in more senior political circles. In the autumn of 1924, MacDonald told Addison that he believed that:

> The loan now being negotiated in pursuance of the Dawes Plan is quite independent of any considerations related to the proposed Anglo-German Commercial Treaty. Nevertheless, it would in public opinion in this country, throw a most unfavourable light on [the] German government if, after our having played a prominent part in the issue of the loan in the face of great difficulties, Germany fails to respond in a manner well in her power.

MacDonald also referred to the British desire to seek a 'genuine economic rapprochement' between Britain and Germany.[27] Ignoring German complaints about the fairness of the Reparation (Recovery) Act, Bennett of the Central European Department minuted that the case for preserving the 26 per cent levy was 'very good'. He argued that Britain would probably never be forced to choose between the 26 per cent export levy and concluding a commercial agreement with Germany. What was more, there was little point in discussing the subject further, 'until we are in a better position to judge whether Germany really means business or whether she is merely bluffing'.[28] Finally, he warned D'Abernon against giving the impression that the British government would 'give way' in the discussion of issues related to the collection of the 26 per cent levy.[29]

The German government, however, interpreted the British intention to conduct commercial relations with Germany through the Reparation (Recovery) Act as well as a more wide ranging agreement as evidence of a lack of trust on the British part. The resulting diplomatic tension severely hampered the negotiation of the commercial agreement and was not alleviated by D'Abernon's activities. The Foreign Office argued that German objections were excessive. As Sir Miles Lampson urged:

> I cannot resist the suspicion that this is again bluff on the part of the Germans and if so it shows a strange lack of psychology. I find a general disposition here to regard the idea of the miscarriage of the

> Commercial Treaty with comparative equanimity. For Germany, on the contrary, I should have thought it was a matter of some moment.[30]

Lampson had consulted the Board of Trade and had concluded that, if a choice had to be made between the Reparation (Recovery) Act and the commercial treaty, the latter would 'have to go'. Lampson then asked D'Abernon whether the Germans would really be 'so foolish as to throw over their first commercial treaty with one of the Great Powers – I almost said the greatest of the Great Powers'. The German government should be informed that if the commercial agreement was not ratified because of 'some comparatively insignificant point', it would confirm the 'belief held in some quarters' that 'the Germans [were] hopeless people' and that it was 'really useless to try to help them!'[31] D'Abernon's opinion about Lampson's observations has not survived but it is likely that he would have agreed with the substance if not the severity of this criticism of the German approach to negotiation. In his diary, he commented: 'In this question as in others the necessity of a *quid pro quo* makes itself felt. The German mind is particularly sensitive on this point and in doubt whether execution of disagreeable obligations on their part will bring about a fair return.'[32]

As D'Abernon makes clear, these observations could be applied as much to the negotiation of the Anglo-German commercial agreement as to the security negotiations or the controversy surrounding the evacuation of the Cologne Zone.

German requirements

The negotiation of the Anglo-German Commercial Agreement revealed how little the British government understood of the rationale behind the German negotiating position. There were, in fact, several reasons why the German government entered into commercial negotiations with Britain in 1924. Despite being superseded by the United States as the world's dominant economic power, Britain was still a major trading nation and a country with which Germany had a long commercial history. In German eyes, Britain's status as a former enemy had little relevance in this context. This was the attitude adopted by the German press to the agreement. An article in *Vorwärts* suggested that the policy of the German government towards improved commercial relations with Britain was not only sensible but indicated that it was Germany rather than Britain that was displaying the healthiest attitude towards burying the remnants of past hostilities. 'It is of very great importance', it trumpeted,

> that both countries have accorded each other absolute most-favoured-nation treatment; before the war this principle was the backbone of European commercial treaties, but since 1918 more and more countries have departed from this sound principle under the influence of intensified protection and wish only to grant limited most-favoured-nation treatment.[33]

Moreover, an agreement that would include the regulation of British commercial activity in Germany could be used as a method of preventing excessive Allied involvement in German affairs. However, the real strength of the German position was that it was the British who most wanted an agreement to be signed. Hard bargains were driven with D'Abernon and his colleagues that often resulted in the negotiations being turned into a German critique of British reparations and commercial legislation.

The negotiations were made more complex because D'Abernon underestimated the negotiating skills of the German delegation. He took particular pride in giving his personal assurance of fair treatment – that he was not merely negotiating as a representative of the British government but as a friend to Germany. Despite all apparent barriers to a successful outcome, D'Abernon was, as ever, optimistic. He told MacDonald that concluding a commercial agreement with Germany would be a straightforward process and that it could be framed in such a way as to allow British interests to predominate.[34] Within a few days of the start of the negotiations, however, it became apparent that D'Abernon's optimism was unfounded. His views during the first week of meetings with the German delegation were also inconsistent. The problem centred around the German government's wish to build a degree of flexibility into the agreement that would allow items to be made exempt if the economic situation in Germany deteriorated. Initially, D'Abernon claimed that granting such latitude would be at the expense of British commercial interests. He told MacDonald that the negotiations could not proceed 'as long as [the Germans] refuse to give adequate guarantees for reasonable treatment of British trade in future'. If they did not, there would be 'no solid ground on which to base a businesslike negotiation'. The British government should make it clear that it had no intention of restricting the types of goods that could be exported to Britain from Germany. This was justified by stating that such a prohibitive act would imply that the British government had no intention of formulating a truly reciprocal commercial agreement and that reassurances in this respect should be given to the German delegation.[35] He pointed out that 90 per cent of German goods were admitted to Britain with no customs duty and blamed 'foreign investors' for conveying an inaccurate impression of British commercial policy and intentions.[36] D'Abernon raised no objections to discussing any misgivings about British attitudes towards the agreement, but made it clear that if the Germans failed to comply with British requirements, the potential consequences for Germany could be severe. Placing the Anglo-German Commercial Treaty in an international context deflected German opinion away from an examination of British objectives. Such tactics were made more compelling through the threat of international ostracism should British requirements not be met. D'Abernon assured MacDonald that this 'gesture of goodwill' would have the full support of the German delegation and was likely to be well received in Berlin. However, in the same dispatch, he told the Prime Minister that there was 'reason to believe that we can carry our point if we are sufficiently vigorous and persistent'.[37]

The ambiguity of D'Abernon's views heightened German mistrust of the motives behind British policy towards Germany, especially as his reassurances often coexisted with much more uncompromising statements concerning British policy. This hardline approach was also followed by Joseph Addison. He told Stresemann that 'the failure of the German delegates to accommodate reasonable requests put forward by the British had produced an unfavourable impression in London, and that if this attitude continued, [it] would leave a similar impression on British public opinion'.[38] Suspecting that D'Abernon was suggesting that British imports should be granted treatment beyond that of most favoured nation, the German delegation refused to guarantee anything further because of the commercial agreements that the German government had concluded with other countries. Undeterred, and reiterating his views on free trade, D'Abernon asked von Schubert if he would be willing to examine the whole position in the light of British assurances, and issue a guarantee regarding the treatment of British commercial interests in Germany.[39]

The German government preferred to adopt a less direct approach. The clearest indication that the Germans did not trust D'Abernon came from an increasing desire to discuss the treaty with other British officials, especially Henry Fountain of the Board of Trade. Appointed, ironically, at D'Abernon's request to assist in the interpretation of technical matters, Fountain was particularly trusted by the Germans because he was unlike 'certain other influential Britons' who concerned themselves with trying to secure 'exceptional treatment of a suspicious nature' for Britain.[40] German fears were driven by a belief that, by being given the responsibility of heading the negotiations himself, D'Abernon's actions would be motivated by a desire to promote British interests rather than a desire to conclude a fair and reciprocal agreement beneficial to both countries. As chief British negotiator, it was natural that D'Abernon should place great emphasis on preserving the British position. But it is fair to say that, had he not given the Germans cause to doubt his motives in the past, they would have had little reason to question his integrity during the negotiations.

Negotiating tactics

D'Abernon's decision to use Number 11 Downing Street and the British embassy in Berlin as the venue for most of the negotiations did little to convince the German delegation of the openness of the British attitude towards the negotiations. The complete failure to hold discussions either on neutral territory or at the offices of a German government department was indicative of particular diplomatic insensitivity. From the outset of the negotiations, the German approach was understandably defensive. The minutes of the first of a series of seven meetings in Berlin in September 1924 illustrates the extent of German misgivings about what was perceived as an attempt by the British to secure preferential treatment for their imports.[41] One of the German delegation, von Stockhammern, advised caution lest 'circumstances' forced Germany to become committed to a policy that would 'make Germany vulnerable to commercial competition from other countries and to foreign exploitation'.[42] He emphasised that the German government wished to make concessions to Britain but did not want to give the impression that these could be achieved through bullying. Von Stockhammern reminded D'Abernon that he had Stresemann's personal support on these matters and that his instructions represented the limit of the German negotiating position.[43] D'Abernon was angered by what he described as excessive German obstinacy and sent a note to von Schubert asking him for guarantees that British goods in Germany would not receive treatment except in a way that was 'reconcilable with a candid appreciation of the advantages of the English free trade attitude'.[44]

Tensions also ran high between D'Abernon and the German government on matters relating to the implementation of individual pieces of

British legislation that affected Britain's commercial relationship with Germany. Greatest disagreement centred on what connection, if any, there should be between the commercial agreement and the Reparation (Recovery) Act. From the outset, D'Abernon and the German government held opposing views.[45] D'Abernon believed that the Act should not form part of the negotiation of the commercial agreement while the German government saw a direct link between a re-drafting of the Act and the implementation of the proposed agreement with Britain. This issue was of such importance that the German delegation was instructed not to sign the commercial agreement until some concessions relating to the future implementation of the Act had been secured. One of the German delegation, Hemmen, summed up this point in a conversation with D'Abernon, stating that the Act was seen as a 'perpetuation of a sanction' and represented 'a very serious discrimination against Germany'. He suggested that the Act should be revised to establish a framework within which cash reparations could be guaranteed without 'the disturbance of trade entailed by the present system'. D'Abernon disagreed, and argued that German objections to the Reparation (Recovery) Act lacked substance. He believed that if German requests were to be met, legislation would have to be passed and that its passage could not be guaranteed until Britain received assurances of 'substantial advantages in return'. For his part, D'Abernon was convinced that this requirement might be met if the German government undertook to abandon any heavy duties and prohibitions on British goods entering Germany.[46]

For two months there was stalemate between the delegations. The impasse was broken when the British government, somewhat uncharacteristically, decided to take a more sympathetic view of the German position than D'Abernon. By the late autumn of 1924, Treasury and Board of Trade reservations were increasing. Concern was expressed that as the date for the expiry of the clause of the Treaty of Versailles guaranteeing most favoured nation status to British goods in Germany approached, an agreement setting out the pattern of future Anglo-German commercial relations had yet to be reached. At a meeting between the German delegation and Winston Churchill, the Chancellor of the Exchequer, at which D'Abernon was present, a statement was read which declared that the British government was willing to consider a future reform of the Reparation (Recovery) Act if the negotiation of the commercial agreement was not further delayed.[47] Von Schubert was not impressed. He insisted that, while under these circumstances the commercial agreement would be valid, ratification would not take place until the controversy over the 26 per cent export levy had been resolved.[48] D'Abernon's objections to this suggestion were stronger. He told Churchill that it would be impossible for the British government to 'hold the commercial treaty up to see whether the negotiations with the agent-general and the Transfer Committee and France and Belgium are accepted'. He thought that it would create an 'absurd position' that would make German acceptance of the commercial treaty 'dependent upon the will of France and Belgium' – to him the worst possible situation.[49] Churchill remained unmoved and instructed all British representatives to make it clear that the negotiation of the commercial agreement was to proceed separately from a review of the Reparation (Recovery) Act.

German objections continued to such an extent that by the closing weeks of 1924, D'Abernon was determined to seek alternative means of persuading the Germans of British good faith. He believed that the German delegation might be more accommodating if an intermediary was appointed. His choice of candidate was Parker Gilbert, the Reparation Agent, a man who certainly possessed an appropriate level of expertise but who was associated with the French-based Reparation Commission. D'Abernon's gesture towards the continuation of the negotiations was either oddly eccentric or profoundly tactless as it was unlikely that the Germans would respond well to an individual based in the capital city of the nation that was thought to have done most to emasculate Germany economically. Subsequent events render the task of working out where D'Abernon's sympathies lay more, rather than less, difficult. What is clear is the exception that the German government took to the suggestion of Gilbert's appointment. D'Abernon saw the dispute over the 26 per cent levy as a specifically German 'problem', so the onus was placed on the German government to make the first move in seeking arbitration. On 14 January 1925, D'Abernon learned that Gilbert wished to meet with the British government to discuss the future of the 26 per cent levy. Von Schubert believed that this process of revision would be swift. He also believed that the Reichstag was poised to accept the new terms of the Act that he hoped would remove all 'discrimination against German goods'.[50] At the same time, von Schubert was sceptical about D'Abernon's motives in seeking this arbitration. Furthermore, he doubted whether Gilbert could be regarded as impartial. As he was based in Paris, von Schubert wondered whether he was a French 'spy'. Equally, he was concerned that the British government was using Gilbert to lull the German government into a false sense of security prior to an attempt to gain major concessions in the commercial agreement negotiations. For this reason, von Schubert expressed concerns about whether Gilbert was familiar with what he termed 'Germany's technical position'.[51] He decided not to leave D'Abernon in any doubt about the extent of his misgivings. He reminded him that, despite Gilbert's appointment, it was still a firm German condition that, before the commercial agreement could be ratified, the question of the 26 per cent levy must be satisfactorily resolved.

Tension between von Schubert and D'Abernon was increased when rumours reached Berlin that the British government had no intention of reappraising the Reparation (Recovery) Act. Von Schubert believed that D'Abernon was not taking the German position seriously. He told him that he intended to send a letter to London to ensure that the British government fully understood the German terms for signing the commercial agreement. D'Abernon drafted this document, in which the German government made assurances of compliance with the terms of the Reparation (Recovery) Act. Nevertheless, von Schubert remained unconvinced that it would be enough, commenting that 'the letter is beautifully written but it is after all only a letter'. Later he told the other members of the German delegation that no satisfactory agreement with the British government was possible because 'the position of the British government [was] completely incomprehensible'.[52] Frustration in Berlin was intensified by Britain's apparent reluctance to agree to accord the Germans the treatment that they expected. While some remained sceptical about United States' involvement in German affairs, the feeling still prevailed that the Americans were likely to treat Germany less harshly than would Britain and France. D'Abernon was forced to admit this after a conversation with the former Secretary of State for Foreign Affairs, von Maltzan.[53] The commercial agreement negotiations highlighted the differences between Britain and Germany rather than providing a sound foundation for the creation of closer relations between the two countries. If a more intimate relationship was to be achieved, the tensions between von Schubert and D'Abernon indicated that much more work needed to be done.

While the British government wished to conclude a commercial agreement with Germany as soon as possible, D'Abernon believed that time should be taken to reflect on how closer relations between the two countries could be brought about in the future.[54] It is clear though that he did not envisage a relationship based on what he termed 'an equal partnership'; rather, Britain would occupy a 'superior' role and this 'superiority' would extend to political and diplomatic relations. In a memorandum on the wider significance of the commercial negotiations, D'Abernon told the German delegation:

> You, who are so much interested in international commerce, must realise that what you do in the near future in a matter of commercial policy will exercise a considerable influence on the future policy of the nations which surround you. Remember this – the commercial negotiations of today will have a marked influence on the political relations of tomorrow. However much it may be desired to divorce business from politics and to keep tariff discussion on purely economic lines, it is impossible for anyone who follows the movements of public opinion in England not to be convinced that the future political relations between the English people and the German people must depend to a large extent upon the facilities for commerce which each country offers the other.[55]

These differences were viewed in London as no more than matters of emphasis, but the trust that was placed in D'Abernon was such that it is possible to refer to British commercial policy towards Germany as *his* policy, even though the British government and D'Abernon continued to view Germany very differently.[56] This tends to reveal yet more contradictions within D'Abernon's position. British commercial policy towards Germany bore the hallmarks of his own views on his country's status as a world power at a time when the MacDonald administration's acceptance of the Dawes Plan seemed to be an admission that Britain was no longer the world's foremost trading nation. The willingness of the British government to sympathise with D'Abernon's views is nevertheless easy to explain. Although faced with the economic realities of the post-war world, British politicians looked back with affection to the days when British interests lay at the heart of so much international activity. If, through D'Abernon, Britain could preserve even a small amount of her former reputation in an era of such profound and rapid change, then so much the better.

Motives behind the agreement

Angela Kaiser has suggested that the Anglo-German Commercial Agreement was part of a general process of German rehabilitation after the war – that D'Abernon's motives were altruistic and that he wished to secure a place for Germany in the international arena based on equality with her former enemies.[57] It is reasonable to suggest that a bilateral commercial treaty between a country with a relatively sound economy and one emerging from several years of economic chaos would be concluded so that the stronger power could help the weaker to the benefit of both parties. Furthermore, she attempts to justify an apparently benign attitude adopted by the British government towards Germany. However, Kaiser misinterprets the motives behind D'Abernon's activities. His views on British commercial relations with Germany were based on two ideas. As already discussed, he believed that Britain's status as an imperial power accorded her a right to conclude a commercial agreement with Germany on terms largely determined and dictated by the British government. Secondly, and somewhat paradoxically, D'Abernon anticipated that while the terms of the agreement would place equal emphasis on the interests of both countries, in reality the interests of Britain would automatically prevail. As he told Grahame: 'The press here... has quite missed the essential point, which is that Germany specifically promises reciprocity for the Free Trade attitude of England. In practice, of course, it will not be carried out to the full extent, but the recognition of the principle is novel.'[58]

Many of D'Abernon's dispatches also suggest that he did not view a commercial agreement between Britain and Germany entirely as an opportunity to further the process of international rehabilitation begun by the Dawes Plan. Instead, he made reference to the 'moral obligation' of the German government to create good conditions for the operation of British commerce within Germany.[59] He believed that the British government was 'entitled to every consideration from the German government', and that the Germans 'would not be so foolish as to run the risk of losing the powerful support we have afforded them by refusing to recognise just claims for fair treatment'.[60]

This sense of superiority mixed with compulsion and obligation was also reflected in D'Abernon's address on 22 September 1924 to the German delegation. As far as he was concerned, the onus was on the Germans to prove themselves worthy trading partners.[61] He believed that Germany should be compelled to offer Britain favourable commercial treatment 'in the interests of those who desire the development in England of feelings of confidence towards Germany'.[62] Towards the end of the negotiations, he explained the general philosophy behind his dealings with the Germans to the King:

> I believe it is the first time that a foreign power has definitely accepted the obligation to make in her tariff some return for the liberal customs attitude of the United Kingdom. It has always been held by foreign negotiators that England was entitled to no counter-concession,

> because her attitude was adopted in self interest. Personally I have always failed to understand why we did not obtain better treatment – why we made no more vigorous effort to obtain it. Although retaliatory duties are excluded by our general policy, English goodwill is sufficiently worth having for a foreign nation to make considerable sacrifices in order to obtain it. I have not hesitated to point this out.[63]

The second idea that underpinned much of D'Abernon's dealings with the Germans was more idiosyncratic but was nonetheless typical of his attitude towards Germany's relations with Britain. As he had stated on numerous occasions, he believed that the German government held British advice in high regard. As a result, the British government would be able to convince the Germans of the existence of an indissoluble bond between Britain and Germany at a time when the American government's involvement in German affairs was beginning to rival that of the British. In this respect, D'Abernon argued that the British government should 'take advantage of our present political influence' to secure most favoured nation treatment for British commerce after 10 January 1925.[64] In September 1924, he wrote:

> The memory of the assistance given to Germany [by Britain] has not faded from the German mind and the severe competition which will occur later has not yet led to any great tension between the commercial communities in the two countries. Our political assistance is still urgently needed. All this may alter. America will play a larger part in German finance, France will cease to be execrated, English trade rivalry will be more acutely felt. So far as one can judge future events, it seems to me probable that the present is the best moment to make our bargain.[65]

At the same time, he hoped that a commercial agreement between the two countries would help diminish German enthusiasm for closer relations with the United States and strengthen the bond with Britain. This reinforced D'Abernon's belief that relations between Britain and Germany were central to post-war European diplomacy and that, through close links with Britain, Germany's future as a major power and trading nation would be secured. After the negotiations were complete, D'Abernon reported that the German government 'attached importance to relations with Britain and that it is recognised that during the last few years we have been a moderating element in *Entente* policy, and that the result of our attitude has been a marked benefit to Germany. It is further admitted that in matters of finance and currency the English experts have been steadily right, and that they saw the true lines of recovery long before any leading authority here. Indeed, I believe that many Germans with inside knowledge would recognise that the recovery of the country would not have been possible but for our advice and for the broad and generous view which we adopted.'[66]

The commercial agreement and American involvement in German affairs

D'Abernon's fears about further American involvement in German affairs beyond the Dawes Plan were reflected in observations about the kinds of people who should be involved in discussion of the commercial agreement. One of the principal objectives of the Dawes Committee had been to distinguish itself from previous attempts to assess the German financial position by focusing primarily on financial affairs and not allowing the political objectives of the interested parties to influence its judgement. D'Abernon had expressed doubts about the advisability of this and, throughout the negotiations of the commercial agreement, remained determined to reverse this trend. Immediately before the discussions began, he had stated: 'However sincere endeavours may be to separate commercial relations from politics and to allow business to develop independently of political feeling or political prejudices ... this is unhealthy and unrealistic.'[67]

D'Abernon insisted that the Anglo-German negotiations had a political as well as a commercial foundation and recommended that senior government officials should be involved at all levels of the consultations. He thought that otherwise the constant need for the German experts to refer to their political masters in Berlin would cause unnecessary delays.[68] More importantly, D'Abernon believed that through the maintenance of a 'political dimension' in the negotiations, he could wield greater influence with the German delegation. He anticipated that his negotiating position would be enhanced if some of the German delegates were known to him personally. D'Abernon was particularly anxious that von Schubert should be included in the German delegation because he had a good knowledge of commercial affairs and because the *Staatssekretär* was willing to act on his advice.[69] His earlier experience of dealing with German financial experts at reparations conferences led him to believe that they were not as conversant with the 'special' nature of Germany's relations with Britain as officials in the *Auswärtiges Amt*.

D'Abernon's idiosyncratic manoeuvres were underpinned by a growing fear that his influence with the German government was declining. As the negotiations progressed, the 'independence' of the German delegation became an increasing source of exasperation to him. As he told his wife in the spring of 1925, 'with Germans here [and] a German (Niemeyer) at the Treasury – a world record for obstinacy has been set up'.[70] Convinced that von Schubert's attitude was inconsistent with that of the German delegation and the German government, he turned increasingly for advice to Germans who he thought took a 'broader view'. D'Abernon was comforted by what he interpreted as Stresemann's commitment to closer relations with Britain. He told the new Foreign Secretary, Austen Chamberlain that the attitude of the Germans

> in September and October was so hostile to any concession of a nature to satisfy us that I regarded it as waste of time to deal further with them on this subject. I decided, therefore, to treat the question with the higher political authorities in the State, and to negotiate it on broad lines. I was fortunate in being able to interest in the negotiation not only... Stresemann, but also Ebert, who at once recognised the far-reaching importance of the occasion.[71]

D'Abernon's dispatches also frequently suggested that Stresemann prized good relations with Britain above all else. In November 1924, he reported that, despite problems over 'small points of detail', 'Stresemann fully realises [the] importance of [the] commercial treaty with England and will do everything in his power to facilitate and conclude same'.[72]

Yet, while there is little doubt that Stresemann favoured a commercial agreement with Britain, he was suspicious about the motives of the British delegation and of the Treasury and Board of Trade experts dispatched to Berlin. He told a rally in Dortmund in the autumn of 1924 that during the commercial negotiations with Britain, he had 'come across curious paradoxes' in which the experts supporting free trade who had been sent to Berlin had implemented high tariffs 'the moment their own products [had] come up for discussion'. The statements that D'Abernon had made on behalf of the British government certainly suggested that this was the case. D'Abernon and the British government clung to ideas that were becoming outmoded even before the war, in an era when many of the values of that period had been destroyed or swept aside. The difficulty of D'Abernon's position provides further evidence of the uncertainty that underpinned much of British policy towards Europe in the 1920s.

Stresemann believed that if Germany's future as one of the major European powers was to be secured and the remaining ghosts of wartime hostility laid to rest, the German government must conclude a multilateral agreement with the Allied powers. He saw the Anglo-German Commercial Agreement as only a part of a continuing process of improved relations with the Allies. As he stated: 'the future historian will be able to say that the year 1924 has marked the turning-point in recent history. After five years of sterile quarrel the necessity of cooperation between the peoples has been recognised.'[73]

In 1924, German foreign policy was predominantly concerned with two issues: solving the long-term economic problems that had dogged Germany since the war, and regaining some authority and respect in international affairs. In the same year, British foreign policy was preoccupied with more defensive measures – as well as finding ways of halting decline. Yet, few observers of Anglo-German relations at this time would have doubted the relative political, economic and military dominance of Britain. All these areas can be measured statistically and through examination of documentation, but none can give a full picture of the psychological mood of the time. Although Germany was the less influential of the two powers, the Germans, particularly Stresemann, were willing to adopt a much more positive and forward-looking attitude towards international relations. Stresemann had few reservations about seizing the initiative in Germany's dealings with other countries, especially the European powers. As the diplomatic agenda gradually moved away from economic issues, the Allies were increasingly forced to come to terms with a German statesman who was not afraid to act as he saw fit and who did not try to avoid controversial decisions.[74]

6
Security Diplomacy, 1924–26

British policy towards the innumerable crises associated with reparations payments, disarmament and international security in the early 1920s was always one of strictly limited involvement. Consideration of the needs of the empire and a belief that the European diplomatic situation was very complex led the British government to conclude that a more flexible policy might result in Britain becoming involved in a wide range of problems that had little bearing on her interests. Increasing emphasis was placed on the work of the League of Nations and reinforcing and improving Britain's relationship with France.[1] The diplomatic crisis of 1923 that had failed to produce British support for the Franco-Belgian invasion of the Ruhr, placed a severe strain on Anglo-French relations. It was for this reason that D'Abernon's attempt to resurrect the Cuno proposals for a security pact based on French undertakings not to use the Rhineland for military purposes had been rejected by the then Prime Minister, Stanley Baldwin.[2] This scheme, first proposed by the German Chancellor in November 1922, suggested that Britain, France, Germany and Italy should agree not to wage war against each other for thirty years without the prior authorisation of a plebiscite.[3] The initiative coincided with a period of international stability greater than any which had existed since the war and which culminated in the signature of the Treaty of Locarno. Signed by France, Germany and Belgium, and guaranteed by Britain and Italy, the principal treaty signed at Locarno in October 1925 confirmed the permanence of the German frontier with France and Belgium and the demilitarisation of the Rhineland, that had been first established under the terms of the Treaty of Versailles. Historians have been quick to associate D'Abernon with this period and have emphasised his apparent involvement in the drafting of the note proposing a security agreement between Britain, France and Germany that the German government sent to London in January 1925 and then to Paris a month later. This note, which is usually seen to be the product of conversations between D'Abernon and Carl von Schubert, *Staatssekretär* at the *Auswärtiges Amt*, between November 1924 and January 1925, restated a number of earlier German proposals that D'Abernon had vainly tried to persuade the British government to adopt. It has been argued that D'Abernon's role was of crucial importance to the development of the note.[4] However, this claim can be challenged. Correspondence between D'Abernon, von Schubert and Stresemann makes it clear that the Stresemann–Luther government intended to conclude a security agreement with the Allies independently of D'Abernon.[5] It is also important to place D'Abernon's actions within the wider debate about the effectiveness of the Treaty of Locarno. While contemporary observers heralded it as the most significant breakthrough in European diplomacy since the war, the verdict of historians has been less positive.[6] It has been criticised as a piece of 'old diplomacy' that failed to contain Hitler's policy of annexation in the 1930s and prevent the outbreak of war in 1939.[7]

Nevertheless, it is still claimed that without D'Abernon's efforts, the German government would not have put forward the proposal and that without his influence, Stresemann would have been much more reluctant to trust Chamberlain and Briand.[8] These ideas come mainly from D'Abernon's own pen as he assumed that a close relationship with Britain lay at the heart of German foreign policy formulation. As it was, D'Abernon's understanding of the dynamics of German foreign policy was fundamentally flawed. Stresemann saw Germany as a strong power militarily, economically and politically. D'Abernon believed she was none of these. During the security negotiations, he continued to regard Germany as a weak, defeated power dependent on Britain for protection against an overbearing France. He also wished to secure the admission of Germany to the League of Nations as a means of improving Britain's relations with Germany in the absence of American interference. D'Abernon also failed to appreciate the importance, both psychologically and diplomatically, of German relations with the Soviet Union. As a result, he found himself increasingly on the margins of the security negotiations.

Origins of the security negotiations

In March 1923, D'Abernon tried to persuade the British and German governments to revive the Cuno proposals as a means of diffusing growing tension between the Allies and Germany. He discussed the relationship between security and reparations with Curzon, suggesting that 'no reparation settlement was possible without previous agreement establishing security'.[9] But Curzon was anxious that Britain should adopt as low a profile as possible during the Ruhr crisis and thus rejected involvement in any situation that might lead to further controversy with France.[10] The response in Germany was equally unenthusiastic. The recent French invasion of German territory did little to create a desire to negotiate with France. It was also bitterly resented that the British government had not come to Germany's assistance to bring the Ruhr occupation to an end. Undeterred, D'Abernon put forward his own proposal for a security agreement in early 1924. He believed that the German government might be willing to sign an agreement with France that undertook not to use the Rhineland for any military purpose.[11] However, the new Prime Minister, Ramsay MacDonald, was wary of limited agreements.[12] He wished to channel his energies into improving the machinery for the arbitration of international disputes that would encompass a means of satisfying French security requirements. He was also convinced that the acceptance of the Dawes Report now enabled the European powers to concentrate their diplomatic efforts on security. In the autumn of 1924, a combination of opportunity and confidence led MacDonald, in conjunction with the French, to take an active role in drafting the Geneva Protocol.[13] This offered an elaborate mechanism for the resolution of international disputes by arbitration and gave power to the Council of the League to ask signatory states to apply sanctions against aggressors.[14] Domestic affairs then intervened, removing the Labour administration from office and preventing MacDonald from taking further action to ensure the Protocol's acceptance.[15] The Conservative administration led by Baldwin was more sceptical about whether it was advisable for Britain to sign the Geneva Protocol. Not all of the government were convinced that Germany was the most likely aggressor in Europe. Leo Amery, the Colonial Secretary, and the Cabinet Secretary, Sir Maurice Hankey, urged caution in signing a bilateral security agreement with France.[16] More scathing comments came from Lord Robert Cecil, the Chancellor of the Duchy of Lancaster, who wrote that while 'we hear a great deal about the necessity for French security, the necessity for security for some other nations in Europe seems no less essential to peace'.[17] Therefore by the winter of 1924, it was by no means clear how far the British government would be prepared to offer support to an initiative for a security pact. What was becoming apparent, however, was that such a proposal was not likely to come from London.

The security issue aroused similar but different passions in Berlin. The eminent *Staatssekretär* at the *Auswärtiges Amt*, von Schubert, passionately believed that greater definition needed to be given to Germany's role in international relations. Both he and Stresemann argued that, as a first stage, emphasis should be placed on German relations with the western European powers because it was in this region that the greatest threats to German security lay. When relations with Britain and France had been put on an acceptable footing, attention could be turned towards the conclusion of an entente with the Soviet Union. In the meantime, Germany must avoid 'the impression of duplicity', but should 'not to be forced away from [her] course'.[18] France was seen as the greatest military threat to German security. Thus it was to the French that most efforts to instigate a dialogue about the development of European security were directed. A reciprocal agreement with France should be signed that would reduce tensions between the two countries and remove the need for the Rhineland to be a demilitarised zone. Britain was to act as a diplomatic facilitator in this process, but would only be consulted when necessary. Good relations with Britain, although desirable, were not a priority, nor were they to be cultivated at the expense of the general German western European security strategy.

D'Abernon read the situation differently. He believed that the relationship he had secured with von Schubert during the negotiation of the Anglo-German Commercial Agreement could be used to gain influence with Stresemann. But this was to be a gradual process. When '*Das Kind*', as D'Abernon and von Schubert named the proposal for a security pact, reached a certain stage in its maturity, then, and only then, was the German Minister for Foreign Affairs to be informed. It is debatable whether D'Abernon succeeded in his objective – a failure that was to be reflected in his growing frustration with von Schubert.[19] Indeed, initial discussions between them were not harmonious. When D'Abernon suggested resurrecting the Cuno proposals, von Schubert thought it improbable that the French would agree to anything that implied that they were as likely as the Germans to start another war.[20] It was also pointless to expect the French to grant Germany full administrative rights in the Rhineland while that very issue remained such a bone of contention in the Ruhr.[21] It is difficult to understand why D'Abernon thought that the contrary was the case.[22] Nevertheless, throughout 1924, he tried to persuade von Schubert to take the initiative and dispatch a note proposing a security agreement between Britain, France and Germany to London. He also continued to try to persuade von Schubert to revive the Cuno proposals. A bilateral security agreement would be much more satisfactory than the multilateral agreements that the French were seeking. D'Abernon also led von Schubert to believe that he possessed inside information about French attitudes of which the British government was unaware and which suggested that his proposed course of action was the most appropriate. Von Schubert thought that D'Abernon was bluffing. At the end of a particularly strenuous conversation, he concluded that, in actuality, D'Abernon did not 'know much' about the situation.[23]

On 14 January 1925, D'Abernon was summoned to the *Auswärtiges Amt.* Once again rejecting the Cuno proposals as a basis for a proposed pact, von Schubert proposed instead to pursue ideas that had been put forward in 1923 by Gaus, the Chief Legal Adviser to the *Auswärtiges Amt,* in which every country with an interest in the Rhineland undertook to guarantee the security of this region. D'Abernon doubted whether the British government would wish to make such a large commitment. However, von Schubert believed that any communication proposing a security pact between Germany and the Allies must make reference to the Rhineland. Unable to persuade von Schubert to abandon this idea, D'Abernon suggested that a note be drafted encompassing both the Cuno and Gaus schemes. This idea proved acceptable to von Schubert.[24] The security proposal that emerged and was sent to the Allies was thus a compromise between the diplomatic agendas of the two men, rather than an unqualified acceptance of a British idea.

The discussions between von Schubert and D'Abernon were also overshadowed by the debate concerning the evacuation of the Cologne Zone. In the spring of 1924, D'Abernon had believed that an agreement timetabling the evacuation of the region could soon be drawn up. Stresemann however, thought it unlikely that the French would sanction a policy that could inhibit their ability to provide military assistance to Poland. Why D'Abernon thought such an agreement would be acceptable to the French is not immediately apparent.[25] On 5 January 1925, however, the German government received Allied notification that the Cologne Zone would not be evacuated because of German violations of the disarmament provisions of the Treaty of Versailles. Stresemann responded by cataloguing the trauma suffered by the German people since the start of the Ruhr occupation.[26] At the same time, he thought that the Rhineland Pact offered the French a means of acknowledging that the Rhineland was German territory and of renouncing the use of military sanctions.[27] A demilitarised Rhineland thus provided one of the best guarantees against another war. Consequently, the future status of this the region should be at the centre of a reciprocal security agreement with the Allies.[28] In all likelihood, the British government would sign a bilateral agreement with France in the first instance, with German interests being considered at a later date.[29] Therefore, the onus was on the German government to remove obstacles that might prevent the improvement of Franco-German relations.

Stresemann was dismayed to hear that the Cologne Zone was not to be evacuated by January 1925, but nevertheless envisaged that negotiations to set a date for the evacuation would start in the near future.[30] This would be more likely if the negotiations for a security pact with the Allies were proceeding well.[31] Furthermore, discussions of a security pact that affected Germany but which took place without German participation would lead to a second diktat settlement.[32] But as the reparations question was now settled and Germany had complied with 'all the undertakings resulting from the present Treaty', the Allied presence in the Rhineland could no longer be justified. D'Abernon was sympathetic but thought Stresemann's suggestion would prove unpopular in France. Stresemann thought D'Abernon too cautious and called for a commission to be created to modify the Rhineland regime after the security pact came into force. D'Abernon agreed.[33] By liaising with the British as closely as possible, Stresemann hoped that a revision of the Treaty of Versailles could begin in the near future. This was the principal reason for his apparent closeness to D'Abernon.

Chamberlain and Stresemann

One of the most important influences that had a bearing on the conduct of the security negotiations in 1925 was the relationship that D'Abernon had with Stresemann and with the British Foreign Secretary, Austen Chamberlain. The suggestion in Chamberlain's thinking that German interests were of secondary importance to those of France was to be the source of much animosity with D'Abernon. It has been argued that by March 1925 D'Abernon was successful in persuading Chamberlain to adopt a proposal for a security pact that placed equal emphasis on German needs.[34] But the extent of D'Abernon's influence over Chamberlain can be questioned. It was not D'Abernon but members of the British government who insisted that Chamberlain should abandon the plan for a bilateral security agreement. Even when Chamberlain publicly embraced a proposal that included Germany, there is little to suggest that it was D'Abernon who had convinced him that the policy was the right one. There is even less evidence to suggest that D'Abernon persuaded Chamberlain of German trustworthiness.

D'Abernon had long believed that Germany's defeat in war and the French government's growing friendship with the new countries in eastern Europe had swung the balance of power in favour of France. He also felt that the French economy was stronger than that of Germany while the difference in population between the two countries suggested that it was France that possessed the larger resource of men fit for military service. This was a particularly eccentric statement as the population of France at this time was significantly smaller than that of Germany. Nevertheless, he pressed for British support for Germany as a necessary counterbalance to French attempts to establish economic and military dominance in Europe. Those who failed to recognise the need for this – and D'Abernon must have had Chamberlain in mind here – were guilty of a 'Rip van Winkle conception' of European diplomacy.[35] D'Abernon set out his argument for a sympathetic treatment of the German case in a memorandum sent to Chamberlain two weeks before the German government dispatched its proposal for a security pact in January 1925. In it he stressed the relative military weaknesses of Germany and claimed that French domination of Europe was currently of a 'far more pronounced and indisputable character' than had been exhibited by Germany even before the First World War.[36] The British government must decide either to support the French idea for a simple guarantee of French frontiers and to continue to regard Germany as 'a permanent enemy', or to ensure that Germany would be included in the negotiation of a security agreement from the outset, thus providing equality of treatment of French and German frontiers. It would be unwise for the British government to believe that an agreement would result in closer Anglo-French relations, since French eyes were firmly fixed on Germany and not on Britain. At the same time, once the French had been persuaded that the Germans did not intend to infringe their territorial integrity, Britain risked 'losing an ally'. With Chamberlain's preferred policy undoubtedly in his mind, D'Abernon advised that if Britain signed a bilateral agreement with France, it would be 'frankly absurd' to expect it to be subsequently extended to include Germany. Warning again of the perils of the British government adopting an excessively accommodating attitude towards France, he cautioned that 'once we are tied by such an obligation, we become satellitic – deprived of independence and authority'.[37] A satisfactory relationship between the Allies and Germany could only be reached when the tensions within Anglo-French relations had been permanently eased.

At the same time, D'Abernon believed that the British government should be prepared to ensure that Germany's future role in European affairs was developed. In particular, he feared that if Germany was 'permanently alienated' from her former enemies, it could result in a German drift towards communism, perhaps facilitated through the conclusion of a second Rapallo-like agreement with the Soviet Union.[38] It was in the 'essential interest' of Britain to 'prevent the breaking up of Germany', for 'as long as Germany [was] a coherent whole, there [was] more or less a balance of power in Europe'.[39] The intensity of his suspicions about communism set him slightly apart from Chamberlain, although several members of the government held similar views, most notably Winston Churchill.[40] D'Abernon also shared the views of many in the Cabinet that Anglo-French relations should be carefully regulated.[41] He was convinced that an exclusive British commitment to France would simply reaffirm the wartime alliance against Germany. This would make the task of creating a lasting peace more difficult and would undermine Britain's reputation as a moderate force in European diplomacy. The conclusion of an Anglo-French agreement would be seen in Berlin as tantamount to the British government condoning a range of other French tactics deployed to bully the Germans since the war. If the British government pursued such a policy, it was inevitable that Britain would become part of an 'anti-German defensive league'.[42] This would undermine the entire commercial and diplomatic foundation of the Anglo-German relationship that he had endeavoured to develop for the past five years. D'Abernon's views were therefore rooted as much in personal pride as they were in a coherent analysis of the dynamics of Britain's relations with France and Germany.

D'Abernon was convinced that the driving force behind the pro-French bias of British foreign policy was Chamberlain himself. While the Foreign Secretary was 'well placed to exercise decisive influence', he allowed his personal prejudices to influence his assessment of European diplomacy. D'Abernon criticised Chamberlain for 'parading' his Francophilia throughout the negotiations and complained that his scepticism about German involvement in a security agreement had made the task of persuading the German government to consider Allied proposals on this matter more difficult.[43] Undercurrents of this nature are less apparent in Chamberlain's correspondence with D'Abernon, primarily because he believed that the intransigent views expressed by D'Abernon were those of the German government and not his own. This lack of certainty about the origin of D'Abernon's statements about security may explain why his role in the negotiation of the Treaty of Locarno has not been subjected to as much historical scrutiny as that of Chamberlain, even allowing for Chamberlain's greater general responsibility for such matters as Foreign Secretary. But as far as Chamberlain was concerned, D'Abernon's apparently close relationship with the German government offered him unparalleled opportunities to influence Stresemann and von Schubert. Furthermore, Chamberlain was convinced that D'Abernon had been the architect of the German note proposing a security pact that had been dispatched to London in January 1925.

Therefore there was a misunderstanding about the extent of D'Abernon's influence in Berlin compounded by the ambassador's misguided belief that the German government relied on his advice. Another difficulty derived from D'Abernon's ability to equal Chamberlain's talent for inflexibility and partisanship. Throughout the security negotiations, he remained firmly wedded to the idea that the greatest threat to European security came from France. The role played by personal prejudice in these discussions can also be seen by examining Chamberlain's attitude towards D'Abernon's opposite number in London, Friedrich Sthamer.[44] The Foreign Secretary often refused to see him, preferring to delegate the task to Sir Miles Lampson of the Central European Department.[45] Significantly, he dealt with French ambassadors and government ministers personally. The lack of personal contact with their German equivalents suggests that he was deliberately keeping his distance.[46] As it was, when it came to seeking information about the policies and activities of the German government, D'Abernon was in one sense the lesser of the two evils.

Stresemann and D'Abernon enjoyed a personally cordial but professionally distant relationship. Edgar Stern-Rubarth, Stresemann's press secretary, described them as pragmatists who developed a rapport because they interpreted the diplomatic situation in Europe in the same way and because 'neither man liked "beating around the bush"'.[47] D'Abernon prided himself on having Stresemann's confidence.[48] As in his dealings with von Schubert, D'Abernon believed that Stresemann placed great emphasis on British advice and on cultivating closer relations with Britain.[49] Clearly D'Abernon was uncertain whether Stresemann was initially convinced of the reliability of British advice but believed that that situation would change once he had gained the trust of the Minister for Foreign Affairs. But it is easy to overstate the degree of intimacy that existed between them. There is a much greater volume of correspondence between D'Abernon and von Schubert than there is between D'Abernon and Stresemann. The German Minister for Foreign Affairs liked to 'give the impression' that relations with D'Abernon were the key to success.[50] He did not seek D'Abernon's advice, but regarded him as a source and conveyor of information. Like Chamberlain, Stresemann pursued his own policy objectives and sometimes D'Abernon became a casualty of the strategies pursued by both men. For the most part, he was happy to delegate responsibility for dealing with D'Abernon to von Schubert in the same way that Chamberlain delegated responsibility for dealing with Sthamer. This reveals much about the attitude of the governments in Berlin and London to these ambassadors accredited to them and the importance each gave to Anglo-German relations.

While D'Abernon found solace in his conversations with von Schubert, Stresemann was anxious how the *Staatssekretär*'s collaboration with D'Abernon would appear in Moscow. He told Brockdorff-Rantzau, the German ambassador in Moscow, that the security initiative was nothing out of the ordinary and had been 'in the air' for some time.[51] However, Stresemann realised that suggesting that the German government wished to sign a security agreement with the Allies would create an unprecedented opportunity to move towards a negotiated revision of the Treaty of Versailles. Making the (false) assumption that D'Abernon had acted with the knowledge and approval of the British government, Stresemann told von Hoesch, the German ambassador in Paris: 'We would therefore scarcely be able to ignore [D'Abernon's] urgings, all the more so as they offer us an opportunity to broach this problem with the Allies in quite an unobtrusive manner.'[52] Indeed, the key to Stresemann's policy in western Europe and to his dealings with D'Abernon was Germany's relationship with France. Like D'Abernon, Stresemann believed that it was France that was most likely to provoke a second world war.[53] He also realised that if Germany wished to gain the reputation of a peace-loving nation, a framework would have to be created for the removal of the historic French fear of German invasion.[54] D'Abernon was again at one with him and saw such statements as an opportunity to cultivate closer links between Britain and Germany.

Yet despite such agreement, the two men did not interpret the role of France in European diplomacy in entirely the same way. D'Abernon was mindful of Chamberlain's strong pro-French sympathies and his reluctance to adopt a tolerant attitude towards German involvement in the security negotiations. As a counterbalance, D'Abernon placed the emphasis of his dealings with Stresemann on those areas of French policy that were most likely to cause controversy in Berlin: reparations and security. To D'Abernon, Stresemann's 'essential policy' was to bring about a state of permanent peace between Germany and France. But as long as France refused not to undertake a repetition of the Ruhr invasion, such an agreement was not possible.[55] What he did not realise was that Stresemann also intended to cultivate a closer relationship with the British and French governments in order to press for the recovery of the Polish Corridor.[56] Beyond that, the Treaty of Locarno could have an adverse effect on Franco-Polish relations by increasing French security on the Rhine and thereby lessening the need for allies in eastern Europe. Germany's western frontier would receive some protection in the event of a Polish attack and be secure if the German government contemplated the use of force to revise the eastern frontiers. The Treaty of Locarno, therefore, offered a potential improvement in Germany's strategic position by reducing the possibility of a war on two fronts.[57]

Dispatch of the German note

One of the dominant features of the security negotiations in the mid-1920s was the impact of Chamberlain's personal opinion about the respective merits of French and German rights to secure their frontiers from attack. He had never entertained the possibility that the most significant security initiative in recent years would come from Germany. Furthermore, the initiative made German involvement in any ensuing discussions unavoidable. Chamberlain's response to the note was defensive. A particular cause of exasperation was the request that accompanied the arrival of the German note in London that its contents should not yet be revealed to the French.[58] D'Abernon favoured such a strategy as it would enable the British government to take the lead in the negotiations and persuade the French of the merits of the initiative. Seeing this as an attempt to undermine the relationship between the British and French governments, Chamberlain expressed his frustration to a fellow Francophile, the Marquess of Crewe. He wrote:

> First they hand a copy of their secret memorandum on a pact to D'Abernon and ask my advice about it, whilst attempting to enforce the condition that I shall say nothing to the French. I repudiated the condition ... and one would have thought that they might have learned the lesson; but they next sent the same memorandum to Herriot with the addition that he must not communicate with me. Herriot very properly responds to my confidence by giving me his confidence. But what earthly object do they think that all this tortuous duplicity would serve?[59]

D'Abernon was sent a copy of the letter and the resulting burst of correspondence set the tone of his public and private communications with Chamberlain about security for the remainder of his embassy. D'Abernon warned that: 'To adopt the view that [the German security note] is a dodge or trick of controversy is not only unjustified by the facts but would be extremely unwise even if it were justified.'[60] He urged a rapid response, prompting an angry retort from Chamberlain that 'any appearance of negotiations between Germany and this country behind the back of France would arouse suspicion and destroy any influence which Britain might have with the government of France'.[61] The priorities of D'Abernon and Chamberlain thus remained seemingly irreconcilable and were made worse by the Germans' misguided decision to dispatch the German security proposal to the British and French capitals separately. On this point, the German government seemed curiously ignorant of Chamberlain's attitude towards European diplomacy and indeed, about the general priorities behind British foreign policy towards Europe since the war. For this, D'Abernon must bear at least partial responsibility.

In urging Chamberlain not to respond impetuously, D'Abernon nevertheless remained dismayed that the British government appeared to be 'so prejudiced against Germany'. He believed that Chamberlain had failed to understand the importance of the German initiative. His disenchantment was such that he anticipated that the German government could no longer 'base any line of policy upon co-operation with London'. The German security proposal would be 'cold-shouldered in favour of an Anglo-French and anti-German agreement' that would demonstrate more clearly than any recent diplomatic initiative that the British government's greatest loyalty was to the protection of French interests.[62] This point marked D'Abernon's lowest ebb during the security negotiations. He feared that his much-desired Anglo-German dominated security agreement was unlikely to be concluded, and that a third party, France, would necessarily adopt a more prominent role in brokering a European security pact. For D'Abernon, as well as for Chamberlain, therefore, the Treaty of Locarno would prove to be a compromise of his preferred policy and one with which he was never entirely satisfied.

It has been suggested that D'Abernon's role in the drafting of the German security note of January 1925 was that of an adviser who had the interests of the German government primarily at heart.[63] This conclusion is partly attributable to D'Abernon's pompous statements about reintegrating Germany into the international community. This is well and good, but D'Abernon was also mindful of the advantages to Britain if a security pact guaranteeing the integrity of France's border with Germany could be signed. This was an aspect of the negotiations that he believed that Chamberlain had at best played down and at worst completely ignored. As it was, D'Abernon thought that, just as it had been appropriate to create a demilitarised zone – an 'iron curtain' – in the Rhineland, so the British government should ensure that the English Channel served the same purpose for Britain.[64] Reiterating his argument about the consequences for Britain of a dominant French presence on the other side of the Channel, D'Abernon urged Chamberlain to 'look facts fully in the face, and not shirk the consideration of disagreeable possibilities as the forces behind the continental bloc idea [were] very considerable'.[65] On 20 July, he wrote that 'it is worthy of note that so far no one has brought forward the idea of guaranteeing the inviolability of the English Channel'.[66] These are the words of one who had not ruled out taking the lead in the conduct of British foreign policy himself. This can partly be explained by D'Abernon's view of balance of power diplomacy which set him apart from Chamberlain, who believed that war would only be avoided if that equilibrium was underpinned by objectives that were common to most nations, such as disarmament and the promotion of the work of the League. Chamberlain found D'Abernon's vision of Europe as a continent possibly on the brink of war too pessimistic and unlikely to improve the prospects for the conclusion of a security pact.[67]

Another aspect of this analysis of diplomatic tactics and timing is the extent to which the Foreign Office was aware of D'Abernon's involvement in the composition of the German security note. It has been suggested that D'Abernon made his plans known to Sir James Headlam-Morley, the Historical Adviser to the Foreign Office.[68] If that is accurate, Chamberlain should not have been surprised to receive the German note. As it was, D'Abernon merely inquired about the historical precedents for the conclusion of security agreements. The British government was therefore unaware of anything other than his general interest in the subject. At no time did Chamberlain, or anyone acting on his instructions, urge D'Abernon to encourage the German government to present a proposal for a security agreement. It was unlikely that anyone within the Foreign Office would have been given permission to approve a step that could have had such a potentially damaging effect on Anglo-French relations.[69]

D'Abernon's surprised response to Chamberlain's hostility is thus difficult to understand. Since it was his intention to persuade the British government of the merits of the German proposal, it is unclear why he believed that a caveat stating that its contents should not be discussed with the French would be palatable to Chamberlain. The situation was made worse by Chamberlain's subsequent discovery that he had not been kept informed by D'Abernon about the latter's diplomatic manoeuvrings in Berlin on this subject. Not only that, a senior member of the British Diplomatic Service appeared to be the principal author of the German security note. Yet throughout the spring of 1925, D'Abernon remained unable to understand how Chamberlain had 'derived so false an impression' of German intentions. He was further forced onto the defensive when concern was expressed in Berlin at Chamberlain's cool response. D'Abernon endeavoured to assure senior German politicians, including the Chancellor, Luther, that Chamberlain would eventually recognise the merits of the proposal and that it would ultimately receive a positive response from London.[70] The realisation of the enormity of the diplomatic task facing him, however, was reflected in his comment that Chamberlain's response had made the German government's efforts to gain Reichstag support to continue the security negotiations 'decidedly more difficult'.[71] Like Lloyd George three years earlier, D'Abernon found that his disregard for diplomatic conventions and procedures ultimately resulted in his being hoist by his own petard. That said, he would have regarded any comparison with Lloyd George as the highest compliment. Such was the complexity of his character.

Von Schubert was by no means confident that sending the security note to London before it was dispatched to Paris was the best course of action. Correctly, he anticipated that it could lead to accusations of trying to drive a wedge between the Allies and would be seen as a deliberate snub to the French. D'Abernon thought no such danger existed. He encouraged von Schubert to write an introduction to the proposal for inclusion with the text stressing the high regard in which the German government held Britain.[72] But as has been suggested, Chamberlain's response to the note was less positive than D'Abernon had led von Schubert to expect. It is difficult to view D'Abernon's dealings with the German government as anything other than idiosyncratic.[73] But von Schubert already had doubts about the soundness of D'Abernon's judgement and almost certainly used this to his advantage during the early days of the security negotiations.[74] Like Stresemann, von Schubert believed that if the security negotiations were to provide a diplomatic lever with the Allies, good relations with France had to be the ultimate objective. He saw his dealings with D'Abernon as an opportunity to test out on the British government ideas that were intended primarily for French consumption. What is more, he had made D'Abernon aware of this.[75] It was also concern about causing offence in Paris that prompted his remark that German consultation with the British could be interpreted as an underhand intrigue against France. D'Abernon's statements about Chamberlain's likely response are thus even more difficult to explain.

There was a lack of consistency in D'Abernon's relations with von Schubert. When the latter requested that the history of the German security proposal be revealed to Sir Eyre Crowe, the Permanent Under-Secretary at the Foreign Office, D'Abernon initially refused. He claimed to be offended by the proposal's suggestion that the German government did not wish to concentrate on the development of a special relationship with Britain but were looking for close allies on continental Europe. It is likely that he realised that Chamberlain would be less than pleased at his taking such a bold initiative without instruction. But he was equally keen that the proposal should still be used as an opportunity for the German government to take the initiative in the security debate. Yet, after some thought, D'Abernon made the odd decision to send the memorandum to Crowe, a well-known sceptic about the motives behind German foreign policy, as an indirect challenge to Chamberlain's pro-French policies and as an opportunity to persuade von Schubert to re-focus his attention on relations with Britain. Von Schubert was aware that there was a more subtle agenda behind D'Abernon's recommendations. He noted: 'Despite [D'Abernon's] statements, I do not exclude the possibility that he has already reported on this matter, but given the practices of the English this will not protect us against their pretending in their reply that [the report D'Abernon was about to dispatch] was in fact the first they had heard of the matter.'[76] Von Schubert's doubts remained. He asked Sthamer to find out what the British government's response was likely to be to the proposal.[77] At the same time, de Margerie, the French ambassador to Berlin, and von Hoesch, were asked to ascertain the likely French response.[78] The Germans had thus committed themselves to pursuing negotiations with the French before they had learned of the British reaction to their security proposal.[79]

A copy of the security note sent to London in January 1925 was dispatched to Paris a month later. Initial French reactions were reported to be favourable but because of considerable right-wing opposition to his government's policies, Herriot, the French Minister for Foreign Affairs, found it difficult to expedite a reply. D'Abernon urged Chamberlain to apply pressure on the French to respond quickly.[80] The German government suspected the adoption of underhand diplomatic tactics. Stresemann, D'Abernon reported, was convinced that the French were stalling in order to gain a psychological advantage over Germany in the negotiations.[81] Chamberlain dismissed such concerns and recommended that the Germans should regard the French reply when it came as 'a not unfriendly response to the German advance'. He gave D'Abernon instructions to pass on to Stresemann outlining the best way to react to the forthcoming French reply. The German government must realise that whatever its content, the French reply would 'open a new chapter' in the negotiations. To ensure a favourable German response in Berlin, British influence should be brought to bear in political circles.[82] D'Abernon thought that the Foreign Secretary had forgotten that the initial impetus in the diplomatic process had come from Germany and not from France. The onus was on the French, and not the Germans, to demonstrate a commitment to an 'improved relationship' and the conclusion of a security agreement.[83]

Von Schubert also hoped for an immediate response to the note.[84] He used D'Abernon as a means of exerting indirect pressure on the French government. He assumed that the ambassador enjoyed a good relationship with Chamberlain and he knew that the British Foreign Secretary liaised closely with the French government. In April, when the French reply was still not forthcoming, D'Abernon was asked to remind Chamberlain of the 'very magnanimous' nature of the German offer. When D'Abernon disclosed that Chamberlain wished the Germans to get in touch with him before replying to French questions, von Schubert's anger increased. Suspecting that the British were now conspiring with the French to create obstacles to future negotiations, he said the German government was becoming 'very averse' to 'confidential conversations... with Britain', because they ultimately became the subject of 'highly indiscreet statements' by Chamberlain.[85]

Von Schubert's scorn was not merely reserved for Chamberlain. Several weeks later, in May 1925, when D'Abernon suggested that the German government might renew the security offer in order to inject fresh life into the negotiations, von Schubert described British and French responses to the German note as 'ludicrous' and accused them of 'performing a wretched operetta to no purpose'.[86] The situation was further complicated when the French government insisted on a date for evacuation of the Cologne Zone being settled as a pre-condition for signing the security pact. Neither von Schubert nor D'Abernon approved of this because they believed that it would excessively prolong the negotiations. Von Schubert also wished to keep the two issues as separate as possible to give the German government leverage with the Allies in the future and because both issues impacted strongly on German relations with the Soviet Union.[87]

The French response

By the end of May, von Schubert was growing impatient at the French government's failure to respond to the German security note and to clarify its position on the future of the Cologne Zone.[88] He told D'Abernon that regarding the security initiative even a preliminary recognition that the German note was 'a sincere endeavour to improve present conditions and arrive at a basis for pacification' would be acceptable.[89] When the French government finally published its response on 16 June, von Schubert's spirits were lowered by the apparent absence of good faith in the tone of the text. He was now 'far from optimistic' about the prospects of a security pact, particularly since the response made it clear that the French government now reserved the right to define what constituted a 'hostile act'. D'Abernon believed the Germans were becoming too bogged down in 'small details' and that the negotiations should move on to the next stage. This was not mere impatience. He feared that von Schubert had formed a 'totally erroneous' view of the underlying intentions of the French note.[90] But D'Abernon failed to persuade the German government to heed his advice. Both von Schubert and Stresemann long continued to believe that the French had shown insufficient willingness to negotiate with Germany on equal and reasonable terms. Von Schubert expressed particular surprise at what he saw as D'Abernon's insensitivity on this issue. He thought it was the height of arrogance to keep the German government waiting for four months and then to reply by 'flinging an ultra-official note in our face'. He was 'astounded' that D'Abernon could not see this.[91]

Relations between D'Abernon and von Schubert continued to be strained as the German government considered its response to the French note. Once again, D'Abernon's diplomatic tactics appear idiosyncratic. Von Schubert was surprised that D'Abernon tried to 'tranquillise [his] apprehensions' by referring to Lampson's conversations with Sthamer as evidence of support for the German position.[92] As suggested earlier, it is doubtful whether von Schubert would have been convinced of the willingness of the British government to give equal consideration to German as to French security requirements. For example, von Schubert thought that the pro-French bias of British diplomacy made it inevitable that Britain would give support to French desires to improve relations with Poland. D'Abernon, on the other hand, thought that the British government had no intention of becoming involved in any such diplomatic initiative. He did, however, suggest that Germany should conclude an arbitration treaty with Poland under French guarantee. This would make Germany 'much better off' because relations between France and Poland were fragile or, as he quaintly put it, 'that of a man who wished to part from his mistress in a mannerly fashion'.[93] Initially D'Abernon wished this suggestion to be held in the strictest confidence. But on reflection, he decided that a more forthright approach was desirable. Seeing an opportunity to test French commitment to the security process, D'Abernon suggested that the Germans should announce that the proposed agreement with Poland would be bilateral. Von Schubert was more cautious. He rejected this idea because he did not believe that France would ever take action against Poland in favour of Germany. As it was, D'Abernon's suggestion proved to be counterproductive because his assessment of the Polish position persuaded von Schubert and Stresemann to give further consideration to signing a mutual assistance treaty with the Soviet Union. Both feared that if France was not allied with Poland, immediate overtures would be made in Moscow to conclude a Russo-French agreement that would scupper much of Stresemann's eastern European agenda. The German government therefore felt that steps had to be taken to ensure that, if the Russians formed an alliance, it would be with Germany rather than with France. Diplomatic contact with von Hoesch was increased to monitor French relations with the Soviet Union. Von Schubert also cultivated closer relations with de Margerie for the same purpose. In a letter to von Hoesch, von Schubert confided his fear that through D'Abernon he was receiving only a 'one-sided' account of the diplomatic intricacies surrounding the security negotiations.[94]

At the heart of von Schubert's fears lay the belief that the German government would no longer receive adequate consultation as the negotiations progressed. In his conversations with D'Abernon, he continually referred to the 'right' of the German government to have 'a voice in the matter' and to the desperate need to avoid a 'cast-iron mould'.[95] He was particularly worried that negotiations were taking place between legal officials of the British and French governments to discuss procedure in the absence of a German representative.[96] D'Abernon endeavoured to reassure him that German interests would be given full consideration and pointed out that, despite German reservations, contact between the legal experts of the principal countries involved was inevitable.[97] He persuaded von Schubert that the conference of jurists was a more effective means of making the German position heard than direct contact with the Foreign Ministers of Britain and France. Recommending the appointment of Gaus as the German representative at such a gathering, D'Abernon 'hinted' that the latter was a 'greater politician' than the British and French experts and consequently the German government would 'enjoy a certain advantage'. D'Abernon was to be proved correct. During the later stages of the security negotiations, Gaus demonstrated his skills as a shrewd negotiator.[98]

Chamberlain's pro-French stance and impatience with the German position made D'Abernon's task of reassuring von Schubert increasingly difficult. The French reply had stressed that the negotiations could not proceed further unless Germany joined the League without making special conditions about membership. This meant in effect that Germany would be admitted without being a member of the Council – a requirement that the Germans had long insisted upon in recognition of Germany's former status as a Great Power. Chamberlain believed that it was 'monstrous' to allege that the French note had misrepresented the German proposal and that it was clear to all that the French were making an 'honest attempt' to further the negotiations.[99] Matters were made worse by the arrival in Berlin of a stream of telegrams from Sthamer chronicling Chamberlain's close relationship with Briand.[100] When von Schubert learnt that Chamberlain remained unenthusiastic about the German security proposals, he summoned D'Abernon to express his dismay. Von Schubert interpreted Chamberlain's complaints that the German government had failed to view the French note as proof that the Allies intended to impose a security agreement on Germany.[101] When D'Abernon later reported that Chamberlain had accused him of becoming too involved in the formulation of German security policy, von Schubert regarded this as evidence of French-led hostility to Germany.[102]

But Chamberlain's assessment of D'Abernon's role at this point in the negotiations was essentially accurate. At the height of von Schubert's concerns about the possible impact of the Chamberlain–Briand relationship on the German position in the security negotiations, D'Abernon told von Schubert that he had in his possession a security note based on recent dialogues between Chamberlain and Briand. Mindful of Chamberlain's warning, D'Abernon hesitated before he revealed its text but realised that if he withheld it, it would confirm German suspicions that the British and French governments were acting independently of Germany. What he failed to realise was that von Schubert was fully aware of his tactics. Von Schubert wrote: 'It is intended in London to take us by surprise with an official note, that Lord D'Abernon knows this very well, but that he wished to keep us guessing.'[103] Stresemann was aware of the way in which statements from right-wing German politicians appeared to the French. Stresemann thought that a plot to undermine the future of the negotiations had been hatched because of French fears about Hindenburg's recent election as German President.[104] German political opinion about the note had polarised between those who were sceptical about the government's policy on security and those who thought an agreement with the Allies remained desirable but that the negotiations had been handled badly. D'Abernon issued a reminder about how much the Luther–Stresemann government had achieved in persuading the Allies of its good faith and how much German efforts were recognised.[105] Once again, he was engaging in wishful thinking. On this occasion, his motives were entirely understandable. Nevertheless, he was stretching the boundaries of the truth to their very limits.

Sensing this, Stresemann made it clear to D'Abernon that he did not share his optimism.[106] He thought that the French note was too detailed to merit discussion and that further consideration would not be given to it until German objections to its contents had been resolved. D'Abernon tried to persuade him to take a more favourable attitude, emphasising the amount of respect that the German government commanded in Britain because of its desire to conclude a security agreement and because the British government recognised the amount of domestic opposition the Germans had had to overcome to participate in the negotiations. It is difficult to know why D'Abernon continued to believe that Stresemann would be reassured by these latter points as Sthamer's dispatches had made the attitude of Chamberlain very clear. Despite this, D'Abernon felt compelled to report that Stresemann was 'determined to press forward [the] pact negotiation with maximum speed and [was] still whole-hearted[ly] behind it'; a striking observation given Stresemann's actual comments. The only conclusion that D'Abernon presented to Chamberlain that genuinely reflected the mood of Stresemann's remarks related to the strength of the opposition his statements on security had encountered in the Reichstag.

Throughout the summer of 1925, Chamberlain attempted to persuade D'Abernon that the French government had never been more 'set on peace' and that never before had Britain 'marked its desire for better relations with Germany or spoken with such generous appreciation of the attitude of the Germans'.[107] At the same time, Chamberlain continued to be exasperated by German reservations about French attitudes towards the security negotiations. He thought that because the German government had voiced objections to the French reply, which had received British approval, the Germans regarded him as a 'dupe'. Once again, he interpreted the German attitude as evidence that their note of January had been sent 'with the hope of creating dissension in the councils of the allies'. D'Abernon was instructed to ensure that Stresemann knew of the 'deplorable impression' that German reactions to the French reply had made in Britain. The onus was now on the Germans to convince the Allies of the sincerity of their commitment to the conclusion of a security pact.[108]

Nevertheless, Chamberlain was reluctant to condemn German statements outright until he had had an opportunity to discuss the progress of the negotiations with the French. In the meantime, he warned D'Abernon not to use the lull in negotiations to embark on another unauthorised initiative. In particular, he should not encourage the Germans to make an 'independent' statement to the French reply. This might be open to 'misunderstanding' and prompt the expressing of a view 'with which the French subsequently found themselves unable to agree and of thus laying themselves open to a charge of disloyalty'. Chamberlain felt confident that in time the German government would see the merits of the French reply, but warned that if they did not, 'the world [would] quickly revise its estimate of the nature and purpose of their original proposals' and suggested that Germany would rightly be accused of 'deliberately repudiating the policy of peace… [that] she herself was the first to propose'.[109]

In July, the German government published its response to the French note. Chamberlain hoped that it would remove any remaining obstacles to direct negotiation, but was disappointed to learn that the French government was not satisfied with its content. His anger, however, was targeted at Berlin and not at Paris. He complained that while the German government had had it in its power 'to write a note which would have enabled me to insist on immediate conversations', a response had been communicated that would 'probably render unavoidable a further reply before any effective progress can be made'.[110] Chamberlain's scepticism about the German government's commitment to the security pact was increasing. He thought that the second note appeared to be on 'a different principle and [had] a wholly different aspect' to that dispatched in January. Now the German government no longer occupied the role of the 'far-seeing contributor to the general cause of peace, but rather that of a somewhat unwilling participant, who acquiesces in a scheme, not because of its intrinsic merits, but merely in the hope that consent will enable him to drive a bargain in other directions'.[111] He despaired of the future of the negotiations when the need to construct a framework for direct dialogue was not shared by the German government. D'Abernon was instructed to inform Luther and Stresemann that if the Allies' desire for direct negotiations was rejected, the responsibility for the collapse of the security negotiations would rest solely with the German government. Chamberlain was 'amazed at the blindness of the Germans to the inevitable consequences of [their] own action' while they asked the Allies for 'patience, forbearance and statesmanship, not to say courage, in [the] face of public opinion in which in effect they avow themselves incapable'.[112] D'Abernon found it difficult to understand Chamberlain's argument. He could see no reason why face-to-face negotiations could not begin immediately.[113] But Chamberlain clearly thought that D'Abernon had not impressed the extent of his displeasure upon the Germans with sufficient force, telling him that 'I fear you do not realise what difficulties they have quite gratuitously created for others as well as themselves.'[114]

Direct negotiation

Chamberlain was now determined to start a process of direct negotiation. On 11 August 1925, he discussed the proposed French reply to the most recent German note with Briand. He later wrote a forceful letter informing D'Abernon that the French note would conclude with 'direct invitations to the Germans to enter in conversations on the basis of this correspondence'. Such an invitation was intended to make the German task of replying more straightforward thus avoiding further animus over the interpretation of text and clause.[115] Chamberlain then suggested that Gaus should come to London to discuss the legal implications of a security agreement with representatives of the Allied governments. Gaus would then communicate the results of these discussions to the German government and would discuss the German response with the Allies. When this process was complete, the way would be clear for a security conference to take place.[116]

Nevertheless, the German government remained unconvinced about the sincerity of British and especially French objectives in seeking a security agreement with Germany. Stresemann felt that unless German objections were met or a timetable for their resolution established, there was little to prevent the Allies imposing an agreement on Germany.

Once again, Chamberlain was not wholly convinced that D'Abernon had conveyed to the German government the gravity of the situation. At the end of August, D'Abernon was asked to explain 'in firm but friendly terms' that the British government did not understand the actions of its German counterpart.[117] A month later, Chamberlain found further grounds for criticising the way that D'Abernon was communicating the British position. The Foreign Secretary had been sent a series of press cuttings from Crewe outlining the 'official' attitude of Stresemann towards the security negotiations. These claimed that D'Abernon had persuaded the Germans to insist on extra French assurances concerning the preservation of Germany's western frontier. It is not clear whether Chamberlain believed these rumours but, as a precaution, he warned D'Abernon against the employment of 'destructive tactics' that might scupper the security negotiations.[118] Should the alleged comments have been made by Stresemann, D'Abernon was to leave him in 'no doubt' that additional conditions of this nature were unacceptable.[119]

In the ensuing weeks, Chamberlain repeatedly wrote about the 'niggling, provocative and crooked' negotiating style of the German government.[120] D'Abernon as ever remained convinced that Chamberlain's attitude was too uncompromising. In particular, he thought that Chamberlain's belief that as soon as German 'overtures are accepted, they begin to whittle away their assurances and to introduce new conditions' was unfair and inaccurate.[121] D'Abernon was frustrated by the difficulties caused for him in Berlin by Chamberlain's negative interpretation of the German approach to the negotiations. He told Luther and Stresemann candidly that Chamberlain was 'too quick to take offence at German actions'.[122]

Beyond Locarno

In October 1925, representatives of the British, French, German and Italian governments met at the Swiss resort of Locarno to sign a series of multilateral and bilateral treaties. Most of those who were involved in the negotiations were to regard the treaties of Locarno as the greatest diplomatic achievement of their careers. However, the Treaty of Locarno – the principal agreement which confirmed the permanence of Germany's western frontiers as defined by the Treaty of Versailles – marked the start of an era when discussions about security and disarmament were foremost in the minds of politicians and diplomats, not the end.

Von Schubert's doubts about the motives behind Allied policy continued throughout the negotiations of 1925. He was surprised at the euphoric response given to the Treaty of Locarno, primarily because he thought that it only fulfilled half of Germany's security agenda in Europe.[123] Unlike D'Abernon, who now thought that Germany was safely within the western European fold, von Schubert began turning his attention towards concluding an entente with the Soviet Union. He told von Hoesch that 'neither East nor West can, nor wish to, tempt us into a real alliance, such as could cause us to abandon our policy of the free hand'.[124] One of von Schubert's closest allies was Sthamer, who interpreted British foreign policy in a different way from D'Abernon. Sthamer was convinced that if the Treaty of Locarno was not counter-balanced by a German rapprochement with the Soviet Union soon, it was only a matter of time before such an option would have to be forsaken. Once Germany had been admitted to the League, there would be a 'regrouping of the European powers to the exclusion of Russia'.[125]

D'Abernon was surprised by von Schubert's enthusiasm to conclude an agreement with the Soviet Union. He was so astounded that when de Margerie told him of von Schubert's preferred policy, he wondered whether the French ambassador's sources were reliable.[126] He asked von Schubert to specify the advantages to Germany of concluding such an agreement. The latter conceded they were not considerable but would prevent the Russians from 'going right away' from German policy. If the Russians were 'at a loose end', they might feel compelled to act in a manner inconsistent with German interests.[127] Nevertheless, von Schubert was anxious to reassure D'Abernon that the negotiation of an agreement with the Soviet Union did not imply any reduction in the German commitment to the Treaty of Locarno. When in April 1926, a draft Russo-German agreement was produced, D'Abernon feared that it would be used as an extension of the Treaty of Rapallo and thus as a means of divorcing Germany from the west. Von Schubert denied an alliance was being contemplated but the spirit of openness created by the Locarno agreements made it necessary for the Allies to be told of Germany's negotiations with the Soviet Union.[128] He then composed a dispatch to Chamberlain for this purpose. D'Abernon however was not convinced. He believed that closer German relations with the Soviet Union would have a negative effect on future Anglo-German relations. Von Schubert admitted that it appeared to be the aim of the Russian government to drive a wedge between Germany and the Allies but assured him that the Russians' tactics were 'too transparent to be taken seriously'. D'Abernon nevertheless, remained gravely concerned.[129]

D'Abernon's concerns increased in the spring of 1926 when rumours were rife of a diplomatic rift between Poland and France. If the Soviet

Union formed an alliance with Poland, Germany would no longer have an eastern buffer against communist infiltration. Such an agreement would also preclude the territorial revision in that area that von Schubert and Stresemann so desired. D'Abernon was thus forced to admit that it would 'be much better if Germany made a treaty with Russia than if Poland did'.[130] He and von Schubert discussed the contents of a draft dispatch to be sent to Chamberlain. Von Schubert was relieved that D'Abernon was now 'completely convinced that our agreement really was fully in line with the Locarno policy'.[131] But D'Abernon had little choice.

Germany and the Soviet Union

The development of a close relationship with the Soviet Union had a particular resonance for the German governments of the 1920s. The memory of Russian friendship in Germany's darkest hours, when the Allies seemed unsure how to implement the Treaty of Versailles, cast a long shadow over the gradual improvement in diplomatic relations between the British, French and German governments, particularly after the conclusion of the Treaty of Rapallo in the spring of 1922. This is a point that D'Abernon never fully comprehended. During the next four years, the Russian government endeavoured to persuade the German government to adhere to the Treaty of Rapallo and to forge closer economic and political relations between the two countries.[132] The Russians were anxious to prevent Germany from joining the League – a body that they thought acted as a focus for anti-communist activity. Stresemann was unwilling to make a formal commitment to the Soviet Union but stated that Germany would only enter the League on conditions that kept the option of a Soviet alliance open. Whether Soviet suspicions could be allayed by discussing a possible commercial rapprochement was debated at the highest political level in Berlin throughout the negotiation of the Treaty of Locarno. The next step was dictated by the Allies as it became increasingly clear that the British and French were determined to link Germany's signature of a security agreement with her admission to the League.[133]

D'Abernon was not involved in the negotiations between Germany and the Soviet Union that culminated in the signature of the Treaty of Berlin in April 1926, which provided a reaffirmation of the Rapallo treaty signed four years earlier, while further extending the range of commercial links between Germany and the Soviet Union. He was familiar with German desires to cultivate closer links with the Russians, but remained confident of the ability of the Allies to steer Germany away from such a course through a satisfactory solution of the reparations question. The German government had been rash to sign the Treaty of Rapallo and had been bullied into doing so by the Soviet government. Faced with a choice between closer links with the Allies or the Soviet Union, he was confident that the German government would always choose the former.[134] D'Abernon was not concerned lest an alliance between Germany and the Soviet Union be used to attack the western Allies because he was convinced of the sincerity of Stresemann and von Schubert's commitment to the Treaty of Locarno. Furthermore, any treaty of mutual assistance would not amount to much because Russians and the Germans did not 'think' about diplomacy in the same way.[135]

It is doubtful in fact whether D'Abernon was ever clear about Stresemann's attitude and policy towards the Soviet Union. This was partly because the German Minister for Foreign Affairs often changed tack at the last minute in order to maintain satisfactory relations with the Russians and with the west, thus depriving the ambassador of the necessary time to inform or consult. Nevertheless, private comments made by D'Abernon suggest that he was unclear about Stresemann's objectives. In a discussion of the Rhineland question, Stresemann told D'Abernon that if the French had invaded the Rhineland in 1923 as well as the Ruhr, 'Germany would have formed a coalition with the Soviet Union, and together [they] would have swept over Europe'. D'Abernon was shocked at this suggestion but dismissed it as unfeasible. Doubts nevertheless lingered in his mind. In the privacy of his diary, he wrote: 'I do not know how far Stresemann was serious in his retrospective threat, but I am pretty convinced that no German Government could have carried out the scheme, however great the temptation.'[136] Despite this, D'Abernon did not feel compelled to convey his misgivings to Chamberlain.

Nevertheless, after the Locarno conference, D'Abernon felt certain that as soon as the security agreement was ratified 'the old danger of a Russo-German alliance versus the western powers may be regarded as obsolete'.[137] When, therefore, he learnt that the German government was continuing to pursue a vigorous policy towards the Soviet Union and intended to conclude a second treaty of neutrality, he believed that such an agreement would incline Germany too far to the east. D'Abernon was anxious that the German government should realise that an alliance with the Soviet Union might not be in Germany's best interests in the long term. He warned that 'what happened once may happen again' because when the Germans were 'disappointed in the West', they were 'apt to turn to the East for consolation and support'.[138]

Even during the final stages of the negotiation of the Treaty of Berlin, D'Abernon remained convinced that Stresemann's desire to conclude an agreement with the Soviet Union was 'because he was afraid not to'.[139] As a result, the psychological effect on D'Abernon of the conclusion of the Russo-German treaty was great.[140] He believed that all of his work since November 1924 had been fundamentally undermined.[141] He was also anxious to ensure that the Treaty of Berlin did not detract from the new spirit of friendship created by the Treaty of Locarno. He admitted that he had been unable to persuade Stresemann to reconsider his position but took some comfort from the fact that Stresemann's attitude towards the Soviet Union did not command unanimous political support within Germany.[142] He was surprised when the German Foreign Affairs Committee passed a unanimous vote in favour of the Treaty of Berlin and was distressed that the Locarno agreements had not been greeted with the same enthusiasm. Faced with accepting this unpalatable fact, he played down its significance, writing: 'Personally, I am sceptical, but rejoice to see that the western powers have taken the fact of the signature quietly and without lapse into nervosity.'[143]

During the remainder of his embassy, D'Abernon did not mastermind any special initiatives and did not offer unusual amounts of advice to either the British or the German governments. When the German delegation returned to Berlin, D'Abernon told Chamberlain privately that he believed that the success of Locarno was solely due to British influence.[144] But it is likely that he was referring to himself and not to Chamberlain. The Foreign Secretary's instinctive attitude towards German security policy is revealed in his correspondence with D'Abernon. He constantly referred to German 'duplicity' both before and after the Treaty of Locarno had been signed. These comments were made more than a decade before his claim that Hitler's occupation of the Rhineland in 1936 vindicated his scepticism about the German commitment to a common European security policy.[145] In his collection of reflections on British politics and European diplomacy, he issued several warnings about the German commitment to peace that proved to be prophetic. In this respect, Chamberlain deserves kinder treatment by historians than he has sometimes received because it was he, and not D'Abernon, who was proved right. The disagreements between Chamberlain and D'Abernon were not just differences of emphasis. They illustrated a fundamental crisis in British foreign policy in the mid-1920s. These two men represented the two sides of a debate that dominated Anglo-European relations after the First World War – how to strike a balance between protecting French security needs and aiding the economic and political regeneration of Germany. Similarly, if the long-term consequences of the Treaty of Locarno to Britain are examined, it is clear that it did not lead to a radical rethinking of Foreign Office policy towards Germany. To D'Abernon, Britain and Germany were natural allies but, with Chamberlain at the Foreign Office, he believed that an agreement should be concluded that would prevent the Foreign Secretary from promoting an anti-German alliance with France. D'Abernon was only to remain in Berlin for another year, while Chamberlain would occupy the post of Foreign Secretary until 1929. Chamberlain was thus in a stronger position to influence the direction of Anglo-European diplomacy in the years that followed. His response to the controversy in 1926 concerning the German government's insistence on being given a permanent seat in the League of Nations Council on admission to the League illustrated that the signature of the Treaty of Locarno had had little effect on his attitude towards Germany.[146] By the early summer of 1926, however, D'Abernon felt that he had been swept aside as Stresemann focused on his own agenda. He accepted that the German government would place as much emphasis on relations with the Soviet Union as with the Allies, but believed that it was important to do all that he could to reinforce Germany's commitment to the western European powers through the Treaty of Locarno. It was with growing disillusionment that D'Abernon devoted much of his energies in the final months of his embassy to securing the admission of Germany to the League of Nations.

7
The Admission of Germany to the League of Nations, 1922–26

The attitude of the British and German governments towards the work of the League of Nations, an organisation that was the very embodiment of the commitment of many of the world's nations to the pursuit of peace at the end of the First World War, illustrates many of the differences between the two countries towards international diplomacy. To the British government, the League was a worthwhile cause but one which, potentially, threatened to embroil Britain in diplomatic conflicts where her interests were not at stake. This was the price of a permanent seat on the League's governing body, the Council, but one that was thought to be worth paying in the same way that the burdensome task of administering the empire offered Britain enormous influence in international diplomacy. At the same time, a balance needed to be struck between the work of the League and the requirements of British foreign policy, particularly regarding European security. It was this debate that the British government was engaged in throughout D'Abernon's embassy and for much of the remainder of the interwar period. In contrast, the German governments that held office between 1920 and 1926 viewed membership of the League as a means to an end – as an opportunity to deal with the Allies on equal terms to secure concessions relating to the security of Germany's frontiers and potential revisions of the Treaty of Versailles. The League was never regarded with the same idealistic enthusiasm in Germany as it was in Britain. Indeed, it was seen by those on the right as a means of perpetuating British and French diplomatic hegemony in Europe and reinforcing the less palatable elements of the peace treaty. Throughout D'Abernon's embassy, League membership remained a German goal, but the enthusiasm with which it was pursued fluctuated according to German perceptions of the Allies' attitude towards Germany's right to a major role in international diplomacy. If the diplomatic negotiations that culminated in the admission of Germany to the League in the autumn of 1926 are examined, D'Abernon emerges as a figure who was often marginalised in Berlin and who found it difficult to believe that Chamberlain ever really intended to treat Germany on equal terms with the Allies. The controversy about the meaning of Article 16 of the League Covenant and the League Council Crisis of 1926 reveal a great deal about British and German attitudes towards involvement in international diplomacy. In particular, Stresemann's insistence that Germany should be given a permanent seat on the League Council suggests that he saw the League as a way of promoting German nationalist goals, and not, as D'Abernon believed, as a means of improving relations with the Allies.

The dilemma that faced the British government and D'Abernon over the 'old' and 'new' diplomacy is reflected in the way that historians have viewed the League. The organisation has been described as a 'modern' institution that favoured 'diplomacy by conference' as a means of resolving international disputes.[1] F.S. Northedge, on the other hand, sees the League as an Allied attempt to preserve the 'old' diplomacy by viewing it as an extension of the nineteenth-century 'congress' system.[2] Because the world that inspired its creation was very different from the world in which it operated, Northedge argues that the League was doomed from the outset. What is more, the Allies were powerless to do anything because they were unaware of the flaws in the system until Europe's problems were so serious that League intervention made little difference. If the League is regarded as a pre-war creation, this has a number of implications for the study of D'Abernon's embassy. The foreign policy of the Luther–Stresemann government had a fundamentally nationalist agenda. Therefore, admission to an international body which was based on a system which Bismarck manipulated to ensure the predominance of Germany in Europe at the end of the nineteenth century was in the Germans' best interests.[3] Consequently, it is doubtful whether D'Abernon, or indeed Briand and Chamberlain, had much influence on Stresemann's League policy. Northedge's argument also presents an opportunity to evaluate Chamberlain's Foreign Secretaryship. His continued refusal to adopt a more 'open' form of diplomacy can be seen as a contributing factor to D'Abernon's resignation.

British policy

Close British consideration of the admission of Germany to the League of Nations had begun in the spring of 1920. During the following two years, the government grew increasingly impatient with the French for creating what appeared to be trivial obstacles to an analysis of the German requests for membership.[4] Austen Chamberlain, then Lord Privy Seal, and Herbert Fisher, a British delegate to the League, believed that Britain should work towards dispelling the German view that the League was 'a machine for executing French policy'. They recommended that 'no stone should be left unturned' to secure the admission of Germany to the League.[5] Sir Eric Drummond, Secretary General of the League, believed however that French interests should be of greater concern to the British government. The French should be made to realise that it was in their interests to 'get Germany inside'. More significantly, he anticipated that if Germany were to become a member of the League, French influence would act as a check on any resurgence of German nationalism.[6] The consensus of opinion in the Cabinet was that France, through her growing friendship with Poland, would help to guarantee a geographical buffer between the Soviet Union and Germany.

When D'Abernon learned of these discussions, he was concerned that the German position was not being given sufficient priority. At a meeting in Downing Street with Lloyd George, Balfour, Chamberlain and Hankey in June 1922, D'Abernon emphasised that the German government wished to join the League to prove that it was committed to a peaceful course and that it had accepted the terms of the Treaty of Versailles.[7] He argued that the main obstacle to achieving this goal was continued and unreasonable French hostility. At D'Abernon's suggestion, Lloyd George agreed to provide Germany with some measure of protection from France should an application for German membership be made. Pressure would be brought to bear on the French to promise not to oppose German entry. D'Abernon felt sure that once this was clear, the German government would apply for immediate admission.[8]

D'Abernon then discussed the League question with the German Chancellor, Wirth. Once again, such conversations pose questions about the extent of D'Abernon's influence in Berlin and illustrate his idiosyncratic approach to the conduct of diplomacy. While Wirth believed that Britain was sympathetic to the German position, he remained concerned by what he termed the 'uncertainty and fragility of [Britain's] support'. Instead of trying to reassure Wirth, D'Abernon stated that Anglo-German relations would be better served if the German government believed that it could 'not count on [Britain] too surely'. Such a policy, D'Abernon anticipated, would ensure that the German government would continue to seek closer relations with Britain. He told Curzon that 'the German steed runs perhaps more kindly if not too self-confident'.[9] Not surprisingly, D'Abernon's tactics did not work. Wirth condemned the League as an 'institution from which Germany has nothing good to expect' and claimed that 'tangible British support for the German case' had not been sufficiently forthcoming.[10] He then sent a letter to Lloyd George outlining German reservations about the League. Lloyd George discussed the question with Balfour who thought that D'Abernon had clearly misjudged German enthusiasm for League membership.[11] Of particular concern was Wirth's assertion that, if Germany entered the League, Britain would 'abandon her to her enemies'. D'Abernon was instructed to assure the German government that this would not happen and to dispel the view that the League operated under French control.[12] Although he told Hankey that Wirth 'had failed to say what he means', D'Abernon had misunderstood German attitudes on this issue.[13] The absence of accurate information from D'Abernon contributed to British difficulties in aiding Germany's admission to the League.

The situation was further aggravated when Balfour outlined his objections to the German position in a memorandum, written after consultation with Saint-Aulaire, the French ambassador to London. It stated that Britain wished to expedite Germany's admission to the League, but conceded that objections had been voiced by both the French and German governments. Balfour stressed that the French were anxious to mollify Germany but that Wirth's views were unacceptable to them. If Germany were to be admitted to the League in September 1922, her government would view the matter with 'very different eyes'. More significantly, Saint-Aulaire had argued that it would threaten Anglo-French relations if Germany entered the League under 'British patronage against French wishes'. Balfour believed that the German government possessed a 'great ignorance of what [the League] has done and what it is doing'. In contrast, the French were 'genuinely convinced' that Germany had fulfilled her obligations under the Treaty of Versailles and intended to observe them in the future. He was perturbed by Wirth's comment that the League was 'completely identified with the Versailles Treaty' and that it was regarded as an 'instrument' to execute that treaty. He concluded that Germany wished to enter the League, to 'upset the Versailles arrangement' and recommended that the British government should dispel the impression that the British were in any sense 'patrons of Germany'.[14]

The beginning of the Ruhr crisis in January 1923 produced mounting reluctance on the part of the British government to offer open support for the admission of Germany to the League. In Berlin, D'Abernon came under pressure from the German government to obtain a British commitment to push ahead with admission. It was made clear to him that any wavering of British support at this time would be construed as condoning the Franco-Belgian occupation.[15] D'Abernon proposed a compromise solution. He suggested that the British government should create a link between the admission of Germany to the League and Allied recognition of German territorial sovereignty. As the Ruhr occupation continued, exchanges between the French and German ambassadors to London and the Foreign Office indicated the difficulty of the British position.[16]

The tensions surrounding this matter were eased through a number of factors. The resolution of the reparations question through the Dawes Plan enabled the French to focus their attention on European security. The new British Prime Minister, Ramsay MacDonald, possessed a less ambiguous enthusiasm for the work of the League than his predecessors, viewing it as an important means of guaranteeing future peace. He believed that both Germany and the Soviet Union ought to join as soon as possible.[17] D'Abernon agreed. He thought that the League could only operate if there was a 'certain balance-of-power guaranteed by Britain' that would ensure that 'French military supremacy [would] not be exaggerated and that German military subjection should not be excessive'.[18] He therefore saw a close link between the admission of Germany to the League and the future of European security. More importantly, D'Abernon viewed the League as an important means of preventing the French bullying Germany. He envisaged a close partnership between the decision-making apparatus of the organisation, the rights its members enjoyed and a general security treaty to promote the German point of view in international diplomacy.

Chamberlain and the League

Chamberlain was less enthusiastic about the League than D'Abernon. During the security negotiations in the spring and summer of 1925, he relished giving speeches at the League headquarters at Geneva. But his visits were little more than a reaffirmation of relations with France and were more about making his mark as Foreign Secretary rather than demonstrating a commitment to the ideals of the League.[19] There were other influential critics of the League in London. A memorandum by Harold Nicolson, a minister at the Foreign Office, on British security policy suggested that while the League was 'a wholly admirable institution', it would be 'unsafe to count upon its authority being sufficient to restrain a Great Power in any case in which that power considers its vital interests to be at state'. He concluded that it was 'vain... to hide the fact that a sense of security cannot, in such vital matters, today emanate from Geneva'.[20] Nicolson believed that there was a close connection between European security and developing the role of the League. This was consistent with the opinion that Chamberlain had held since the war and was one reason why it had been possible to persuade him to abandon a bilateral security agreement in favour of a framework that included Germany. Nicolson anticipated that the multilateral security agreement would provide a basic commitment to avoid war in the future as a means of solving international disputes. From that, he hoped that much more specific issues could be addressed. One of the most important was providing further ways of reassuring France that the threat of a German attack had been permanently removed.[21]

As his Foreign Secretaryship progressed, Chamberlain grew increasingly uninterested in the League. He believed that it had a potentially large role to play in influencing international relations but was equally convinced that Britain's foreign policy should be determined in London and not in Geneva. He anticipated that it should be possible to create a basis on which Britain could negotiate with Germany on the issue of security and the question of admission to the League and believed that British cooperation was essential to the successful conclusion of both matters. He also hoped that by securing the admission of Germany, the danger of war in the east would be reduced and the French commitment to Poland strengthened.[22] However, he was disconcerted that the Germans appeared not only to be dictating the agenda of the security negotiations and insisting on special conditions for admission, but that they wished the process to take place at breakneck speed. He interpreted this as a tactic to obtain concessions from the Allies without giving time for due consideration and reflection.[23]

In the early summer of 1925, Chamberlain continued to warn the Germans against insisting on special concessions before admission to the League. He also became convinced that the text of the proposed security agreement should contain a clause committing Germany to seek admission.[24] D'Abernon did not agree, thinking that it would be counter-productive to apply pressure on the German government in this way. He was concerned that it would make Stresemann's task in obtaining support in the Reichstag for the security pact still more difficult. D'Abernon anticipated that the admission of Germany after such an agreement had been signed would occur naturally and that no further consideration of Germany's status within the League would be necessary.[25] He also believed that Britain should use German admission as a means of preserving political influence in Germany.

After the Locarno agreements had been signed, Chamberlain continued to accuse the German government of lacking a commitment to the spirit and operation of the security pact. He complained that the Germans too often resorted to 'ever-growing demands put forward as ultimatums'.[26] In a typical dispatch on the subject, he told D'Abernon:

> I do feel most strongly that Germany has not done her share towards confirmation of the new relationship. I try to make all allowances for the difficulties of the [German] Government and I do not attempt to apportion blame, but if you exonerate the Government it can only be at the expense of the German nation or at least of German political parties. You know how much we conceded after Locarno in the endeavour to make the task of the Government easy and these seem to me to be matters in which the Government ought to have been able to act whatever their parliamentary difficulties in regard to the entry of Germany into the League.[27]

German attitudes towards League membership

German policy towards the League was much less complex. The early governments of the Weimar Republic believed that it was important to be a member. As the British and French played a leading role in its activities, German membership would afford an opportunity to negotiate in a forum dedicated to the promotion of peace and reconciliation. Germany should be admitted to the League as soon as certain issues had been addressed. Membership of the League was viewed as a way of proving, or at least suggesting, that German militarism and aggression were a thing of the past. At the same time, those on the right of German politics saw membership as an opportunity to debate the terms of the Treaty of Versailles with the Allies on equal terms. Consequently, it was logical and necessary that Germany, one of the world's Great Powers, should be given a permanent seat on the principal governing body of the League, its Council. As Britain and France dominated this body, attaining such a position was viewed as an important step towards an equality of status between Germany and her former enemies. Stresemann was therefore anxious to pursue League membership, especially during and after the negotiation of the Treaty of Locarno. The prospect of German membership also gave him diplomatic leverage with the Russians, who opposed such a move root and branch as evidence of Allied attempts to 'corrupt' Germany.

It had been widely believed that if the Allies intended to use the League as a means of banishing war, the vanquished as well as the victorious powers should immediately be included as members.[28] When, however, it became clear that the French government would not offer unqualified support for German admission, doubts about Allied policy began to emerge. Matters were exacerbated by the loss of much of Upper Silesia to Poland in a plebiscite in 1921.[29] To a broad spectrum of German opinion, this indicated that League policy was not impartial and that it was a body dedicated to the promotion of French interests. Britain was viewed with less suspicion, but with insufficient trust to enable D'Abernon to persuade those with whom he came into contact that Britain would treat Germany fairly if she were to gain admission.[30]

By the beginning of 1924, German attitudes towards the League had begun to change. This was due primarily to Stresemann's influence. He viewed the role of the League in international diplomacy in two ways: as 'the union of the nations under the sole purpose of the maintenance of peace and the furtherance of all humanitarian ideals' and as 'a new diplomatic method of national representation'.[31] Membership would give Germany greater opportunity to negotiate a revision of the Treaty of Versailles. If a dialogue were to take place, it would be advantageous if Germany was not just a member of the League but was there on an equal footing with the Allies. Members should be made to realise that the absence of a German delegation left the League unable to 'regulate European affairs' adequately. He complained that insufficient attention had been paid by the Allies to the potential German contribution to European political affairs.[32] Consequently, Germany would not join the League until other issues relating to the European security question had been resolved. Thus he justified the right of Germany to set the agenda for the resolution of the entire security question. This gave him a strong negotiating position but greatly annoyed Chamberlain.[33]

Stresemann searched for a formula which would allow Germany not only to sign a security pact with the Allies and join the League but also to work towards revision of the Treaty of Versailles and the reinforcement of relations with the Soviet Union.[34] In his famous letter to the former German Crown Prince, Stresemann wrote:

> Our anxiety on behalf of Germans abroad is an argument in favour of joining the League ... In Geneva we shall speak on behalf of German civilisation as a whole, because the whole of the Germanic world sees in us its refuge and protector.[35]

D'Abernon's view of the German position overlooked the nationalist undertones of Stresemann's declarations. He dismissed his comments on Germany's right to be regarded as a Great Power as political rhetoric and reported simply that 'solid progress' had been made regarding the admission of Germany and that the government had decided to make a formal application to join the League.[36] As the security negotiations progressed, it became apparent that D'Abernon had failed to understand the connection in Stresemann's mind between the admission of Germany to the League and a reappraisal of the terms of the Treaty of Versailles.[37]

Germany, the League and the Soviet Union

German policy towards the League had a great bearing on relations with the Soviet Union. Stresemann believed that the League question offered an opportunity to develop Russo-German relations but that until the question of membership had been settled, no lasting rapprochement with the Soviet Union could be reached. He also knew that he could use German statements about League membership to extract concessions from both the Soviet Union and the Allies and play them off against each other. The German Cabinet met on 21 March 1925 and agreed that entry into the League must not cause a breach with the Soviet Union. The Russians applied continuous pressure on Stresemann to abandon his policy. They feared that once inside the League, Germany would be drawn into an anti-Russian bloc under the leadership of France. Stresemann refused to accept this argument. He believed that the diversity of countries within the League combined with a 'growing weariness of French predominance' would protect German interests and could result in the powers 'group[ing] themselves round Germany'.[38] He also rejected the Russian contention that it would be impossible for the German government to conclude a satisfactory agreement with the Soviet Union and embrace the terms of the League Covenant simultaneously. Stresemann used this latter point to reassure the Allies of Germany's commitment to the security process. During the Locarno meeting in October 1925, he amused Chamberlain by dismissing the notion of an anti-Russian combination within the League as being as absurd as saying that D'Abernon was the 'dictator of Berlin'.[39] This joke did of course contain a serious point; D'Abernon's advice and relations with Britain were not at the heart of the German foreign policy decision-making process.

The Allies regarded the Covenant of the League as a means of preventing European affairs being dominated by the interests of any one country or bloc of countries and as an important way of maintaining peace. The Germans saw it as an Allied statement about the treatment Germany would receive on entering the League.[40] In London and in Paris, the Covenant was not regarded as a subject for debate or negotiation, while the German government thought of its articles as open for discussion and possible amendment. The latter wished to negotiate an 'opt-out' from articles with which they were unable or unwilling to comply. These differences of approach not only slowed down the admission of Germany to the League, but had a general bearing on German relations with the Allies. At a time when D'Abernon and others imbued with the spirit of Locarno were working towards greater harmony between the Allies and Germany, the often intransigent stance that was taken on matters relating to the Covenant reinforced those prejudices that had so damaged relations since the war. There were nevertheless wider issues to be considered. While the Germans regarded themselves as a special case, the Allies had to calculate the effect of setting such a precedent. If Germany were to be allowed to join the League under special conditions, the authority of the body as a whole could be undermined as other countries may also have felt inclined to set out their conditions for membership.

Article 16

The bitterest exchanges concerned the meaning of Article 16 and its bearing on Germany.[41] Stresemann argued that the first paragraph, with its reference to severing commercial and financial contact with a Covenant-breaking state in the event of war, posed a potential threat to Germany's long-term economic recovery.[42] But it was the second and third paragraphs which were the most controversial. Considerable doubt was expressed in Berlin about the ability of Germany to contribute to a League military force because of the disarmament clauses of the Treaty of Versailles. The Allies had completely disregarded this point. To those on Germany's political right, this suggested that the Allies continued to regard Germany as a threat to the security of Europe. Stresemann also feared the consequences of being obliged to grant troops from member states (marshalled primarily by France) a right to march through (*durchmarsch*) Germany to defend Poland against possible future Russian attack.[43] He believed that should such a situation arise, it would compromise his entire foreign policy by forcing him to abandon Germany's 'neutral' status between the Allies and the Soviet Union. Stresemann had to strike a delicate balance. He was fully aware that the main Russian objection to German admission to the League was that the Allies would insist that the Germany would become part of a western anti-communist bloc.

D'Abernon's conversations with von Schubert and Stresemann reveal the growing German preoccupation with the effect that admission to the League would have on relations with the Soviet Union. In February 1925, D'Abernon had a number of discussions with von Schubert on this subject, in the course of which D'Abernon was handed a 'very confidential' memorandum on the future of Russo-German relations. He cannot have been pleased by its contents. It expressed scepticism about previous League decisions concerning Germany and about the consequences of Article 16, and concluded that:

> The Soviet Government would in all probability regard the acceptance of the obligation arising out of Article 16 without reserve as a proof that Germany in an eventual conflict would take the side of the western powers against Russia. They would adjust their whole policy, including their economic policy *vis-à-vis* Germany accordingly. Germany is of course just a little bound in the question of the League of Nations *vis-à-vis* the Soviet Government as she is in any other political question. This freedom of decision does not at the same time absolve German policy from the obligation of investigating carefully if and how far an interruption of German-Russian relations would be in accordance with Germany's interests, all the more as such an interruption would inevitably follow the abandonment of neutrality.[44]

The Germans feared being obliged to participate in sanctions against the Soviet Union and the 'development on German soil of operations over which they would have no say' – a clear reference to the possibility of a *durchmarsch*.[45]

D'Abernon was convinced that the way to maintain German enthusiasm for admission to the League was to discredit Russian statements criticising Germany's dealings with the Allies regarding security. But he found this almost impossible to do, reporting that 'Russian influence is still being exercised, almost violently, against Germany entering the League'.[46] Matters were made still worse when a month later D'Abernon heard reports about conversations between Sir Eric Drummond and Stresemann. From these, it emerged that the German government was not only enthusiastic about reaching a rapprochement with the Soviet Union, but that the Allies were viewed as the 'enemy of the German cause' because of their insistence on acceptance of Article 16.

The intransigence of the Allies, Stresemann claimed, provided proof that Germany was regarded as a 'second class power'.[47]

Drummond later told D'Abernon that he was convinced that Stresemann did not wish to pursue German admission to the League.[48] D'Abernon was horrified. He feared that the security initiative contained with the German note of January 1925 would sink without trace before it had been given full consideration. Realising that von Schubert and Stresemann usually spoke with one voice on foreign affairs, he was amazed that the former could favour close relations with Britain while elsewhere sanctioning a policy that was likely to destroy this objective. D'Abernon believed that a 'stern warning' should be issued to the government in Berlin to make it realise that its first loyalties lay to the Allies. It is not clear from where he thought this warning should come as the negotiations with von Schubert that resulted in the security note had taken place without authorisation from the British government. He was not in a position to appeal to anything other than the goodwill of Stresemann and von Schubert. This was not enough, nor was it reasonable for him to have expected it to be. Nevertheless, D'Abernon believed it was now imperative to secure German admission to the League as soon as possible. Once that had been achieved, but only then, could a discussion take place about the implications of Article 16 for Germany. Yet, not surprisingly, D'Abernon found the Germans stubborn and impervious to such pleas. During a number of increasingly frosty meetings with Luther, Stresemann and von Schubert on 9 and 10 March, he warned that the German attitude was 'something akin to [asking for] a specially reduced subscription on entering a club' and should be abandoned immediately.[49]

Relations between D'Abernon and the German government improved almost immediately, but not because the Germans were overcome by the force of his argument. The League Council's reply to the German note of December 1924 requesting admission to the League arrived in Berlin. Stresemann was pleased with its content, describing it as 'fairly satisfactory, courteous and accommodating in form'.[50] He told D'Abernon that it formed a good basis for further discussion and that a more positive response would be forthcoming if existing League members were encouraged to instigate the proceedings. As a result, D'Abernon proposed a conference between the Allies and Germany to discuss the wider implications of Article 16. Stresemann regarded this as an opportunity to discuss not only the League question but military control and the evacuation of the occupied territories. Much to D'Abernon's pleasure, he readily assented.[51] But D'Abernon's efforts were scuppered by news from London. In a long series of dispatches based on meetings with Chamberlain, Tyrrell and Lampson, Sthamer warned Stresemann against assuming that the British would adopt a more sympathetic attitude than the French towards the German position regarding the interpretation of Article 16. He also thought it unlikely that they would ever agree to modify it. What was more, British policy had the sole purpose of 'restricting Germany's political independence and gaining influence over Germany's attitude towards Russia'.[52] Heeding Sthamer's advice, Stresemann became increasingly convinced that the British and French governments spoke as one on security matters and that it was Chamberlain who tended to follow the French lead. He thought that if the French could be persuaded to take a more sympathetic attitude towards the German case, British support was likely to follow. To this end, he held a number of interviews with the French ambassador, de Margerie, in the late spring of 1925.[53] D'Abernon was not consulted.

On 10 October 1925, a compromise on Article 16 was finally reached by a team of Allied and German jurists. At the Locarno conference, the Allies agreed to take account of Germany's geographical position should German responsibilities as a member of the League threaten to compromise the conduct of her foreign policy.[54] Stresemann and von Schubert were pleased because it maintained the element of freedom with which they wished to pursue their policy towards the Allies and the Soviet Union.[55] In conversations with Briand and Chamberlain, Stresemann emphasised Russian mistrust of the League. To the Allies this implied a perceptible German shift away from closer relations with the Soviet Union. Nevertheless, despite the apparent resolution of the issue, conversations between D'Abernon and von Schubert in the spring of 1926 continued to be dominated by discussions about Article 16. When admission to the League was not forthcoming in March, von Schubert warned D'Abernon of Germany's increasing vulnerability to Russian diplomacy. The German government had been placed under considerable pressure by the Russians to abandon admission but had consistently rejected the idea that the League, dominated by Britain, was a 'coalition against Russia'. However, Germany 'did not intend to conduct an anti-Russian policy'. This argument had already been made on a number of occasions, especially to the British government. At the same time, it was not in Germany's interests to alienate the Soviet Union completely. While German assurances about the practical significance of Article 16 had dominated the correspondence between Berlin and Moscow for some time, the Russians were insisting that a separate agreement with Germany should be concluded. Von Schubert denied categorically that the German government had any intention of signing a treaty of neutrality with the Soviet Union. In paving the way for the news of the Treaty of Berlin, he clearly wished D'Abernon to think that the Germans had had the agreement forced upon them. The onus was therefore on the Allies to do all in their power to keep Germany within the western fold. Von Schubert warned that if Germany did not gain admission to the League in September, she 'might run the risk of falling very thoroughly between two stools'. D'Abernon was furious and argued that if a Russo-German treaty was signed it would have 'very disagreeable consequences for [Germany's] relations with the League'.[56] He believed that the German government should make a choice: ally Germany closely with either the western European powers or with the Soviet Union. While the consequences of the latter were almost too dire to contemplate, D'Abernon was coming increasingly to the conclusion that German foreign policy in Europe could not operate effectively when pursued on two 'fronts'.

British policy towards German requests for exemption from Article 16 further demonstrated Chamberlain's inflexible attitude towards Germany.[57] He believed that an absolute acceptance of the Covenant was a requirement for admission to the League and that no exceptions could be made.[58] He thought that Germany's reservations would be best addressed once she became a member of the League. This point he strongly impressed on D'Abernon.[59] In January 1925, Chamberlain had told Sthamer that it was inappropriate to attach conditions when applying for League membership. He also pointed out that the League Council took the domestic circumstances of individual countries into account before making demands upon them. Throughout these conversations, Chamberlain became increasingly irritated by the German position. At the end of a particularly 'tortuous' meeting, he lost his patience. Reporting the conversation to D'Abernon, he noted: 'I confessed my inability to understand the German mind. Germany was offered a seat at the Council of the League of Nations and refused to take it.'[60]

Feeling that Chamberlain did not understand the German position, D'Abernon set out his interpretation in a long letter. Its content, however, suggests that he himself had an imperfect grasp of German policy and the psychology behind it. D'Abernon claimed that the main reason why Germany had thus far not joined the League was because objections to Article 16 had not been met. He believed that this 'threat' had receded because Germany had been assured of a seat on the Council. He thought that the Germans now feared that entry into the League would result in a break with the Soviet Union. Curiously, he argued that German confidence in the Soviet Union was waning and that the most opportune time for the Allies to push for German entry had been reached. He thought it important to remove the fear of German 'diplomatic isolation' and recommended that a gesture of Allied goodwill should be forthcoming. Admission to the League would be made more palatable if it coincided with a cessation of military control and the evacuation of the Cologne Zone.[61] None of these suggestions proved acceptable to Chamberlain; nor were they likely to have been given his close working relationship with the French government over the security negotiations. Much still had to be done to convince the French that the Cologne Zone should be evacuated and there was the question of whether the Germans could be trusted to enter into the spirit of this gesture should it be forthcoming.

D'Abernon was not without British critics away from Whitehall. Some British diplomats believed that he was not doing enough to convey the British position. London, a member of the British delegation to the League of Nations, discussed the German attitude towards Article 16 with Drummond. He was astounded that the German government continued to make conditions before joining the League and that D'Abernon was apparently so sympathetic to them. London asked:

> Does D'Abernon realise that unless they join the League on the same footing as other Great Powers nothing can come of their proposals? Without unconditional entry into the League there can be no possibility of any pact. If they are not prepared to express their willingness to do this we shall make no progress.[62]

When Chamberlain met Stresemann at Locarno, he was concerned that the issues relating to German admission to the League would threaten the conclusion of the proposed security agreement. Chamberlain once again stated that Article 16 was 'easy to interpret' but diluted his comments by observing that the ability of the League to enforce it had been significantly undermined because the United States had refused to join. While the deployment of military sanctions still remained an option, their nature and range had not yet been established. Thus Chamberlain and Briand agreed to do what they had never intended to do – they issued a statement recognising that Germany, as a League member, was in a special position.[63]

In British minds, the future of European security was directly linked to the success or failure of the work of the League. It was logical, when so much time was devoted to improving relations between victors and vanquished, that efforts should be made to ensure that Germany was also admitted to the League as soon as possible. Officially, the right of Germany to be regarded as a Great Power was not an issue for the Allies. Once obstacles such as the Article 16 controversy had been removed, there was in theory nothing to prevent the admission of Germany to the League as a permanent member of the Council. This was, after all, a fundamental part of the Treaty of Locarno. But the diplomacy that took place between Britain, France and Germany regarding German admission to the League in 1926 suggests that Chamberlain's commitment to the 'spirit of Locarno' was less than complete. In particular, the complex process that led him to try to secure diplomatic concessions for France at each stage of the admission process in the spring of 1926 placed a severe strain on relations between each of the signatory powers of the Treaty of Locarno. The League Council crisis in the spring of 1926 can be viewed as an indirect commentary by the Allies on Germany's right to be regarded as a Great Power.

The League Council crisis

A matter of only a few months after the Locarno conference, the British and French governments were considering the claims of powers other than Germany to a seat on the League Council before German admission had been secured. Briand was anxious to give consideration to Poland's desire for Council membership. Pressure had been brought to bear on him by the Polish government to provide further security guarantees, as the Treaty of Locarno had left open the question of Germany's eastern borders. At the same time, Briand had no desire to abandon the German case. In January 1926, he suggested to Chamberlain that the claims of Poland and Germany should be put forward simultaneously. He argued that if both countries were members of the League Council, the Polish government would be able to negotiate with the Germans on equal terms and not be forced to rely on France to put forward their case. This would reinforce the Locarno agreement by diminishing yet another potentially difficult problem.

Chamberlain's response was favourable. In an attempt to convince his Cabinet colleagues, he wrote:

> My own disposition ... is to support the claim of Poland. I think that by doing so we shall best serve the cause of peace and, as far as I can judge from the opinion of other powers represented on the Council,

> we shall be acting in accordance with the general wish. We might find ourselves isolated if we adopted an attitude of opposition.[64]

However, objection was widespread. The Foreign Office advised against supporting the Polish case. Waterlow believed that it would swell the Council to such a size that its activities would be inhibited.[65] Lampson argued that 'to let Poland in [was] ... almost indefensible'.[66] More vocal criticism came from the League of Nations Union, headed by Gilbert Murray, which mounted a sustained campaign commanding considerable press support. Cabinet opposition was led by Lord Robert Cecil, Chancellor of the Duchy of Lancaster, who warned that the admission of Poland would have 'very far-reaching effects' that would ultimately undermine the future of the League.[67] He recommended that the forthcoming meeting of the League Assembly in March should be exclusively concerned with the admission of Germany. If it was necessary to admit a second power to the Council then that country should be Spain with British and French support being given to Poland to become a non-permanent member.[68]

Chamberlain also came under attack from Berlin. Complaints were voiced through Sthamer rather than through D'Abernon. Sthamer reported concerns about the potential diminution of the status of the League Council should powers with 'no claim to greatness' be admitted as permanent members. The Germans believed that the only powers currently outside the League which were of sufficient international standing to be admitted on the same terms as Germany were the United States and the Soviet Union. Chamberlain ignored this point and assured Sthamer that 'Germany's position as a Great Power could not be affected by the election or non-election to the Council of any other State; that a nation like Germany was a Great Power even on the morrow of defeat and would always be a Great Power in whatever assembly she took part.'[69] Sthamer suggested that extending membership of the Council beyond Germany would in fact be 'contrary to Locarno'. Chamberlain argued that it was important to develop the 'work of Locarno' so that the size and membership of the League Council should be such as to maintain international security.[70]

D'Abernon's reports from Berlin made little impression on Chamberlain. During a visit to the German capital by Drummond, Stresemann and D'Abernon discussed the implications of extending the League Council beyond the inclusion of Germany. D'Abernon tried to propose a compromise, suggesting that German objections to Spain becoming a permanent member were 'somewhat less vehement' than those against Poland.[71] Aware of Chamberlain's likely hostility to this idea, he endeavoured to cushion the blow by stressing that the Germans were not being intentionally 'contrariwise', but believed that any extensions to the League Council should be made only when the German position was assured.[72] His efforts had little effect. Chamberlain claimed to be much 'disturbed' by the idea of abandoning Poland in favour of Spain and once again chastised Stresemann for displaying an apparent lack of commitment to the Locarno agreements.[73]

Chamberlain found himself increasingly isolated. On 18 February 1926, Viscount Grey of Falloden, the much respected former Foreign Secretary, published a letter in *The Times* expressing total opposition to Chamberlain's view.[74] On the same day, Chamberlain received a letter from the King expressing support for Grey's position. The Swedish government, holder of a non-permanent seat on the League Council, also issued a statement opposing any enlargement beyond Germany. Against such powerful adversaries, and opposed by much of the Cabinet, Chamberlain had little choice but to back down. Once again he used a letter to D'Abernon to vent his frustration. Its contents almost completely contradicted the substance of his letter of the previous day. He now wrote: 'I do not believe that there is the slightest chance of this solution being adopted by the Council, whose unanimity is required, nor does it seem to me very probable that Poland would secure the necessary majority in the Assembly even if the Council had agreed.'[75]

The Foreign Secretary blamed his predicament on the Germans. He felt sure that the reason why he had not been able to secure Cabinet approval was because the Germans had misunderstood the intentions behind French support for the Polish claim. He accused the Germans of adopting a short-sighted attitude that had resulted in an opportunity for the resolution of German disputes with Poland being lost. Once again, he vented his spleen to D'Abernon, writing: 'Why should [the Germans] at their very entry into the League and even before they have entered begin to threaten that, unless they have their way, they won't play?'[76] D'Abernon was irritated by Chamberlain's attitude. He believed that his comments about the German government were unfair and that he had only himself to blame for his present position. He regarded Chamberlain's climb-down as a victory for German tenacity, noting 'I doubt whether – if Germany had not protested so strongly against the extension of the Council – there would have been any effective check to that proposal.'[77]

At the same time, D'Abernon realised that the situation was more complex. Chamberlain's comments about Germany and Poland during the previous few months confirmed that he still lacked a basic sympathy for German attitudes and policies. D'Abernon thought it 'superficial in the extreme' to suggest that Polish and German permanent membership of the League Council would bring about an amicable resolution of the tensions that existed between them. He believed that Chamberlain's attitude showed that British politicians needed to be purged of their hostility to Germany if the Locarno agreements were to survive and if the German government were to think it worthwhile applying for admission to the League.[78]

D'Abernon felt his comments were further justified when Chamberlain's abandonment of the Polish claim was rapidly followed by a declaration of support for the Spanish candidature.[79] Despite his earlier report that such a suggestion would be acceptable to the Germans, D'Abernon found this rapid change ludicrous, noting that if the Spanish claim was recognised, 'cats will, in future, scratch duchesses in order to be admitted to their tea-parties'.[80] Tension within the British Cabinet also ran high. Despite having been told initially that they would have a 'free hand' at the forthcoming meeting of the League Assembly, Chamberlain and Tyrrell were now dispatched to Geneva with very narrow instructions. No change in the composition of the Council was to be sanctioned which delayed the admission of Germany. The convention that only Great Powers should be permanent members of the Council should be maintained. Finally, neither Poland nor Brazil should be made permanent members, but Poland should be given a non-permanent seat as soon as possible.[81] Tyrrell, Crowe's successor as Permanent Under-Secretary and the man whom Curzon had been so determined not to appoint as ambassador to Berlin, knew how much such a course of action would frustrate Chamberlain. Tyrrell wrote:

> People here are beginning to rub their eyes and to ask themselves whether they have not been carried too far in their zeal for the League, and whether it was desirable to send you out tied hand and foot to Germany. It has been one of the most ill-informed and mischievous ramps that I have ever seen in the domain of foreign affairs, and I hope that its repercussions will not be beyond repair.[82]

Because he believed that Chamberlain was not committed to promoting the German cause, D'Abernon held little hope that the meeting of the League Assembly would produce anything positive for Germany. He thought that Briand and Chamberlain's promotion of the Polish candidature had done much to 'discredit' the League and had significantly 'diminish[ed] the prestige of the great Powers'. He was fearful that if the German application encountered too much opposition, the German government would be placed in such a difficult position at home that the entire question of League admission would have to be reviewed.[83]

The negotiations at Geneva in March 1926 were long and tortuous. The French and Polish delegations recognised that Germany and Sweden were opposed to the Polish claim but asked that Poland should immediately be given a non-permanent seat. Once again Chamberlain complained about the Germans, telling D'Abernon: 'The Germans knew they had all the cards in their hands and were unwilling to concede anything. [They] were perfectly well aware that I was in their pocket and that my vote could be dictated by them.'[84]

There then followed a series of negotiations aimed at providing Germany with 'compensation' for the replacement of Sweden by Poland as a non-permanent member of the League Council. Czechoslovakia, another of the newly emerged states in eastern Europe, was asked to forego a non-permanent seat in favour of a less 'controversial' country. Briand and Chamberlain had, however, neglected the Spanish and Brazilian candidatures that were opposed by Sweden and Germany. The Spanish government indicated that it would not veto German membership of the Council, but would consider withdrawing from the League altogether if it went ahead. Brazil went further and threatened to block German admission. In view of this deadlock, the Assembly of the League was adjourned on 16 March 1926 until September.[85]

Once more Chamberlain's severest critics were British. The tireless defender of the League and its ideals, Lord Robert Cecil, again went on to the offensive. He believed that Chamberlain had supported the adjournment motion too soon and was convinced that if the matter had been more fully discussed, there was a possibility that Brazil might have relented. Annoyed also about Chamberlain's failure to consult him more fully while in Geneva, he protested that there had 'never been a more impotent conclusion'. Consequently, it was 'no wonder the enemies of the League are chortling with joy'.[86] D'Abernon too was becoming increasingly pessimistic. While he was confident that Germany would be admitted to the League in September, he believed that the best chance for the German government to influence the allocation of permanent and non-permanent seats on the Council had now passed. He predicted a decline in the status of the Council and with it the League as a whole. The League was having to pay too high a price for Chamberlain's idiosyncratic beliefs.[87] He was particularly upset by a letter from Tyrrell expressing pleasure that Germany had not been admitted.[88] Contemplating resignation, D'Abernon wrote: 'If the tranquillity of Europe produced by Locarno is at all proportionate to the dullification of negotiations here, Europe had gained a great deal.'[89]

Between March and September 1926 attempts to break the deadlock were made by a League Committee chaired by Giuseppe Motta, the Swiss Foreign Minister. In a further telling comment on Chamberlain's position, the Cabinet now appointed Cecil as sole British representative. Cecil presented a number of papers arguing that all meetings of the Committee should be conducted in public in order to avoid the 'cosiness' that had been such a feature of the negotiations at Locarno.[90] Cecil and the Cabinet therefore rejected Chamberlain's diplomatic methods and apparently undermined his ability to reinforce his success at the Locarno conference.

The Motta Committee drew up a plan to conciliate Spain, Brazil and Poland by recommending the creation of three semi-permanent seats on the League Council. These powers would not be required to resign after three years, as was the norm, but would have to secure a two-thirds vote in the League Assembly to guarantee re-election. The Spanish and Brazilian governments were unimpressed by this compromise and duly withdrew from the League. Poland on the other hand accepted the Motta proposal. With the removal of the Brazilian threat, the way was now open for Germany to be accepted into the League at the next meeting of the General Assembly. D'Abernon was relieved. He believed that unless the Committee's findings had been favourable, the German government would have withdrawn the application for League membership.[91] When Germany was admitted to the League and granted a permanent seat on the Council in September, D'Abernon greeted the news with pleasure:

> While this result has been practically certain for some weeks, it is a relief to have confirmation of a final settlement. Though second in importance to Locarno the entry of Germany into the League of Nations is nonetheless an outstanding achievement of statesmanship.[92]

The German government viewed the situation differently. Stresemann's policy had centred around his wish to ensure that when Germany became a permanent member of the League Council, no similar seats would be created for other powers in the foreseeable future. Germany, he believed, was in a unique position as a Great Power recently fallen on 'hard times'.[93] He also anticipated that he would have a much better chance of influencing the Allies if the League Council remained comparatively small. His greatest concern related to the consequences to Germany if Briand and Chamberlain's promotion of the Polish claim had proved successful.[94] Stresemann feared that, as Poland was a close ally of France and as Chamberlain tended to follow the French lead, German grievances regarding the Treaty of Versailles would stand little chance of being addressed. He was also convinced that behind the Allies' promotion of the Polish candidature was a French plot to minimise German influence once Germany was in the League. D'Abernon responded by sending a number of long dispatches outlining the German position. Yet he seems to have been oblivious to the depth of Stresemann's reservations, noting with characteristic over-optimism that the 'whole business [would] blow over rapidly'.[95]

Stresemann then received news that the French government intended to promote the Polish candidature at the next session of the League Assembly. He summoned D'Abernon and told him that, if that happened, the German application for admission would have to be reviewed.[96] Von Hoesch was later instructed to oppose the idea and to declare that the entire process of German admission to the League had proceeded on a 'false basis and under a misunderstanding'.[97] It therefore seemed likely that German admission would not take place until September at the earliest. At a meeting on 19 February, D'Abernon was struck by Stresemann's resolution. He reported that he had 'pressed him closely but he [had] asserted with vigour that there could be no doubt as to the whole country being unanimous'. Despite this, Stresemann 'did not consider any compromise solution could be found'.[98] On the one hand, Stresemann wished to condemn Allied support for the Polish candidature. On the other, he did not wish to give the Allies too much ammunition to use against him while he was completing the negotiation of the Russo-German agreement. Stresemann also recognised that, by being selective in the information he revealed to Britain and France, he could manipulate the diplomatic situation to Germany's advantage. He and von Schubert studiously avoided lengthy conversations with D'Abernon and the French ambassador to Berlin, but told Brockdorff-Rantzau:

> Since, in our view, publication of the German–Russian treaty would have to follow immediately upon signature, it would be concluded from our having signed before Geneva that we regard our entry into the League, which after all is the real occasion for the treaty, as a matter of complete certainty. This would prejudice to our disadvantage the diplomatic struggle over the question of the Council

> seats which is now in progress and which has by no means been decided yet.[99]

D'Abernon was becoming increasingly intolerant of Stresemann's attitude. When the German application for admission to the League proved unsuccessful in March 1926, he was convinced that the deadlock had been caused as much by German stubbornness as by other factors. He rejected Stresemann's claim that the Germans had been 'innocent bystanders' at Geneva and regretted his inability to persuade the German delegation to take a more 'moderate course'.[100]

When Stresemann returned from Geneva, D'Abernon stressed that German disappointment should not be used as an excuse to abandon the Treaty of Locarno. The fragility of the treaty was however only too visible. Stresemann believed that the Geneva expedition had 'menaced' his entire League policy.[101] He was also aware that the delay in admission had direct consequences for reduction of the Allied garrison in the Second and Third Zones of the Rhineland that had been promised for when the Locarno Pact actually came into force, that is, when Germany entered the League. He was particularly critical of Chamberlain's activities in Geneva and stressed that the 'bright spot' in the negotiations had been Briand's attitude.[102] Stresemann thought Chamberlain 'too much of the schoolmaster' who did not regard the League as a 'temple of peace, but a market where nations were bought and sold'.[103]

Concerned about the future of the German application to the League and even of the Locarno agreements themselves, D'Abernon emphasised that Stresemann was anxious not to break away from the Locarno powers.[104] He was concerned about the impact of events in Geneva on Russo-German relations. But he had little first-hand knowledge of German policy towards the Soviet Union. He relied instead on his powers of deduction rather than on direct information. D'Abernon thought that before the meeting of the League Assembly, there had been a 'vague intention to give the Soviet Union some sort of consolation for her failure to prevent Germany's entry into the League'. One option that had been considered was a treaty of neutrality, but he reported that 'nothing very concrete' had been decided upon. D'Abernon believed that as Germany still remained outside the League, the signature of a treaty with the Soviet Union would 'incline the balance too much to the east'. Consequently, the Germans would ultimately reject closer relations with the Soviet Union because 'the desire in dominant circles [was] still to maintain a certain preponderance of the western inclination'.[105]

Meanwhile, Stresemann was becoming convinced that the League was incapable of protecting German interests. He had also come under pressure from nationalist elements to abandon his League policy. In a speech in Stuttgart on 19 April 1926, he declared that the League was no longer a body that could represent German interests in a satisfactory manner. He thought there was little reason to doubt that the League would 'continue to render Germany injustice after injustice' and insisted that, in joining, Germany should not only be assured of a permanent seat on the Council, but be given the right to administer colonies and made exempt from making any declaration of moral responsibility for the Great War.[106] At the same time, he summoned D'Abernon to discuss Britain's attitude towards German admission to the League. He not only believed that the British government had abandoned Germany to the mercy of the French, but doubted the sincerity of Briand's sympathy for the German application.[107] This change in Stresemann's attitude towards Briand, when only a short time earlier he had been described as the 'bright spot' of the Locarno negotiations, illustrates the continued fragility of Germany's relationship with France.

When Spain and Brazil announced their withdrawal from the League, Stresemann was relieved because it removed the threat of a second veto. But he was concerned when Chamberlain tried to persuade the Spanish to reconsider their position. He told D'Abernon: 'As matters stand we must count on the fact that every concession to Spain would also be applied to Poland, and that this might give rise to difficulties for Geneva that could not be overlooked.'[108] Stresemann therefore doubted whether the German application would be given a more favourable hearing in September. D'Abernon shared his misgivings, observing: 'The occurrence of any incident must be avoided, for [it] was perfectly clear that the whole policy inaugurated at Locarno could not be carried on if Geneva came to nothing this time.'[109] In the end, it was the nationalist threat to the stability of the Luther government rather than Allied pressure that forced Stresemann to reconsider German League policy.[110] He told D'Abernon that the German government should receive a satisfactory guarantee from the Allies regarding the reduction of the troops of occupation, but agreed to abandon his other demands until Germany had joined the League of Nations.[111] The modification of his views was interpreted by the German nationalists as an act of betrayal. Yet Stresemann was conscious that any attempt to appease them would almost certainly be interpreted by the Allies as a threat to the Locarno agreements.[112]

Germany joins the League

In September 1926 Germany became a member of the League of Nations. It was an event that should have been of momentous significance but one which has merited comparatively little historical attention. This can be partly explained in terms of hindsight. Hitler withdrew Germany from the League, and the consequences of his rejection of its ideals have been more than adequately chronicled in the numerous histories of the origins and course of the Second World War. It is also important to examine the motives of the politicians in the mid-1920s and the general attitude of the governments they represented to international security and the commitments that this entailed. To Stresemann Germany's admission to the League, together with the Treaty of Locarno, provided a basis for revitalising Germany's role in European affairs and altering her relationship with the Allies. Unlike D'Abernon, he did not regard the security process as the end of a process of diplomatic negotiation but the start. Nor did he feel obliged to commit Germany exclusively to closer relations with the west. He also used the prospect of German admission to an international body widely seen to be dominated by the Allied powers as a potent diplomatic weapon in his dealings with the Russians. In his League diplomacy Stresemann showed a strength of purpose and determination that few outside German government circles understood.

The British position was in many ways more clearly defined but gave the impression of weakness and compromise rather than strength. Since the end of the war, the British government had believed that Germany should become a member of the League as soon as possible. As had often been the case in the past, the key to understanding British policy lay with France. Throughout the 1920s, the great debate both in Downing Street and in the Foreign Office was how far Britain should be guided by French attitudes towards the admission of Germany to the League. It was a dilemma that remained unresolved and was never more apparent than during Chamberlain's very public isolation in the spring of 1926. As a tactician Chamberlain was the very antithesis of Stresemann. He prided himself on the firmness of his beliefs. For him diplomatic alliances went much further than practical expediency.[113] The country that Chamberlain represented as Foreign Secretary in the mid-1920s had begun to lose her influence in international affairs and saw in the League a means of holding on to a leading role in world affairs in the future. Yet the formulation of League policy was dogged by intrusions from other areas, particularly imperial affairs and, again, the perpetual matter of relations with France. By 1926 it is debatable whether Britain's role in European affairs was more clearly defined than it had been eight years earlier at the signing of the Armistice.

Resignation

A month after Germany was admitted to the League, D'Abernon resigned. He believed that this event had set the final seal on the Treaty of Locarno and secured a basis for closer Allied relations with Germany. In one of the final entries in his diary, he drew up a checklist of his objectives as ambassador to Berlin and concluded that he had achieved all of them.[114] But his mood was not euphoric. His dispatches in the final year of his embassy suggest a man powerlessly watching a sequence of events unfolding before him with a mixture of disapproval and disbelief. Yet, at the same time, he remained convinced that the Germans would ultimately see the error of their ways and pursue a foreign policy more consistent with his views. By 1926 it was clear that this was not going to happen. He did not share the German government's belief that the Treaty of Berlin could coexist easily with the Treaty of Locarno. He also failed to understand the complex strategy behind Stresemann's policy towards the Allies both before and after Locarno. Like many contemporary German writers, D'Abernon believed that Stresemann was a 'good European' – that his dearest wish was that the Allies would forgive Germany for causing the war and enable reconciliation to take place.

When D'Abernon had suggested resignation in the past, pressure had been put on him in London to reconsider. In the autumn of 1926 this did not happen. By that time, the differences between Chamberlain and D'Abernon over Allied policy towards Germany were becoming irreconcilable. Chamberlain had experienced a great deal of criticism in British political circles for his often single-minded pursuit of closer relations with the French. In this respect, he saw D'Abernon as a further source of pressure. The Foreign Secretary only dealt with the Germans because he believed that he had little choice. D'Abernon's detailed knowledge of German affairs was a source to be drawn on when necessary. This, of course, was not unusual or unethical, but once the German security question had been resolved to his satisfaction, Chamberlain had little need for D'Abernon and therefore made scant reference to him. D'Abernon had also become disenchanted. He suspected that during the security negotiations Chamberlain had been less than enthusiastic about the need to include Germany. He saw the League Council crisis as a further confirmation of his pro-French sympathies and as evidence that Chamberlain was not wholly committed to the terms and the 'spirit' of the Treaty of Locarno. His resignation was prompted more by a general sense of disillusionment than by satisfaction at the completion of a task.

Conclusion

When D'Abernon was appointed ambassador to Berlin in June 1920, Germany and the Allies were in the grip of the debate about the implementation of the Treaty of Versailles. Relations between Britain, France and Germany were tense, as considerable doubts remained about the interpretation of the clauses of the treaty relating to the payment of reparations and to disarmament. No country would have countenanced the resumption of military hostilities but a pervading pessimism remained about the likelihood of maintaining peace and encouraging the creation of bonds of trust and mutual friendship. It was also necessary to face the consequences of the most wide-ranging war in modern history that had had a devastating effect on the fabric and psychological well-being of the nations that had fought it. Empires had fallen, old certainties had been challenged and in many cases swept away. It was not clear what would emerge to take the place of the pre-war order, or whether Europe would disintegrate into anarchy. The democratic powers had won the war and the new countries that were emerging from the ruins of the former empires were predominantly democratic in nature. Nevertheless, democracy as a system of government was vulnerable to attack from communism and from reactionary counter-revolutionaries. Nowhere was this more true than in the Weimar Republic. This gave a particular significance to the Allies' decision to resume diplomatic relations with Germany during the first six months of 1920. The ability to maintain a stable and effective democratic government in Germany was seen as a test of their commitment to democratic principles. The location of the country in the centre of the European landmass also gave Germany a strategic significance dividing the well-established democratic regimes in the west from the newer countries and the potential communist threat in the east.

When D'Abernon resigned six years later, the relationship between Germany and the Allies was somewhat different. The prolonged and often acrimonious debate about reparations payments, which had often threatened to undermine the peace, had apparently been resolved through the Dawes Plan. The debate about the demilitarisation of the Rhineland was making perceptible if slow progress, while the negotiation and conclusion of the Treaty of Locarno appeared to open up a period of unparalleled closeness between the Allies and Germany. The signing of the treaty was viewed as the high point of the careers of both D'Abernon and Chamberlain and as a means of banishing any lasting remnants of wartime hostility. The admission of Germany to the League of Nations provided the logical dénouement to this process of reconciliation and friendship between victors and vanquished. Additionally, it provided D'Abernon with a natural point on which to relinquish his post as ambassador to Berlin. It is not difficult to understand why he found it so desirable and so easy to capitalise on his association with these events and to assume the unofficial title of an 'ambassador of peace'. This book has aimed to assess whether he was justified in taking as much credit as he did for the success of these diplomatic initiatives. It has asked whether they would have taken place without his help and, indeed, whether they would have been more successful had he not been involved. The image conveyed of D'Abernon's activities is thus inevitably somewhat negative as it seeks to challenge several studies that have been made of his embassy that happily accept his own assessment of his effectiveness. It is certainly tempting to view an embassy that ended with the successful completion of a major diplomatic initiative as an overall success.

Britain's attitude towards Germany in the first two years of peace is often characterised as one of benevolence in the face of French intransigence regarding the implementation of the Treaty of Versailles. Lloyd George has been contrasted with Clemenceau, and still more with Poincaré. However, the circumstances that led to D'Abernon's appointment suggest that the British government was wary about resuming diplomatic relations with Germany after the First World War and of acting out of kilter with the other Allied powers. The establishment of D'Abernon in Berlin did little to diminish this hesitancy. Even had he been the most talented of diplomats, it is doubtful whether he would have been able to help clarify the British government's policies on the 'German Question'. As it was, his idiosyncratic attitude towards the relationship between the British and German governments exacerbated an already difficult situation.

This point about the need to establish a clear strategy in foreign policy after the war was lost less on the Germans than it was on the British. During his embassy, the German ministers with whom D'Abernon came into contact had a much clearer and more decisive attitude towards the conduct of foreign policy. This stemmed from the practical need for a defeated nation to construct diplomatic bridges with stronger, more influential countries as quickly as possible. In Germany, this plan of action was rendered even more possible and desirable because the commercial infrastructure of the country had survived the war largely intact, adding an incentive to find new markets and to improve relations with existing trading partners. This self-confidence was evident in the work of German officials at senior levels. It was what drove the work of civil servants like Carl Bergmann and underpinned the rationale behind the strategy of all the German Ministers for Foreign Affairs of the period, especially Rathenau and Stresemann.

D'Abernon's period as ambassador to Berlin also serves as a reminder of the impact that an individual's personality can have on the conduct of diplomacy; that the closeness or otherwise of diplomatic relations can depend on the quirks of human nature and the strength of the rapport that individuals may or may not develop. No amount of international discussion or treaty signing can legislate for this. D'Abernon's personality was particularly complex and the extent to which his eccentricity and intellectual idiosyncrasies impacted on his activities has formed an important part of this assessment of his effectiveness as an ambassador. He shared many of the values and beliefs of his generation – the generation to which all the key British and German political figures with whom he came into contact also belonged. Yet at the same time, his independence of mind led him to consider and even briefly embrace some of the newer ideas that were emerging and which criticised accepted wisdoms. This was most clearly evident in his views on commercial and economic policy, especially in relation to the ideas of Keynes. He agreed with Keynes's views but he could not accept the full implications of their implementation. He was essentially a conservative who recognised the need for change but was only prepared to accept it if it came with an advantage to Britain and helped to preserve her status as a Great Power.

But D'Abernon was often guilty of overestimating the extent of his influence both in Berlin and London. This was his principal failing. A diplomat cannot operate effectively if he is unable to form an accurate impression of what is going on around him and what the priorities are of the government to which he was accredited. D'Abernon tended to see what he wanted to see or what he thought he ought to have been able to see. His view of Germany was one in which the German government recognised and accepted the defeat of 1918 and where the country was dominated by ministers and officials willing to rely heavily on British advice on how to become accepted once again as an economically strong and peace-loving member of the comity of nations. It was through such a paternalistic attitude that he most clearly revealed the origins of his views on Britain's role in world affairs, rooted as they were in an era when British imperial influence was at its height. D'Abernon's comments on this subject made in 1880 remained essentially unchanged forty-six years later. In this at least he was consistent. He was, like many of his generation, wedded to a pre-war perception of Britain's rightful role in world affairs. This was so entrenched in his mind that he was unable (or unwilling) to modify his views from experience. His dealings with the very independent-minded Bergmann at the Brussels conference in 1920 gave him no insight into how to interpret the thought processes and actions of the equally able von Schubert four years later when they were discussing the conclusion of the Anglo-German Commercial Agreement. Yet the issues that D'Abernon was discussing with von Schubert and Bergmann were not so different for this to have been the case. The payment of reparations was always a commercial as well as a financial matter for both countries and part of the rationale for the agreement of 1924 was to stabilise relations between the two countries so that the British share of payments under the Dawes scheme could be smoothly administered.

D'Abernon's embassy in Berlin suggests that the role of the ambassador in post-war diplomacy lacked clarity. On the one hand, the desire to prevent another war was such as to create a strong impetus for different and more effective means of conducting diplomacy and with it a new form of diplomat. On the other, it was not clear what shape that new system should take and what role traditional forms of diplomatic representation would adopt. The complexities of the debates about reparations opened up an obvious role for men with expertise in commerce and finance and it is clear from Foreign Office and Treasury correspondence that that knowledge was appreciated, even if it was only grudgingly acknowledged. However, it would be misleading to claim that D'Abernon's embassy was unique in this respect. During the 1920s, the British government augmented the staff of all its key embassies with experts from a number of walks of life, notably soldiers seconded to advise on matters relating to disarmament, security and military strategy. Nevertheless, it would also be misleading to regard D'Abernon's embassy as part of a general trend. He was one of a number of ambassadors who were appointed to a senior diplomatic post during the 1920s specifically because of their knowledge of the world outside that of the career diplomat. Another, Sir Auckland Geddes, did much to ease the tension between the British and American governments between 1921 and 1923 over the issue of war debts but made little impact on either side of the Atlantic in any other respect. After 1922, this interest in the role of the expert diplomat rapidly diminished. This was partly because the principal champion of the use of experts in international diplomacy – Lloyd George – had fallen from office, but also because government departments were gaining confidence in their ability to interpret and understand events without outside assistance, having selected their own in-house experts. The most influential examples were J.M. Keynes and Ralph Hawtry at the Treasury. Thus, there was an absence of requests from the Foreign Office, the Treasury and the Board of Trade for D'Abernon's assistance in interpreting the hyperinflation that beset Germany between 1921 and 1923 and the subsequent collapse in the value of the mark. As the decade progressed, the major issues forming the central part of D'Abernon's brief had either diminished in importance or had apparently been resolved. International confidence in the ability of the Dawes Plan to provide the most effective solution to the reparations problem led to a return to more traditional styles of diplomatic contact. This is most clearly evident in the negotiations surrounding British involvement in the Treaty of Locarno, where both D'Abernon and Chamberlain resorted to secret diplomacy to try to achieve their objectives, and with limited success. Their relationship, in turn, also revealed much about the flaws of this style of diplomacy, leading as it did to strong personal resentments and the creation of individual agendas.

There were other considerations that influenced the British government's attitude towards secret diplomacy. The Foreign Office never ceased to regard it as the best way to conduct British relations with foreign powers. Outsiders such as D'Abernon, who became members of the Diplomatic Service without being career diplomats, were never fully integrated. This was partly due to an innate conservatism, but also reflected the new conference diplomacy in which these experts operated in an era when British influence appeared to be diminishing. Placing trust in such individuals might, it was feared, lead to a further decline in Britain's fortunes and give the French and the Americans the opportunity, for different reasons, to take advantage of the situation. Foreign Office faith in the fundamental soundness of the pre-war or secret approach to diplomacy was also a matter of principle and a gesture of defiance at a time when its work and values appeared to be challenged by Lloyd George during the first two years of D'Abernon's embassy. D'Abernon was in one sense a pawn in the efforts of the Foreign Office to minimise the impact of the Prime Minister's enthusiasm for the new conference diplomacy on the conduct of foreign policy. He was thus appointed to work within a diplomatic system that the Foreign Office ultimately believed would discredit itself. This offers an explanation of why D'Abernon's appointment was made for an initial period of only two years as it was widely hoped and believed that within that time, Lloyd George would be hoist by his own petard.

The attitude of the Weimar governments to post-war diplomatic practices was much more consistent. The radical restructuring and operational changes undergone by the *Auswärtiges Amt* under the Schüler reforms of 1918 were much more wide-ranging than anything undertaken by the British Foreign Office before the Eden reforms of 1943. They were born out of a need to consolidate and streamline the conduct of German diplomacy and were forward looking. It is not clear whether Edmund Schüler actually anticipated a German defeat in the First World War, but he recognised that when peace did come, it could only be maintained if an acceptable economic settlement was negotiated. All of the principal German politicians and diplomats with whom D'Abernon came into contact readily embraced this point. This is reflected in the selection of Sthamer as ambassador to London before D'Abernon's appointment was announced and in the appointment of Wiedfeldt as ambassador to Washington – financial experts dispatched to the two countries with which Germany had closest economic and commercial relations. The commitment to the use of experts to conduct diplomacy in Germany went further than the selection of diplomats. Parallels can be drawn between the independence of mind and action displayed by Sir John Bradbury and Carl Bergmann during the reparations conferences at Brussels and Paris in 1920 and 1921. But there is no British equivalent to von Schubert. Both Crowe and Tyrrell were fully committed to a rapid return to the pre-war approach to the conduct of diplomacy. Von Schubert, by contrast, was much more comfortable negotiating the Anglo-German commercial agreement in full and open discussion with the British delegation than he was in his conversations with D'Abernon concerning the security proposal that ultimately formed the basis of the Treaty of Locarno. Von Schubert's thoughts on the security negotiations suggest a man who was profoundly suspicious both of D'Abernon's motives and of his desire to play an elaborate game of bluff and double bluff with Chamberlain and Briand. Stresemann also found such an approach to diplomacy tiresome, although both he and von Schubert were as aware as anyone of the advantages of playing off one diplomatic camp against another. Stresemann was nevertheless happy to leave the minutiae of the negotiations to von Schubert and was, like Lloyd George, more in his element in the conference arena. Defeat at the end of the First World War also made it expedient to adopt an approach towards diplomacy that gave the greatest opportunity for commercial and economic advantage to Germany. The new diplomacy appeared to offer a means to this end. The governments of the Weimar period also operated in a political system that, officially at least, disassociated itself from the pre-war traditions and practices that had had such a ruinous effect on the country. As one of the victorious powers, and one faced with little prospect of constitutional or social revolution at the end of the war, Britain had neither the need nor the desire to undergo such a profound process of review and reflection. Thus pre-war and post-war approaches to diplomacy coexisted for the first four years of peace, with serious consequences for the ability of the British government to conduct a coherent policy towards European affairs, especially as they affected relations with France and Germany.

Elspeth O'Riordan's recent study of British foreign policy during the Ruhr crisis has demonstrated how important a good relationship with France was for Britain during the early 1920s.[1] For good or ill, the British government was always reluctant to break away from France over the implementation of the main provisions of the Treaty of Versailles. Yet, as the decade progressed, Britain's relations with France improved, reaching a high point in the close association between Chamberlain and Briand. Franco-German relations lacked the same degree of cordiality but were amicable enough to enable Stresemann to improve his relations with the British and French governments at the Locarno conference. Nevertheless, D'Abernon's embassy reveals the extent to which prejudices left over from the war existed in the diplomacy between these three countries. He was typical of a number of politicians and diplomats from Britain, France and Germany who believed that to be pro-French automatically implied hostility to Germany, and vice versa. It is not easy to see how peace in Europe could have been secured while such ideas not only existed but were allowed to prevail. It was only in the League of Nations that such notions were rejected and yet the work of this body was often dismissed as excessively idealistic by the very countries, sometimes the very politicians, that had helped to establish it. D'Abernon was not committed to Germany joining the League simply because he shared the vision of the peaceful world that was so central to its mission. He was more concerned that outside it, Germany would continue to be vulnerable to French bullying and that the British government would be endlessly obliged to intervene to defuse the tension between the two countries.

D'Abernon was therefore an internationalist merely as a means to an end. He was never an idealist in the manner of Lord Robert Cecil or Gilbert Murray, but he did believe that the League could serve a purpose in preserving international peace – but only after the terms of that peace had been thrashed out by politicians and diplomats who lived in what could be termed the real world. Nevertheless he failed to appreciate the concerns that occupied the minds of statesmen whose *Realpolitik* was very publicly evident. It is doubtful, for example, whether D'Abernon ever appreciated the significance of geography to German foreign policy – how it was both a blessing and a curse to Weimar politicians that Germany was literally at the centre of northern Europe. His sense of history also seems to have been less than complete, or at best selective – his diaries contain considerably more references to the perils of revived Bonapartism than to the threat of resurgent Wilhelmine nationalism. He believed that Germany lacked the will as well as the means to make war. He also appears to have been curiously ignorant of any strategy behind German foreign policy beyond what he deemed to be the supreme importance of establishing a close relationship with Britain. But even this assessment was not entirely justified. His attitude towards those German officials and politicians with whom he came into contact suggests that he tended to talk rather than listen to them. He failed to appreciate the rationale behind German relations with both the Soviet Union and the United States. Like many British people in public life, he was too quick to caricature the Russians as rabid revolutionaries whose sole mission was to destabilise the fabric of European society. As it was, all German leaders since the Middle Ages had appreciated the need for an entente in the east as a means of stabilising the region and of exerting diplomatic pressure on the countries of south-east Europe, especially in the Balkans. After the First World War, a Russo-German alliance had the further attraction of counteracting the effects of the international ostracism suffered because these two countries were the foci of the two events that had destabilised Europe – the revolution of 1917 and the war itself. For different but not wholly unrelated reasons, D'Abernon deemed the Americans to be untrustworthy because they were engaged in a policy of insidious economic rather than ideological imperialism. Within the context of Anglo-German relations, the price that had to be paid here was a diminished British role in Germany's economic recovery together with the painful realisation that the United States had replaced Britain as the world's most commercially successful nation. The American dimension was rendered even more painful because Britain was beholden to the United States through the massive sums borrowed to finance the war. Demonisation of American involvement in German affairs was therefore much more subtle than D'Abernon's critique of the objectives of Russian foreign policy. But a question remains as to what he thought was the alternative. The British government did not have the resources to finance the stabilisation of the German economy alone. This was evident to all in government circles, especially the Treasury and the Board of Trade, with whom he was in contact, and should also have been apparent to him through his own knowledge of the operation of international finance.

D'Abernon styled himself through his embassy diary as 'an ambassador of peace'. As the diary was published at the end of the 1920s and the early 1930s, it would be unfair to dismiss his claim in the light of subsequent events in German history, when the Locarno treaty and indeed the Treaty of Versailles failed to contain Hitler. D'Abernon would, of course, have liked the title to be associated with his work in persuading the German government to trust the Allies, especially during the security negotiations. But this self-description is presumptuous. He was no more effective than other British ambassadors in improving diplomatic relations between the major European powers. The Marquess of Crewe, for example, in Paris, did much to defuse the tension between the French and German governments concerning the implementation of the MICUM agreements. This was an important achievement, as it was much more likely that these two countries would go to war again over an economic dispute than anything else. As it was, D'Abernon happened to bear witness to and be a peripheral player in the conclusion of the most important international treaty since the peace treaties that had ended the war. The Treaty of Locarno did not come about through his efforts as it is clear that both the British and German governments already had the conclusion of such an agreement on their agendas. What was more, both von Schubert and Chamberlain thought that his judgement and understanding were suspect and occasionally flawed. The passage of time did not change Chamberlain's view of D'Abernon's ability to understand the finer nuances of British foreign policy concerning security during the last three years of his embassy. When commenting on the manuscript of the third volume of *An Ambassador of Peace* in the autumn of 1930, Chamberlain bluntly told

D'Abernon: 'I think you scarcely appreciated the difficulties of the British Government and of the Foreign Secretary in the first few months of Baldwin's Government.'[2] So much for the euphoria that permeated their correspondence in October 1925. The present assessment of D'Abernon's embassy also questions whether Richard Grayson's contention that Chamberlain was not as anti-German as others have claimed is sustainable.[3] Chamberlain's correspondence with D'Abernon suggests he had little patience with what he thought were the Germans' stalling tactics during the security negotiations of the spring and summer of 1925. He was also unclear whether it was D'Abernon who was putting them up to such actions. It could be said that they brought out the worst in each other. However, their views on where the priorities of the British government should lie in foreign policy provide a useful case study in the impact of personality on diplomacy and on the debate that raged within the Foreign Office throughout the 1920s about whether it was France or Germany that had the greater claim to British protection.

Notes

Preface

1. P. Neville: *Appeasing Hitler. The Diplomacy of Sir Nevile Henderson, 1937–39* (London: Palgrave, 2000).
2. A. Kaiser: 'Lord D'Abernon und die Entstehungsgeschichte der Locarno-Verträge', *Vierteljahrshefte für Zeitgeschichte*, 34(2), 1986; *Lord D'Abernon und die englische Deutschlandpolitik, 1920–1926* (Frankfurt: Peter Lang, 1989).
3. E. Stern-Rubarth: *Three Men Tried…Austen Chamberlain, Stresemann, Briand and their Fight for a New Europe* (London: Duckworth, 1939), 76–7.
4. Stern-Rubarth, 36.
5. Marchioness Curzon: *Reminiscences* (London: Hutchinson, 1955), 130. Emphasis in the original. Helen Duncombe was one of three daughters of the First Earl of Feversham who were famous Edwardian beauties.

Introduction

1. A. Wolfers: *Britain and France between Two Wars. Conflicting Strategies of Peace since Versailles* (New York: Harcourt, 1940); W.M. Jordan: *Great Britain, France and the German Problem, 1919–1939* (London: Oxford University Press, 1943).
2. L. Zimmerman: *Deutsche Aussenpolitik in der Ära der Weimarer Republik* (Göttingen: Musterschmidit Verlag, 1958); L. Dehio: *Germany and World Politics in the Twentieth Century* (London, 1959); F. Fischer: *Griff nach der Weltmacht*, Third Edition (Düsseldorf, 1962).
3. M. Gilbert: *The Roots of Appeasement* (London: Weidenfeld and Nicolson, 1966); F.S. Northedge: *The Troubled Giant. Britain among the Great Powers, 1916–1939* (London: Bell, 1966).
4. B. Bond: *British Military Policy between the Two World Wars* (Oxford: Oxford University Press, 1980); J.R. Ferris: *The Evolution of British Strategic Policy, 1919–1926* (London: Macmillan, 1989).
5. Useful introductions to this subject include D.C. Watt: *Personalities and Policies: Studies in the Formation of British Foreign Policy in the Twentieth Century* (London: Longman, 1965); C.J. Lowe and M.L. Dockrill: *The Mirage of Power: British Foreign Policy 1914–1922*, Vol. II (London: Routledge, 1972).
6. D.G. Boadle: *Winston Churchill and the German Question in British Foreign Policy, 1918–1922* (The Hague: Martinus Nijhoff, 1973); see also C. Stamm: *Lloyd George zwischen Innen-und Aussenpolitik: Die britische Deutschlandpolitik, 1921–1922* (Cologne: Verlag Wissenschaft und Politik, 1977).
7. M.L. Dockrill and J.D. Goold: *Peace without Promise: Britain and the Peace Conferences, 1919–1923* (London: Archon, 1981): see also A. Orde: *Great Britain and International Security, 1920–1926* (London: Royal Historical Society, 1978), 64–78.

8. A. von Vallentin: 'Lord D'Abernons Anteil an Deutscher Geschichte', *Europäische Revue*, 1(5), 1927; A. Vagts: 'Lord D'Abernon', *Europäische Gespräche*, 1(2), 1930.
9. A. von Vallentin, 327–9.
10. Many have appeared in *Documents on British Foreign Policy*, First Series, Vols IV–XXVII, and Series Ia, Vols I and II, published by HMSO at various times since 1968.
11. Minutes of Cabinet meetings of the numerous coalition governments of the Weimar period have also been published. These are listed in the German Published Primary Source section in the bibliography.
12. F.G. Stambrook: '"Das Kind" – Lord D'Abernon and the Origin of the Locarno Pact', *Central European History*, 1(2), 1968.
13. J. Jacobson: *Locarno Diplomacy. Germany and the West, 1925–1929* (Princeton: Princeton University Press, 1972).
14. A. Kaiser: 'Lord D'Abernon und die Entstehungsgeschichte der Locarno-Verträge', *Vierteljahreshefte für Zeitgeschichte*, 34(2), 1986; A. Kaiser: *Lord D'Abernon und die englische Deutschlandpolitik, 1920–1926* (Frankfurt: Peter Lang, 1989).

1 The Making of an Ambassador

1. For the sake of clarity and consistency, he will be referred to throughout the book as Lord D'Abernon. He became Baron D'Abernon in 1914 and was created Viscount D'Abernon in January 1926 in recognition of his role in the conclusion of the Treaty of Locarno.
2. It is possible that Roger D'Abernon came from Aberon, near Lisieux in Normandy.
3. D. Yates: 'The Manor House, Stoke D'Abernon', *Surrey County Journal*, 3(2), 1952 provides a useful summary of the history of the house.
4. See 'Notes of my life for future reference', 1882, British Library Additional Manuscripts (BL Add MSS) 48945, D'Abernon Papers.
5. Ibid.
6. Ibid.
7. *Handbook of Modern Greek* (London: Macmillan, 1879). It was subsequently translated into German (*Neugriechische Grammatik* (Leipzig, 1881)) by D. Sanders. The manuscript of the English original is in BL Add MSS 48928, D'Abernon Papers.
8. *An Ambassador of Peace*, 25 June 1920, I (London: Hodder and Stoughton, 1929), 53–4.
9. Memorandum, 14 Sept. 1880, BL Add MSS 48922, D'Abernon Papers.
10. D'Abernon to Goschen, 9 Aug. 1880, BL Add MSS 48922, D'Abernon Papers; same to same, 21 Oct. 1880.
11. See for example, Goschen to D'Abernon, 7 Aug. 1880, BL Add MSS 48922, D'Abernon Papers; same to same, 15 March 1889.
12. D'Abernon to Goschen, 27 May 1887, BL Add MSS 48922, D'Abernon Papers.
13. Contained in BL Add MSS 48961, D'Abernon Papers.
14. Baring to D'Abernon, 29 May 1887, BL Add MSS 48929, D'Abernon Papers.

15. 'Diary of period as Financial Advisor to the Egyptian government, November 30 1883–September 1884', 21 Dec. 1883, BL Add MSS 48948, D'Abernon Papers.
16. Ibid., 5 Jan. 1884, BL Add MSS 48948, D'Abernon Papers.
17. Ibid., 20 July 1884, BL Add MSS 48948, D'Abernon Papers.
18. Ibid.
19. Ibid.
20. Ibid., 29 Aug. 1884.
21. Evans to D'Abernon, 24 Oct. 1891, BL Add MSS 48929, D'Abernon Papers.
22. See report in *L'Eclair*, 16 May 1921, discussed in D'Abernon to Curzon, 20 May 1921, PRO/FO371/C10881/416/18; Phipps to Curzon, 18 July 1923, PRO/FO371/8643/C12453/1/18.
23. D'Abernon to Goschen, 20 Feb. 1890, BL Add MSS 48922, D'Abernon Papers.
24. 15 Feb. 1906, J. Vincent (ed.): *The Crawford Papers. The Journals of David Lindsay Twenty-Seventh Earl of Crawford and Tenth Earl of Balcarres, 1871–1940, during the Years 1892–1940* (Manchester: Manchester University Press, 1984), 92.
25. *The Times*, 22 June 1914, 9.
26. D'Abernon was godfather to Violet Asquith's daughter, Cressida Bonham Carter. Lady D'Abernon was godmother to Raymond Asquith's daughter, Helen.
27. Margot Asquith to D'Abernon, 11 Nov. 1909, BL Add MSS 48928, D'Abernon Papers.
28. *The Times*, 4 April 1912, 8. Sir Charles Owens was general manager of the London and South-Western Railway and a member of the War Railway Council. Sir Rider Haggard was an expert on the economics of farming and the history of agriculture.
29. *The Times*, 30 Nov. 1912, 5.
30. *The Times*, 13 April 1914, 7.
31. *The Times*, 2 Feb. 1916, 6.
32. J. Grigg: *Lloyd George: from Peace to War 1912–1916* (London: Methuen, 1997), 236–7. Cameron Hazlehurst sees the establishment of the Board as a means of boosting Asquith's popularity when it appeared that the war was not likely to come to a rapid end. C. Hazlehurst: *Politicians at War* (London: Jonathan Cape, 1971), 210–15.
33. M.E. Rose: 'The Success of Social Reform: the Central Control Board (Liquor Traffic) 1916–1922', in M.R.D. Foot (ed.): *War and Society* (London: Elek, 1973).
34. See the extensive correspondence concerning the structure and operation of the Board in PRO/Home Office (HO)/185/263; J. Turner: 'State Purchase of the Liquor Trade in the First World War', *Historical Journal*, 23(3), 1980, 589–615.
35. *The Times*, 25 Sept. 1915, 7.
36. Ibid.
37. *The Times*, 23 Nov. 1915, 5.
38. *The Times*, 13 July 1916, 5.
39. *The Times*, 19 April 1916, 5.
40. *The Times*, 11 May 1916, 3.
41. *The Times*, 20 Dec. 1917, 3.

42. Speech by D'Abernon entitled 'Future Regulation of Drink Trade', made at the Manchester Town Hall, 15 February 1918, cited in *The Times*, 16 Feb. 1918, 3.
43. *The Times*, 26 Oct. 1918, 3.
44. Cited in *The Times*, 4 Nov. 1918, 3.
45. *The Times*, 28 Nov. 1918, 7.
46. D'Abernon, letter to *The Times*, 8 April 1919, 8.
47. *The Times*, 31 May 1919, 4.
48. *The Times*, 26 May 1919, 17.
49. *British Secretary's Notes of a Conference, Held at Lympne on Sunday, June 20, 1920, at 10.55 am, Documents on British Foreign Policy*, First Series, VIII, 310–18.
50. Boadle, 9–55.
51. A. Orde: *Great Britain and International Security, 1920–1926* (London: Royal Historical Society, 1978), 84.
52. Curzon to Lloyd George, undated (probably early March 1920), House of Lords Record Office (HLRO), Lloyd George Papers, F/12/3/10.
53. K.O. Morgan: *Consensus and Disunity: the Lloyd George Coalition Government, 1918–1922* (Oxford: Oxford University Press, 1979), 140–3; cf. M. Trachtenberg: *Reparations in World Politics: France and European Economic Diplomacy, 1916–1923* (New York: Columbia University Press, 1980), 145–76.
54. Minute by Waterlow, 21 Oct. 1920, on Derby to Curzon, 20 Oct. 1920, PRO/FO371/4728/C9246/8/18; W.A. McDougall: *France's Rhineland Diplomacy, 1914–1924: the Last Bid for a Balance of Power in Europe* (Princeton: Princeton University Press, 1978), 232; *An Ambassador of Peace*, I, 28 Oct. 1920 (London: Hodder and Stoughton, 1929), 80.
55. G. Johnson: 'Curzon, Lloyd George and the Control of British Foreign Policy, 1919–1922: a Reassessment', *Diplomacy and Statecraft*, 11(3), 2000.
56. Z. Steiner: *The Foreign Office and Foreign Policy, 1898–1914* (Cambridge: Cambridge University Press, 1969); A. Sharp: 'The Foreign Office in Eclipse, 1919–1922', *History*, 61(2), 1976; E. Maisel: *The Foreign Office and Foreign Policy, 1919–1926* (Brighton: University of Sussex Press, 1994).
57. *Fifth Report of the Royal Commission on the Civil Service*, Cmd. 7748, 7749, London, 1914, cited in A. Sharp: 'Lord Curzon and the Foreign Office', in R. Bullen (ed.): *The Foreign Office, 1782–1982* (New York: University of America Press, 1984), 67.
58. *Notes of a Meeting of the Heads of Delegations of the Five Great Powers Held in M. Pichon's Room at the Quai d'Orsay, Paris, on Friday, July 25, 1919, at 3.30pm*, in *Documents on British Foreign Policy*, First Series, I, 194.
59. Memorandum by Lord E. Percy, 2 July 1919, in *Documents on British Foreign Policy*, First Series, VI, 17–18.
60. *Notes of a Meeting of the Heads of Delegations of the Five Great Powers Held in M. Pichon's Room, Quai d'Orsay, Paris, on Saturday, October 25, 1919, at 10.30am*, in *Documents on British Foreign Policy*, First Series, II, 68.
61. Note by the British Delegation for Submission to the Allied Supreme Council, 24 Oct. 1919, after a *Meeting of the Heads of Delegations of the Five Great Powers Held at the Quai d'Orsay, Paris, October 25 1919*, in *Documents on British Foreign Policy*, First Series, Vol. I, 76–7; II, 340. This trend was also evident in Germany. In February 1920, the Müller government dispatched a financial expert, Friedrich Sthamer, as ambassador to London.

62. Note by the British Delegation for Submission to the Supreme Council, 24 Oct. 1919 in *Notes of a Meeting of the Heads of Delegations of the Five Great Powers Held in M. Pichon's Room, Quai d'Orsay, Paris, on Saturday, October 25, 1919, at 10.30am*, in *Documents on British Foreign Policy*, First Series, II, 76–7.
63. Undated report of the Allied Supreme Council, quoted in *Documents on British Foreign Policy*, First Series, II, 339–40.
64. Nothing appears to have survived in the Foreign Office archive which explains Kilmarnock's selection.
65. *British Secretary's Notes of an Allied Conference Held at 10, Downing Street, London, SW1, on Monday, March 1, 1920 at 4pm*, in *Documents on British Foreign Policy*, First Series, VII, 330–1.
66. Ibid., 331.
67. *British Secretary's Notes of an Allied Conference Held at 10, Downing Street, London, SW1, on Wednesday, March 3, 1920 at 11am*, in *Documents on British Foreign Policy*, First Series, VII, 365.
68. Ibid., 336.
69. *British Secretary's Notes of a Conference, Held at Lympne, on Sunday, June 20, 1920, at 10.55am*, in *Documents on British Foreign Policy*, First Series, VIII, 312–13.
70. *British Secretary's Notes of a Meeting of the Supreme Council, Held at the Villa Belle, Boulogne, on Monday, June 21, 1920, at 12.30pm*, in *Documents on British Foreign Policy*, First Series, VIII, 343–4.
71. Undated Minute *c.* 9 June 1920, Public Record Office (PRO), Foreign Office (FO) 371/3769/W202512/198916/17.
72. Minute by Waterlow, 13 Nov. 1920, cited in Sharp, 'The Foreign Office in Eclipse, 1919–1922', 213–14.
73. *British Secretary's Notes of an Allied Conference Held at 10, Downing Street, London, SW1, on Monday, March 1, 1920 at 4pm*, in *Documents on British Foreign Policy*, First Series, VII, 334.
74. Churchill to Lloyd George, 24 March 1920, HLRO, Lloyd George Papers, F/9/2/20; Boadle, 136, 144–5.
75. R. Vansittart: *The Mist Procession* (London: Hutchinson, 1958), 253.
76. The 'Garden Suburb', which included Lord Northcliffe, Edward Grigg and Philip Kerr and was widely criticised by contemporaries as it appeared to have the status of a second Cabinet.
77. Curzon to Geddes, 27 May 1920, Oriental and India Office Library (OIOL) Eur F 112/206, Curzon Papers.
78. Cf. Morgan, 113–14. Exacerbated by the often cool relationship between Hardinge and Curzon.
79. D'Abernon had made a positive impression on Balfour while both were in Paris during the peace conference. D'Abernon attended dinners at the British embassy in Paris at which the peace settlement with Germany was discussed. He would therefore have been aware of the rationale behind British policy towards Germany. There are numerous references in the diary of the British ambassador to Paris, Lord Derby, in 920 DER (17) 28/1/3–4, Liverpool Record Office, Derby Papers.
80. Diary, 9 July 1920, Liverpool Record Office, Papers of the 17th Earl of Derby, 920 DER (17) 28/1/7.
81. Journal, 29 Aug. 1920, Churchill College Cambridge, Kennedy Papers, LKEN 2.

82. See, for example, D'Abernon to Curzon, 2 July 1920, PRO/FO371/4739/C549/45/18.
83. Vansittart, 253.
84. Diary, 9 July 1920, Liverpool Record Office, Papers of the 17th Earl of Derby, 920 DER (17) 28/1/7.
85. Derby to Curzon, 5 March 1920, OIOL, Curzon Papers, Eur F 112/197.
86. *The Times*, 25 June 1920.
87. Steed to Curzon, 23 Feb. 1920, OIOL, Curzon Papers, Eur F 112/218.
88. Information about *The Times*'s attitude towards Lloyd George's treatment of the Foreign Office and the circumstances of D'Abernon's appointment can be found in the journal of Aubrey Kennedy, the newspaper's Berlin correspondent. Journal, Churchill College Archive Centre, Kennedy Papers, LKEN 2.
89. Leader, *The Times*, 29 June 1920.
90. *The Times*, 2 July 1920.
91. Cited in *The Times*, 2 July 1920.
92. Hardinge was later appointed ambassador to Paris, 1920–22.
93. Hardinge to Curzon, 19 April 1920, OIOL, Curzon Papers, Eur F/112/119.
94. Later ambassador to Madrid, 1924–28, and ambassador to Berlin, 1928–33.
95. Hardinge to Rumbold, 13 July 1920, 43, Cambridge University Library, Hardinge Papers.
96. Rumbold to Hardinge, 24 July 1920, Cambridge University Library, Hardinge Papers, 43.
97. See D'Abernon's *Eighteenth Decisive Battle of the World* (London: Hodder and Stoughton, 1931), which chronicles his period as head of the inter-Allied mission. See also Norman Davis: *White Eagle. Red Star. The Polish-Soviet War 1919–1920* (London: Orbis, 1983).
98. *An Ambassador of Peace*, I (London: Hodder and Stoughton, 1929), 19–23.
99. Curzon to Lloyd George, 20 July 1920, HLRO, Lloyd George Papers, F/13/1/1.
100. Rumbold to Hardinge, 28 Aug. 1920, Cambridge University Library, Hardinge Papers, 43.
101. Ibid.
102. Hardinge to Rumbold, 4 Sept. 1920, Cambridge University Library, Hardinge Papers, 43. See also M. Gilbert: *Sir Horace Rumbold: Portrait of a Diplomat* (London: Heinemann, 1973), 203–15.
103. Kennedy to Wickham Steed, 15 Aug. 1920, Churchill College Archive Centre, Kennedy Papers, LKEN 1.
104. Johnson, op. cit.
105. See, for example, minute by Lampson, 18 Nov. 1922, on 'Relations between the British Delegation to the Reparation Commission and the Treasury and the Foreign Office', 14 Nov. 1922, PRO/FO371/7487/C15635/99/18.
106. Ibid.
107. Crowe to Curzon, 22 Dec. 1922, OIOL, Curzon Papers, Eur F 112/229. A minute by Curzon of the same day indicates his assent. See also Lady Curzon, 210.
108. H. Nicolson: *Curzon: the Last Phase* (London: Constable, 1934), 274.
109. *An Ambassador of Peace*, I, 25 June 1920, 53–4.
110. D'Abernon to Lloyd George, 16 Jan. 1926, HLRO, Lloyd George Papers, G/5/10/4.

111. *An Ambassador of Peace*, I, 48.
112. Hankey to Lloyd George, 6 June 1922, HLRO, Lloyd George Papers, F/26/1/40. Hankey's emphasis.
113. *An Ambassador of Peace*, III (London: Hodder and Stoughton, 1931), 31.
114. For example, the eighteen extracts that D'Abernon sent from his diary to Hankey and Lloyd George between 7 July and 30 Sept. 1921 contained in HLRO, Lloyd George Papers, F/54/1/32–51.
115. McDougall, 232.
116. Derby to Curzon, 22 July 1920, Liverpool Record Office, Papers of the 17th Earl of Derby, 920 DER (17) 28/2/4.
117. Review of *An Ambassador of Peace*, I, in the *New Statesman*, 26 Jan. 1930, 499.
118. Nicolson, 42–3, 193; Morgan, 114.
119. Derby to Curzon, 22 July 1920, OIOL, Curzon Papers, Eur F 112/198A.

2 The Debate about Reparations, 1920–22

1. D. Felix: 'Reparations Reconsidered with a Vengeance', *Central European History*, 4(2), 1971; S. Marks: 'Reparations Reconsidered: a Rejoinder', *Central European History*, 5(2), 1972, 359.
2. S.A. Schuker: 'Finance and Foreign Policy in the Era of the German Inflation: British, French and German Strategies for Economic Reconstruction after the First World War', in O. Büsch and G. Feldman (eds): *Historische Prozesse der deutschen Inflation 1914–1924: Ein Tagungsbericht* (Berlin: de Gruyter, 1978), 346; B. Kent: *The Spoils of War: the Politics, Economics and Diplomacy of Reparations, 1918–1932* (Oxford: Oxford University Press, 1991), 250–67.
3. J.-N. Jeanney: 'De la spéculation financière comme arme diplomatique. À propos de la première "bataille du franc" (Novembre 1923–Mars 1924)', *Relations Internationales*, 5(1), 1978.
4. A. Kaiser: 'Lord D'Abernon und die Entstehungsgeschichte der Locarno-Verträge', *Vierteljahrshefte für Zeitgeschichte*, 34(2), 1986.
5. J.M. Keynes: *The Economic Consequences of the Peace* (London: Macmillan, 1920).
6. Marks, Felix: *Walter Rathenau and the Weimar Republic. The Politics of Reparations* (Baltimore: Johns Hopkins University Press, 1971), 67–87.
7. Foreign Office correspondence about the San Remo conference can be found in PRO/FO371/8654.
8. See also Sir Maurice Hankey's notes in PRO/CAB 63 and the Foreign Office discussion of the Agreement in Memorandum by Waterlow, 5 July 1920, PRO/FO371/4726/C704/8/18.
9. These can be found in the following Foreign Office 371 files in the Public Records Office: 4728–30, 4739, 4743, 4774–5, 4806–7. D'Abernon also discussed the Spa conference in *An Ambassador of Peace*, I (London: Hodder and Stoughton, 1929), 56–68.
10. D'Abernon and Curzon, 9 Dec. 1920, PRO/FO371/4730/C13512/8/18; *Akten zur deutschen Auswärtigen Politik*, Serie A iv, No. 72 (Göttingen: Vandenhoeck und Ruprecht, 1982); P. Wulf (ed.): *Das Kabinett Fehrenbach, 25 Juni 1920 bis 4 Mai 1921* (Boppard am Rhein: Harald Boldt, 1972), No. 131.

11. D'Abernon to Curzon, 9 Dec. 1920, PRO/FO371/4730/C13512/8/18.
12. Hardinge to Curzon, 12 Dec. 1920, PRO/FO371/4730/C13798/8/18.
13. M. Trachtenberg: *Reparations in World Politics: France and European Economic Diplomacy, 1916–1923* (New York: Columbia University Press, 1980), 181–2; *An Ambassador of Peace*, I, 77–8. See also C. Schulkin: *Lost Opportunity: the Reparation Question and the Failure of the European Recovery Effort* (Princeton: Princeton University Press, 1976), 305–6. Schulkin is mistaken in stating (p. 305) that D'Abernon received no instructions. They are in PRO/FO371/4730/C13331/8/18, dated 8 Dec. 1920, and were approved by the Cabinet on 6 Dec. 1920, CAB 23/23/66/1.
14. An assessment of German attitudes at the Brussels conference can be found in P. Wulf: *Hugo Stinnes. Wirtschaft und Politik, 1918–1924* (Stuttgart: Klett-Cotta, 1979), 241–53. Cf. Kaiser's account of D'Abernon's conversations with Bergmann, Kaiser, 58–65.
15. Bergmann later became principal German delegate to the Reparation Commission.
16. *Akten zur deutschen Auswärtigen Politik*, Serie A iv, No. 85.
17. *An Ambassador of Peace*, I, 16 Dec. 1920, 101; *Memorandum on Position of Brussels Conference at the Christmas Adjournment*, communicated in D'Abernon to Curzon, 3 Jan. 1921, PRO/FO371/5934/C94/94/18. Kaiser states that D'Abernon had a great influence on Bergmann's thinking at the Brussels conference, Kaiser, 512.
18. Ibid., 101. Bergmann also feared that if the Boulogne figure was accepted, it would result in the fall of the German government, Trachtenberg, 183.
19. C. Bergmann: *A History of Reparations* (London: Ernest Benn, 1927), 49.
20. Ibid., 47–8.
21. Ibid., 50.
22. *Secret Memorandum of an Interview with Bergmann, December 18 1920*, OIOL, Eur F 112/202, Curzon Papers; Wulf (ed.), *Das Kabinett Fehrenbach*, No. 145.
23. *An Ambassador of Peace*, I, 18 Dec. 1920, 102.
24. 21 Dec. 1920, diary BL Add MSS, 48953A, D'Abernon Papers. Bergmann's account of the meeting can be found in Undated Memorandum by Bergmann, German Foreign Ministry (GFM) 3375/D735577–9. See also Bergmann to von Simons, 21 Dec. 1920, GFM 3375/D735570.
25. Bergmann, 51.
26. Wulf (ed.), *Das Kabinett Fehrenbach*, No. 145.
27. 28 Dec. 1920, BL Add MSS 48953A, D'Abernon Papers.
28. *An Ambassador of Peace*, I, 31 Dec. 1921, 241.
29. Bradbury to Chamberlain, 19 Jan. 1921, PRO/T104/269.
30. Von Simons to Bergmann, 1 Jan. 1921, T-120/1635/D735589ff, cited in Trachtenberg, 183.
31. Wulf (ed.), *Das Kabinett Fehrenbach*, No. 145.
32. Wulf, *Hugo Stinnes*, 249; Trachtenberg, 155–91.
33. The most comprehensive analysis of the Seydoux Plan can be found in Trachtenberg, 155–91. See also G. Soutou: 'Die deutschen Reparationen und das Seydoux-Project, 1920–1921', *Vierteljahrshefte für Zeitgeschichte*, 23(2), 1975.
34. Bergmann, 52.
35. D'Abernon to Curzon, 19 Jan. 1921, PRO/FO371/5961/C15232/386/18. The main points of this conversation are contained in *Summary of the Various*

Proposals for a Settlement of the Reparations Question Made at Boulogne, Paris and London, June 1920–February 1922, enclosed in Foreign Office Memorandum dated 16 March 1921, PRO/FO371/6018/C5580/2740/18.

36. *Memorandum of an Interview with Herr Bergmann, January 18 1921.*
37. *'Adherence to the Paris Agreement? A semi-official Reuter's message', Berliner Tageblatt,* 14 Feb. 1921, communicated in D'Abernon to Curzon, 14 Feb. 1921, PRO/FO371/6015/C3586/2740/18.
38. *Summaries of Statements Made by the German Delegates at the Conference in December 1920 on the Question of Reparations,* communicated in D'Abernon to Curzon, 20 Dec. 1920, PRO/FO371/4730/C14695/8/18.
39. This stated that Germany would pay approximately 1,800,000 tons of coal per month to the Allies. Foreign Office correspondence can be found in PRO/FO371 4728–30, 4739, 4743, 4774–5, 4806–7.
40. Bradbury to Chamberlain, 19 Jan. 1921, PRO/T194/269.
41. *German Currency: its Collapse and Recovery, 1920–26,* The Presidential Address of the Right Hon. Viscount D'Abernon, G.C.B., G.C.M.G. Delivered to the Royal Statistical Society, 16 Nov. 1926, reprinted in the *Journal of the Royal Statistical Society,* 80(1), 1927, 2.
42. See G.C. Peden: *Keynes, the Treasury and British Economic Policy* (London: Macmillan, 1988), 22–3; Kaiser, 42, 528. Keynes's views were not without support within the Treasury. See Memorandum by Sir Basil Blackett, 22 Nov. 1921, *German Reparations: the Need for a Readjustment of the Present Scheme of Payments,* PRO/FO371/6038/C22283/2740/18.
43. D'Abernon, *German Currency: its Collapse and Recovery, 1920–26,* 4.
44. Grahame to Curzon, 15 Dec. 1920, PRO/FO371/4730/C13969/8/18.
45. 13 Dec. 1920, diary, BL Add MSS 48953A, D'Abernon Papers.
46. Wulf (ed.), *Das Kabinett Fehrenbach,* No. 142; *Akten zur deutschen Auswärtigen Politik,* Serie A iv, No. 85.
47. *An Ambassador of Peace,* I, 28 Dec. 1920, 107.
48. *An Ambassador of Peace,* I, 8 Jan. 1921, 109.
49. Diary, 8 Jan. 1921, communicated in D'Abernon to Curzon, 10 Jan. 1921, PRO/FO371/5934/C1048/94/18.
50. Addison to Waterlow, 15 Dec. 1920, PRO/FO371/4730/C14367/8/18.
51. *An Ambassador of Peace,* I, 31 Dec. 1921, 241.
52. Hardinge to Curzon, 11 Jan. 1921, PRO/FO371/5934/C827/94/18.
53. See for example the comments cited in Mendl to Tyrrell, 1 May 1921, PRO/FO371/357/P826/2/117 and in D'Abernon to Curzon, 20 May 1921, PRO/FO371/5971/C10881/416/18.
54. The entries published in *An Ambassador of Peace,* I, 117–18 give conflicting opinions as to whether Loucheur or Doumer was the author of the scheme, despite reference in D'Abernon's unpublished diary to *Translation of a Note by M. Doumer, French Minister of Finance,* BL Add MSS 48953A, D'Abernon Papers. See also D. Lloyd George: *The Truth about Reparations and War-Debts* (London: Heinemann, 1932), 33–53.
55. *Translation of a Note by M. Doumer.*
56. *An Ambassador of Peace,* I, 24 Jan. 1921, 115; Wulf (ed.), *Das Kabinett Fehrenbach,* No. 165.
57. Bradbury to Chamberlain, 19 Jan. 1921, PRO/T104/269; *Akten zur deutschen Auswärtigen Politik,* Serie A iv, No. 133.

58. See *Summary of the various proposals for a settlement of the Reparation Question made at Boulogne, Paris and London, June 1920–February 1921*, communicated as a Foreign Office Memorandum, 16 March 1921, PRO/FO371/6018/C5580/2740/18. Trachtenberg, 55–191.
59. Kilmarnock to Curzon, 26 Jan. 1921, PRO/FO371/5961/C1957/386/18.
60. Summary of speech by von Simons in the Reichstag, 1 Feb. 1921, communicated in Kilmarnock to Curzon, 2 Feb.1921, HLRO, F/54/1/8, Lloyd George Papers.
61. D'Abernon to Curzon, 4 Feb. 1921, BL Add MSS 48924A, D'Abernon Papers; *Akten zur deutschen Auswärtigen Politik*, Serie A, iv, No. 157.
62. D'Abernon to Boveri, 11 Feb. 1921, HLRO, F/54/1/12, Lloyd George Papers.
63. The article appeared in the *Berliner Tageblatt* on 5 Feb. 1921. A summary can be found in D'Abernon to Curzon, 5 Feb. 1921, PRO/T160/38.
64. 3 Feb. 1921, diary, BL Add MSS 48953A, D'Abernon Papers; Wulf (ed.), *Das Kabinett Fehrenbach*, No. 166.
65. 10 Feb. 1921, diary, BL Add MSS 48953A, D'Abernon Papers.
66. A summary can be found in D'Abernon to Curzon, 14 Feb. 1921, PRO/FO371/5963/C3414/386/18.
67. D'Abernon to Curzon, 18 Feb. 1921, PRO/FO371/5963/C3859/386/18; Wulf (ed.), *Das Kabinett Fehrenbach*, No. 181.
68. Marc Trachtenberg has pointed out that the German government's attitude towards resolving the reparations question differed from that of German industrialists. D'Abernon's dealings with both supports this contention. Trachtenberg, 187–8.
69. See also *Akten zur deutschen Auswärtigen Politik*, Serie A iv, No. 169.
70. *An Ambassador of Peace*, I, 4 March 1921, 134; von Simons to Fehrenbach, 6 March 1921, GFM 3398/D737146/7.
71. Diary, 6 March 1921, Churchill College Cambridge, HNKY 1/6, Hankey Papers.
72. Communicated in Cheetham to Curzon, 8 March 1921, PRO/FO371/6016/C4965/2740/18.
73. *An Ambassador of Peace*, I, 10 March 1921, 130.

3 From Rapallo to the Ruhr Crisis, 1922–24

1. E.Y. O'Riordan: *Britain and the Ruhr Crisis* (London: Palgrave – now Palgrave Macmillan, 2001).
2. *An Ambassador of Peace*, I, 23 April 1922 (London: Hodder and Stoughton, 1929), 296–8.
3. D'Abernon to Curzon, 23 April 1922, BL Add MSS 48924B, D'Abernon Papers.
4. D'Abernon to Curzon, 24 April 1922, BL Add MSS 48924B, D'Abernon Papers.
5. D'Abernon to Curzon, 29 April 1922, BL Add MSS 48924B, D'Abernon Papers.
6. D'Abernon to Curzon, 24 April 1922.
7. See also D. Gilmour: *Curzon* (London: John Murray, 1994), 528.
8. D'Abernon to Curzon, 7 July 1922, BL Add MSS, D'Abernon Papers, is typical of a large number of dispatches which emphasise this point.

9. D'Abernon to Curzon, 12 July 1922, BL Add MSS 48924B, D'Abernon Papers.
10. Viscount D'Abernon: 'German Currency: its Collapse and Recovery, 1920–1926', *Journal of the Royal Statistical Society*, 80(1), 1927.
11. O'Riordan, 25.
12. See, for example, *An Ambassador of Peace*, II, 3 Oct. 1923 (London: Hodder and Stoughton, 1930), 263–4.
13. Neville Chamberlain's diary, entry 27 July 1923, Birmingham University Library, Neville Chamberlain Papers; Crowe to Phipps, 24 Nov. 1923, Tyrrell to Phipps, 18 Dec. 1923, Churchill College Archive Centre, PHPP 2/3, 2/12, Phipps Papers. See also J.R. Ferris: *The Evolution of British Strategic Policy, 1919–1926* (London: Macmillan Press – now Palgrave Macmillan, 1989), 127.
14. Curzon to Kilmarnock, 11 Jan. 1923, PRO/FO371/8707/C1563/313/18.
15. Cited in S. Moore: *Peace without Victory for the Allies, 1918–1932* (Providence, RI: Berg, 1994), 165–6.
16. Curzon to Derby, 1 April 1920, OIOL, Eur F112/240, Curzon Papers.
17. Curzon to D'Abernon, 22 Feb. 1923, BL Add MSS, 48925A, D'Abernon Papers.
18. Ferris, 129.
19. D'Abernon to Curzon, 17 April 1923, PRO/FO371/8729/C7315/313/18.
20. Memorandum by Cadogan, 19 July 1923, OIOL, Eur F112/241, Curzon Papers.
21. The substance of the German government's response is discussed in D'Abernon to Curzon, 23 July 1923, BL Add MSS 48925B, D'Abernon Papers.
22. Julian Piggott to Lampson, 20 Jan. 1923, PRO/FO371/8706, cited in F.L. Carsten: *Britain and the Weimar Republic* (London: Batsford, 1984), 126.
23. Curzon to Kilmarnock, 11 Jan. 1923. Kilmarnock had been appointed in 1922.
24. Curzon to Grahame, 26 March 1923, OIOL Eur F 112/240, Curzon Papers.
25. O'Riordan, 61.
26. *An Ambassador of Peace*, II, 25 Jan. 1923, 161–2.
27. D'Abernon to the King, 26 Jan. 1923, BL Add MSS 48922A, D'Abernon Papers; H. Rupieper: *The Cuno Government and Reparations 1922–1923: Politics and Economics* (The Hague: Martinus Nijhoff, 1979), 11.
28. *An Ambassador of Peace*, II, 9.
29. *An Ambassador of Peace*, II, 21 Jan. 1923, 159–60; Kaiser, 125.
30. D'Abernon to Curzon, 12 April 1923, PRO/FO371/8727/C6880/313/18.
31. D'Abernon to Curzon, 16 Jan. 1923, PRO/FO371/8704/C1146/313/18.
32. D'Abernon to the King, 26 Jan. 1923, BL Add MSS 48922A, D'Abernon Papers.
33. The main points of this report were: that immediate stabilisation of the German economy was possible without external assistance; the establishment of equilibrium in the German economy was a necessary requirement for the stabilisation of the mark; that a foreign loan to aid the stabilisation was not a necessary requirement; that no scheme of stabilisation would be practicable unless accompanied with a solution of the reparations question; that a moratorium on reparations payments was a necessary precondition to budgetary equilibrium.
34. *Akten zur deutschen Auswärtigen Politik*, Serie A vi, No. 291.
35. D'Abernon to Curzon, 6 Jan. 1923, PRO/FO371/8702/C318/313/18.
36. D'Abernon to Curzon, 24 Jan. 1923.

37. D'Abernon to Curzon, 21 Feb. 1923, BL Add MSS 48925A, D'Abernon Papers; Thurstan to D'Abernon, 18 Feb. 1923, communicated in Thurstan to Curzon, 18 Feb. 1923, PRO/FO371/8715/C3301/313/18.
38. D'Abernon to Curzon, 4 Jan. 1923, PRO/FO371/8703/C759/313/18.
39. D'Abernon to Curzon, 3 March 1923, PRO/FO371/8720/C4460/313/18.
40. O'Riordan, 149.
41. *An Ambassador of Peace*, II, 24.
42. Ibid., 27 Oct. 1922, 117–18.
43. D'Abernon to Curzon, 23 April 1922, BL Add MSS 48924B, D'Abernon Papers.
44. *An Ambassador of Peace*, 28 Oct. 1922, II, 118–19.
45. Warren Fisher to Baldwin, 19 July 1923, PRO/T172/1309.
46. See for example Curzon's minutes of 26 Jan. 1923 on a communication from the Reparation Commission to the Foreign Office about the organisation of the Paris conference of that year, PRO/FO371/8628/C1633/1/18.
47. Bradbury to Baldwin, 25 April 1923, communicated in Niemeyer to Lampson, PRO/FO371/86733/C7649/1/18. Bradbury was referring to the disagreement between Britain and France at the Paris conference of 1923 over which proposals to put to the German government.
48. *An Ambassador of Peace*, II, 11 June 1923, 222.
49. Moore, 170–3.
50. Memorandum on the Pledge of the French Government not to act independently of their Allies, 16 Nov. 1923, OIOL, Eur F112/240, Curzon Papers.
51. For example Minute by Crowe, 4 July 1923, on Addison to Lampson, 26 June 1923, PRO/FO371/8641/C11392/1/18.
52. D'Abernon was made aware of this by Curzon. Curzon to D'Abernon, 6 May 1923, PRO/FO371/8634/C8044/1/18.
53. H. Nicolson: *Curzon: the Last Phase* (London: Constable, 1934), 274.
54. Note by Curzon, 6 Jan. 1923, transmitted in Curzon to D'Abernon, 8 Jan. 1923, PRO/FO371/8626/C449/1/18.
55. Memorandum by Lampson, 4 Jan. 1923, PRO/FO371/8626/C466/1/18.
56. Debate in the Reichstag, speech by Stresemann, 10 Aug. 1923, communicated in D'Abernon to Curzon, 11 Aug. 1923, PRO/FO371/8699/C14067/203/18; E.D. Erdmann and M. Vogt (eds): *Die Kabinette Stresemann I und II, 13 August 1923 bis 6 Oktober 1923 bis 30 November 1923*, I (Boppard am Rhein: Harald Boldt, 1978), No. 8.
57. Minute by Lampson, 17 Jan. 1923, on D'Abernon to Curzon, 15 Jan. 1923, PRO/FO371/8627/C882/1/18.
58. D'Abernon to Curzon, 20 April 1923, PRO/FO371/8633/C7580/1/18.
59. See a sequence of documents communicated in D'Abernon to Curzon, 18 Sept. 1923, PRO/FO371/8656/C16264/1/18.
60. D'Abernon to Curzon, 4 Jan. 1923, PRO/FO371/8625/C233/1/18; *Memorandum on Sir Eyre Crowe's note respecting German Reparations*, enclosed in D'Abernon to Curzon, 6 Jan. 1923, PRO/FO371/8627/C594/1/18.
61. D'Abernon to Curzon, 22 April 1923, PRO/FO371/8728/C7177/313/18. See also extract from the *Lokal Anzeiger*, 23 April 1923.
62. Phipps to Curzon, 24 April 1923, *Documents on British Foreign Policy*, First Series, XXI, 223.
63. Curzon to D'Abernon, 25 April 1923, BL Add MSS 48925B, D'Abernon Papers.

64. *An Ambassador of Peace*, II, 3 May 1923, 207.
65. D'Abernon to Curzon, 4 May 1923, BL Add MSS 48925B, D'Abernon Papers. Stambrook cites this remark out of context, suggesting that it was an attempt to convince the German government of Allied good faith. F.G. Stambrook: '"Das Kind" – Lord D'Abernon and the Origins of the Locarno Pact', *Central European History*, 1(2), 1968, 238.
66. D'Abernon to Curzon, 8 Aug. 1923, PRO/FO371/8738/C13770/313/18. The Cabinet debate on funding passive resistance can be found in K.H. Harbeck (ed.): *Das Kabinett Cuno, 22 November 1922 bis 12 August 1923* (Boppard am Rhein: Harald Boldt, 1968), No. 6; Kaiser, 137.
67. O'Riordan, 40.
68. Crewe to Lindsay, 24 Jan. 1923, PRO/FO371/8792/C1653/1652/18. Crewe's emphasis. This dispatch also communicated the text of an article from *Le Matin* of 21 Jan. 1923, entitled *Sir Edgar Vincent alias Lord D'Abernon*.
69. Minute by Lampson, 25 Jan. 1923, on *Memorandum respecting French attacks on Lord D'Abernon*, 25 Jan. 1923, PRO/FO371/8792/C1653/1652/18.
70. Crewe to Curzon, 28 Jan. 1923, PRO/FO371/8792/C1720/1652/18.
71. D'Abernon to Curzon, 31 Jan. 1923, PRO/FO371/8792/C2270/1652/18.
72. *Daily Mail*, 3 Aug. 1923.
73. *Daily Mail*, 8 Aug. 1923.
74. The note contained 55 articles.
75. Earl of Ronaldshay: *The Life of Lord Curzon*, III (London: Ernest Benn, 1928), 359.
76. D'Abernon to Curzon, 11 Aug. 1923, BL Add MSS 48925B, D'Abernon Papers.
77. D'Abernon to Curzon, 14 Aug. 1923, BL Add MSS 48925B, D'Abernon Papers.
78. D'Abernon to Curzon, 23 Aug. 1923, BL Add MSS 48925B, D'Abernon Papers.
79. Jones contains a useful assessment of the activities of the MICUM.
80. The initiative was not the first of its kind. An attempt to create closer economic links between France and Germany had been made as early as 1921, resulting in the Wiesbaden Agreement.
81. *An Ambassador of Peace*, 25 Dec. 1923, II, 286.
82. O'Riordan, 109.
83. Foreign Office to D'Abernon, 26 Sept. 1923, PRO/FO371/8744/C17453/313/18.
84. D'Abernon to Curzon, 4 Nov. 1923, PRO/FO371/8748/C19013/313/18.
85. Curzon to D'Abernon, 7 Nov. 1923, PRO/FO371/8748/C19013/313/18
86. *An Ambassador of Peace*, I, 51.
87. Ibid., 5 Oct. 1923, II, 262–3.
88. D'Abernon to Curzon, 15 Nov. 1923, PRO/FO371/8749/C2015/313/18. Also included in this dispatch is D'Abernon's letter to Stresemann, 12 Nov. 1923 and Stresemann's reply of 14 Nov.
89. Curzon to D'Abernon, 21 Dec. 1923, *Documents on British Foreign Policy*, First Series, XXI, 731.
90. Cf. D'Abernon to Curzon, 1 Sept. 1923, BL Add MSS 48925B, D'Abernon Papers.
91. Curzon to D'Abernon, 4 Jan. 1923, *Documents on British Foreign Policy*, First Series, XXI, 734.
92. Von Schubert to Sthamer, 9 Jan. 1924, German Foreign Ministry, 3116/D640810–11.

4 The Challenge of the United States, 1922–24

1. A. DeConde: *A History of American Foreign Policy*, Third Edition, II (New York: Scribner, 1978).
2. D'Abernon to the King, 18 August 1921, BL Add MSS 48922A, D'Abernon Papers.
3. S.A. Schuker: *The End of French Predominance in Europe. The Financial Crisis of 1924 and the Adoption of the Dawes Plan* (Chapel Hill: University of North Carolina Press, 1976); M.P. Leffler: *America's Pursuit of European Stability and French Security, 1919–1933* (Chapel Hill: University of North Carolina Press, 1979).
4. Diary, 27 July 1922, BL Add MSS 48954, D'Abernon Papers.
5. M.L. Dockrill and J.D. Goold: *Peace without Promise: Britain and the Peace Conferences, 1919–1923* (London: Archon, 1981); B. Kent: *The Spoils of War: the Politics, Economics and Diplomacy of Reparation, 1918–1932* (Oxford: Oxford University Press, 1991).
6. The British government had borrowed heavily from the United States to help finance the war effort – a sum of almost £1000 million. In 1922, the British government, faced with economic recession, requested a moratorium but the Harding administration refused. See B.J.C. McKercher: *The Second Baldwin Government and the United States, 1924–1929: Attitudes and Diplomacy* (Cambridge: Cambridge University Press, 1984), 1–8.
7. McKercher, 8.
8. The German perspective on these negotiations can be found in Bernhard Dernburg: 'The Moribund Peace Treaty', *Berliner Tageblatt*, 23 May 1920, communicated in Kilmarnock to Curzon, 27 May 1920, HLRO, F/54/1/1, Lloyd George Papers.
9. K.O. Morgan: *Consensus and Disunity: the Lloyd George Coalition Government 1918–1922* (Oxford: Oxford University Press, 1979), 318.
10. Cited in diary, 28 March 1923, BL Add MSS 48955, D'Abernon Papers.
11. Germany: Annual Report, 1921, D'Abernon to Curzon, 2 Feb. 1922, PRO/FO371/7556/C2067/2067/18. See also Schulze-Bidlingmaier (ed.): *Die Kabinette Wirth I und II, 10 Mai 1921 bis 26 Oktober 1921, 26 Oktober 1921 bis 22 November 1922* (Boppard am Rhein: Harald Boldt, 1973), I, No. 54.
12. D'Abernon to the King, 18 Aug. 1921, BL Add MSS 48922A, D'Abernon Papers; *An Ambassador of Peace*, I (London: Hodder and Stoughton, 1929), 18–19. These latter observations were written before the Wall Street Crash.
13. *An Ambassador of Peace*, I, 30 Sept. 1921, 214.
14. Diary, 31 Dec. 1921, BL Add MSS 48953B, D'Abernon Papers.
15. Ambassador to Berlin from Feb. 1922 to Feb. 1925, subsequently ambassador to London.
16. Diary, 29 June 1922, BL Add MSS 48954, D'Abernon Papers.
17. K.P. Jones: 'Alanson Houghton and the Ruhr Crisis: the Diplomacy of Power and Morality', in K.P. Jones (ed.): *U.S. Diplomats in Europe, 1919–1941* (Princeton: Princeton University Press, 1981), 26.
18. *An Ambassador of Peace*, I, 19–20.
19. Speech made before the Manchester Chamber of Commerce, 22 April 1927, cited in B. Willson: *America's Ambassadors to England, 1785–1828* (London: Macmillan, 1928), 485.

20. Diary, 26 Aug. 1922, BL Add MSS 48954, D'Abernon Papers.
21. *An Ambassador of Peace*, I, 31 Dec. 1921, 241.
22. Communicated in D'Abernon to Curzon, 24 Dec. 1921, PRO/FO371/5980/C23886/416/18.
23. D'Abernon to Curzon, 1 April 1921, PRO/FO371/6022/C6958/2740/18.
24. Schulze-Bidlingmaier, I, No. 54.
25. D'Abernon to the King, 18 Aug. 1921, BL Add MSS, 48922A, D'Abernon Papers.
26. Ibid.
27. *Germany: Annual Report, 1921*. Cf. Schulze-Bidlingmaier, I. No. 54.
28. Berg, 77–8.
29. Jones, 26.
30. D. Felix: *Walther Rathenau and the Weimar Republic. The Politics of Reparations* (Baltimore: Johns Hopkins University Press, 1971).
31. Cited in Berg, 83; cf. also *An Ambassador of Peace*, I, 4 April 1922, 291.
32. Diamond, 446–7.
33. Ironically, it was Lloyd George who played a large part in encouraging Wiedfeldt's mission. See *An Ambassador of Peace*, I, 9 March 1922, 270.
34. Extract from the *New York Times*, 30 Dec. 1922, communicated in Geddes to Curzon, 5 Jan. 1923, PRO/FO371/8627/C692/1/18. A. Kaiser: *Lord D'Abernon und die englische Deutschlandpolitik, 1920–1926* (Frankfurt: Peter Lang, 1989), 92–3.
35. See British Delegation, Reparation Commission to Treasury, 30 Nov. 1923, PRO/FO371/8662/C20802/1/18; *Annual Report on Germany 1923*, communicated in D'Abernon to Chamberlain, 26 Dec. 1924, PRO/FO371/10726/C370/370/18.
36. Dawes, 85–7.
37. The text can be found in *Report of the First Expert Reparation Committee, 8 April 1924*, PRO/FO371/9739/C5870/70/18.
38. *Summary of Negotiations concerning the Application of the Dawes Report*, PRO/30/69/130, MacDonald Papers.
39. Foreign Office record of Chequers talks, April 1924, cited in D. Marquand: *Ramsay MacDonald* (London: Jonathan Cape, 1972), 340.
40. MacDonald to Massingham, 12 Aug. 1924, PRO/30/69/2, MacDonald Papers.
41. MacDonald to D'Abernon, 3 June 1924, PRO/FO371/9747/C9000/70/18.
42. Diary, 3 Feb. 1924, PRO/30/69/1753, MacDonald Papers.
43. *An Ambassador of Peace*, 20 Feb. 1924, III, 55.
44. *An Ambassador of Peace*, III, 31.
45. Ibid., 65.
46. D'Abernon to MacDonald, 15 April 1924, *Documents on British Foreign Policy*, First Series, XXVI, 638.
47. MacDonald to D'Abernon, 19 April 1924, *Documents on British Foreign Policy*, First Series, XXVI, 648.
48. D'Abernon to MacDonald, 15 April 1924, 639.
49. D'Abernon to MacDonald, 22 April 1924, PRO/FO371/9742/C6815/70/18. Finlayson's technical memorandum was forwarded with this dispatch.
50. D'Abernon to MacDonald, 22 April 1924.
51. MacDonald to D'Abernon, 29 May 1924, *Documents on British Foreign Policy*, First Series, XXVI, 712.

52. *Memorandum by Herr von Schubert on the Execution of the Experts' Report*, 2 May 1924, communicated in D'Abernon to MacDonald, 2 May 1924, PRO/FO371/9743/C7382/70/18. Department III dealt with relations with Britain, the United States and Turkey.
53. Leffler, 92–3.
54. D'Abernon to MacDonald, 18 April 1924, PRO/FO371/9741/C6467/70/18. Cf. *Akten zur deutschen Auswärtigen Politik*, Series B Iii, No. 136.
55. D'Abernon to MacDonald, 2 May 1924, PRO/FO371/9743/C7387/70/18.
56. *Memorandum by Herr von Schubert on the Execution of the Experts' Report*. For an account of D'Abernon's meeting with von Schubert, W. Weidenfeld: *Die Englandpolitik Gustav Stresemanns: theoretische und praktische Aspekte der Aussenpolitik* (Mainz, 1972), 254.
57. A. Cassels: 'Repairing the *Entente Cordiale* and the New Diplomacy', *Historical Journal*, 23(3), 1980, 142–6. The second protocol can be found in *Franco-British Memorandum Concerning the Application of the Dawes Scheme, Drawn up at Paris on 9 July 1924*, PRO/FO371/9750/C11043/70/18.
58. Memorandum by von Schubert, 10 July 1924, German Foreign Ministry (GFM) 4492/E099313; von Schubert to D'Abernon, 1 July 1924, communicated in D'Abernon to MacDonald, 1 July 1924, PRO/FO371/9749/C1038/70/18.
59. *An Ambassador of Peace*, 11 July 1924, III, 78–9.
60. Weidenfeld makes no mention of this or of D'Abernon's subsequent meeting with Stresemann on 11 July 1924, Weidenfeld, 260–1.
61. 'Extract from *Die Zeit* of June 7 1924: Dr Stresemann's speech in the Reichstag, June 6 1924', communicated in D'Abernon to MacDonald, 12 June 1924, PRO/FO371/9747/ C9637/70/18.
62. Cited in Berg, 83.
63. 'Extract from *Die Zeit* of June 7 1924: Dr Stresemann's speech in the Reichstag, June 6 1924', communicated in D'Abernon to MacDonald, 12 June 1924, PRO/FO371/9747/ C9637/70/18.
64. D'Abernon to MacDonald, 22 June 1924, BL Add MSS 48926A, D'Abernon Papers; *Government Statement Made before the Reichstag, June 4 1924*, communicated in D'Abernon to MacDonald, 6 June 1924, PRO/FO371/9747/C9229/70/18.
65. D'Abernon to MacDonald, 11 July 1924, *Documents on British Foreign Policy*, First Series, XXVI, 788.
66. Reported in Sthamer to MacDonald, 16 July 1924, PRO/FO371/9751/C11571/70/18.
67. *An Ambassador of Peace*, III, 20 March 1924, 59–61.
68. D'Abernon to MacDonald, 11 July 1924, PRO/FO371/9751/C11500/70/18. D'Abernon had made this point the previous day, see Memorandum by Stresemann, 10 July 1924, GFM 3398/D739938–40.
69. Memorandum by von Schubert, 23 July 1924, GFM, 4492/E0993676–7.
70. Memorandum by Stresemann, 10 July 1924. See Stresemann to von Hoesch, 13 July 1924, in A. Hartung (ed.): *Gustav Stresemann 'Schriften'* (Berlin, 1976), 321–4.
71. *Memorandum by von Maltzan on a Conversation with Lord D'Abernon*, 14 July 1924, GFM 4492/E099235–7; Weidenfeld, 261. On 23 July, he recommended that the German government should send a delegation to London as

assurances that the conference would have a strong diplomatic basis had been received from the Allies.

72. D'Abernon to Chamberlain, 8 Nov. 1924, PRO/FO371/9804/C17265/737/18.

5 The Anglo-German Commercial Agreement, 1924–25

1. Article 268. It stated that: 'For a period of five years from the coming into force of the present Treaty... the Allied and Associated Powers reserve the right to require Germany to accord freedom from customs duty, on importation into German customs territory, to natural products and manufactured articles.' *The Treaty of Peace between the Allied and Associated Powers and Germany* (London: HMSO, 1919), 129–30.
2. J.W. Angell: *The Recovery of Germany* (New York: Yale University Press, 1929).
3. Ibid., 3.
4. See B. Kent: *The Spoils of War: the Politics, Economics and Diplomacy of Reparation, 1918–1932* (Oxford: Oxford University Press, 1991), 150.
5. J.M. Keynes: *Economic Consequences of the Peace*, 32–3, cited in R.G. Hawtrey: 'Germany's Part in European Economic Life', in P.W. Bidwell (ed.): *Germany's Contribution to European Economic Life* (Paris: M. Rivière, 1949), 134.
6. H. James: *The German Slump: Politics and Economics, 1924–36* (Oxford: Oxford University Press, 1986), 162–3.
7. S. Marks: 'Reparations Reconsidered; a Reminder', *Central European History*, 2(1), 1969; 'Reparations Reconsidered; a Rejoinder', *Central European History*, 5(2), 1972; D. Felix: 'Reparations Reconsidered with a Vengeance', *Central European History*, 61(2), 1971.
8. Angell, 2–3.
9. Marks: 'Reparations Reconsidered'.
10. Memorandum respecting a Commercial Treaty with Germany, 7 Nov. 1924, PRO/FO371/9791/C17139/330/18.
11. This Act was repealed in 1925 before the Anglo-German Commercial Agreement was ratified. See *Safeguarding of Industries – Procedures and Enquiries*, Cmd. 2327, HMSO, London 1925. The British delegation insisted that the British government reserved the right to reinstate the Act should the value of the German currency further deteriorate. Note by Mr Fountain respecting Discussions at Berlin on the Question of an Anglo-German Commercial Treaty, 30 Sept. 1924, PRO/FO371/10721/C5791/124/18.
12. C. Stamm: *Lloyd George zwischen Innen-und Aussenpolitik: Die britische Deutschlandpolitik, 1921–1922* (Cologne: Verlag Wissenschaft und Politik, 1977), 84–9.
13. T. Balderston: *The Origins and Course of the German Economic Crisis, 1923–1932* (Berlin, 1993), 91.
14. Memorandum respecting a Commercial Treaty with Germany.
15. Note by Mr Fountain.
16. D'Abernon to Stresemann, 23 Jan. 1924, communicated in D'Abernon to MacDonald, 25 Jan. 1925, PRO/FO371/9729/C1623/25/18.
17. See, for example, 'Treasury Memorandum on the Effect of MICUM Deliveries, &c., on Finance of the Experts' Scheme', 14 July 1924, PRO/FO371/9750/C11276/70/18.

18. Note by Sir Eyre Crowe, 19 May 1924, PRO/FO371/9765/C8143/79/18.
19. Board of Trade to the Foreign Office, 6 June 1924, PRO/T160/200/F.7629/1.
20. D'Abernon to MacDonald, 3 July 1924, PRO/FO371/10721/C5791/124/18. This Article stated:

    Limited liability and other companies and associations already or hereafter to be organised in accordance with the laws in force or in the territories of either contracting party, are authorised, in the territories of the other, to exercise their rights and appear in the courts either as plaintiffs or defendants, subject to the laws of such other party, and they shall enjoy the benefits accorded to this treaty to the subject or citizens of the first party.

    Furthermore, each of the contracting parties undertakes to place no obstacle in the way of such companies and associations which may desire to carry on in its territories, whether through the establishment of branches or otherwise, any description of business which the companies and associations or subjects or citizens of any other foreign country are or may be permitted to carry on.

    In no case shall the treatment accorded by either contracting party or companies and associations organised in accordance with the laws in force in the territories of the other be less favourable in respect of any matter whatever than that accorded to companies and associations of the most favoured foreign country.

    Negotiations leading up to the Signature of the Anglo-German Commercial Treaty of Dec. 2 1924, PRO/FO371/10721/C5791/124/18.
21. Board of Trade to the Foreign Office, 17 July 1924, PRO/FO371/10721/C5791/124/18.
22. Fountain to MacDonald, 17 July 1924, PRO/FO371/10721/C5791/124/18; MacDonald to D'Abernon, 23 July 1924, PRO/FO371/10721/C5791/124/18.
23. Balderston, 91.
24. Memorandum by Thelwall, 2 May 1924, communicated in D'Abernon to MacDonald, 2 May 1924, PRO/FO371/9790/C7383/330/18; 'Report Respecting Proposed Commercial Treaty between England and Germany', communicated in D'Abernon to MacDonald, 8 Sept. 1924, PRO/FO371/9790/C14404/330/18.
25. MacDonald to D'Abernon, 20 Aug. 1924, *Documents on British Foreign Policy*, First Series, XXVI, 846.
26. Minute by Baillie, 19 Nov. 1924, on D'Abernon to MacDonald, 8 Sept. 1924, PRO/FO371/9790/C14404/30/18. Note that there is more than a two month gap between the date of the dispatch and the date of the Foreign Office minute.
27. MacDonald to Addison, 3 Oct. 1924, PRO/FO371/10721/C5791/124/18.
28. Minute by Bennett, 12 Nov. 1924, on D'Abernon to Chamberlain, 11 Nov. 1924, PRO/FO371/9791/C17092/330/18.
29. Minute by Lampson, 17 Nov. 1924, on D'Abernon to Chamberlain, 11 Nov. 1924, PRO/FO371/9791/C17092/330/18.
30. Lampson to D'Abernon, 27 Jan. 1925, PRO/FO371/10720/C777/124/18. He was referring to Chamberlain's attitude towards the German government. Chamberlain to D'Abernon, 9 Jan. 1925, AC 52/250, University of Birmingham, Austen Chamberlain Papers.

31. Ibid.
32. *An Ambassador of Peace*, 15 Jan. 1925, III, 122.
33. *Vorwärts*, 21 Dec. 1924, communicated in D'Abernon to Chamberlain, 3 Jan. 1925, PRO/FO371/10720/C264/124/18.
34. D'Abernon to MacDonald, 25 Sept. 1924, PRO/FO371/10721/C5791/124/18; Memorandum by von Schubert, 24 Oct. 1924, German Foreign Ministry (GFM) 4481/E091777–9.
35. Ibid.
36. Viscount D'Abernon: 'German Currency: its Collapse and Recovery 1920–1926', *Journal of the Royal Statistical Society*, 80(1), 1927.
37. D'Abernon to MacDonald, 25 Sept. 1924.
38. Addison to MacDonald, 6 Oct. 1924, PRO/T160/200/F.7629/1.
39. Notes on Proposed Commercial Treaty, 27 Oct. 1924, communicated in D'Abernon to MacDonald, 29 Oct. 1924, PRO/FO371/10721/C5791/124/18.
40. D'Abernon to MacDonald, 10 Sept. 1924, PRO/FO371/9790/C14349/330/18.
41. These meetings were also attended by Fountain of the Board of Trade and Addison, Kavanagh, Knox and Thelwall of the embassy staff. The Germans were represented by Hemmen and de Haas of the *Auswärtiges Amt*, and von Stockhammern, a German expert.
42. Minutes of Meetings held at His Majesty's Embassy, Berlin, for the Preliminary Discussion with German Experts of a Future Treaty of Commerce: First Meeting, 22 Sept. 1924, communicated in D'Abernon to MacDonald, 27 Sept. 1924, PRO/FO371/9790/C15269/330/18.
43. D'Abernon to MacDonald, 24 Oct. 1924, PRO/FO371/9790/C16547/330/18.
44. Notes on Proposed Commercial Treaty, 27 Oct. 1924.
45. W. Weidenfeld: *Die Englandspolitik Gustav Stresemanns: theoretische und praktische Aspekte der Aussenpolitik* (Mainz, 1972), 236–8.
46. Minutes of Meetings held at His Majesty's Embassy, Berlin.
47. Proceedings of a Deputation received by the Chancellor of the Exchequer in the Treasury on Thursday, 27 Nov. 1924, at 5.30pm, PRO/FO371/9792/C18128/330/18. Sthamer had also sent a private letter to D'Abernon on this date outlining the German position, Sthamer to D'Abernon, 27 Nov. 1924, GFM 4481/E091979–80; Sthamer to *Auswärtiges Amt*, 28 Nov. 1924, GFM 4481/E091961.
48. Memorandum by von Schubert, 10 Nov. 1924, GFM 4481/E091497–9; D'Abernon to Chamberlain, 11 Nov. 1924, PRO/FO371/9791/C17092/330/18.
49. Proceedings of a Deputation.
50. Von Schubert to D'Abernon, 14 Jan. 1925, GFM 4481/E092305; D'Abernon to von Schubert, 14 Jan. 1925, communicated in D'Abernon to Lampson, 14 Jan. 1925, PRO/FO371/10720/C777/124/18.
51. Memorandum by von Schubert, 29 Jan. 1925, GFM 4481/E092302–3.
52. Von Schubert to Ritter, de Haas and Hemmen, 3 April 1924, GFM 4481/E092187–9.
53. *An Ambassador of Peace*, 28 Dec. 1924, III, 119–20.
54. Note by Mr Fountain.
55. Notes on Proposed Commercial Treaty.
56. Communications between the Board of Trade and the Foreign Office about the commercial agreement made respectful reference to D'Abernon's opinion. See the note of 6 June 1924, PRO/T160/200/F.7629/1.

57. A. Kaiser: *Lord D'Abernon und die englische Deutschlandpolitik, 1920–1926* (Frankfurt: Peter Lang, 1989), 159–60.
58. D'Abernon to Grahame, 24 Dec. 1924, BL Add MSS 48927A, D'Abernon Papers.
59. D'Abernon to MacDonald, 8 Sept. 1924, PRO/FO371/9790/C14404/330/18.
60. Report respecting proposed Commercial Treaty between England and Germany, communicated in D'Abernon to MacDonald, 8 Sept. 1924, PRO/FO371/9790/C14404/330/18.
61. This attitude was dictated very much by the circumstances of the time as Germany already had a very long history of commercial relations with Britain.
62. 'Lord D'Abernon's Address to German Delegates', 22 Sept. 1924, communicated in D'Abernon to MacDonald, 25 Sept. 1924, PRO/FO371/9790/C15132/330/18.
63. D'Abernon to the King, 14 Nov. 1924, BL Add MSS 48922A, D'Abernon Papers.
64. D'Abernon to MacDonald, 2 May 1924, PRO/FO371/9790/C7383/330/18.
65. D'Abernon to MacDonald, 8 Sept. 1924, PRO/FO371/9790/C14404/330/18.
66. D'Abernon to Chamberlain, 15 Nov. 1924, PRO/FO371/9804/C17551/737/18.
67. Lord D'Abernon's Address to German Delegates.
68. D'Abernon to MacDonald, 24 Oct. 1924, PRO/FO371/9790/C16547/330/18.
69. D'Abernon to MacDonald, 14 June 1924, PRO/FO371/9790/C9763/280/18.
70. D'Abernon to Lady D'Abernon, 3 April 1925, BL Add MSS 48936, D'Abernon Papers.
71. D'Abernon to Chamberlain, 8 Nov. 1924, PRO/FO371/9791/C17157/330/18.
72. D'Abernon to Chamberlain, 18 Nov. 1924, PRO/FO371/9804/C17461/737/18.
73. Speech by Stresemann at a convention of the *Volkspartei* at Dortmund, 13 Nov. 1924, communicated in D'Abernon to Chamberlain, 15 Nov. 1924, PRO/FO371/9804/C17430/737/18.
74. D'Abernon's description of the relative standing of Germany and Britain in commercial affairs after the First World War. D'Abernon to MacDonald, 10 Sept. 1924, PRO/FO371/9790/C14349/330/18.

6 Security Diplomacy, 1924–26

1. A. Wolfers: *Britain and France between Two Wars. Conflicting Strategies of Peace since Versailles* (New York: Harcourt, 1940), 207.
2. D'Abernon outlined its history in D'Abernon to MacDonald, 5 Feb. 1924, cited F.G. Stambrook: '"Das Kind" – Lord D'Abernon and the Origins of the Locarno Pact', *Central European History*, 1, 1968, 241. This proposal went beyond Articles 42–44 of the Treaty of Versailles, which stated that the Rhineland should be demilitarised for a fifteen year period.
3. G. Johnson: 'Lord D'Abernon, Austen Chamberlain and the Origin of the Treaty of Locarno', *Electronic Journal of International History*, 1(1), 2000.
4. Stambrook, 242.
5. G. Johnson: '"Das Kind" Revisited: Lord D'Abernon and German Security Policy, 1922–1925', *Contemporary European History*, 9(2), 2000.

6. G. Grün: 'Locarno: Idea and Reality', *International Affairs*, 31(1), 1955.
7. J. Jacobson: *Locarno Diplomacy. Germany and the West 1925–1929* (Princeton: Princeton University Press, 1972).
8. There are numerous examples, although the most noteworthy are Angela Kaiser, 'Lord D'Abernon und die Entstehungsgeschichte der Locarno-Verträge', *Vierteljahrshefte für Zeitgeschichte*, 34(2), 1986; *Lord D'Abernon und die englische Deutschlandpolitik, 1920–1926* (Frankfurt: Peter Lang, 1989).
9. A. Chamberlain: *Down the Years* (London: Cassell, 1935), 157.
10. This can most clearly be seen in a statement that Curzon read to both Houses of Parliament on 12 July 1923, OIOL, Eur F/112/241, Curzon Papers.
11. D'Abernon to MacDonald, 5 Feb.1924, cited in Stambrook, 241.
12. R. Marquand: *Ramsay MacDonald* (London: Jonathan Cape, 1977), 354–6.
13. The full title of the proposed agreement was the 'Protocol for the Pacific Settlement of International Disputes'. See Institute of International Affairs: *Survey of International Affairs* (Oxford: Oxford University Press, 1924), 1–64.
14. Although the decision whether or not to take military action was to be left to the discretion of individual states.
15. Chamberlain's comments on MacDonald's foreign policy can be found in Chamberlain to Mrs Carnegie, 11 Sept. 1924, cited in D. Johnson: 'Austen Chamberlain and the Locarno Agreements', *University of Birmingham Historical Journal*, 8, 1961, 65.
16. Memorandum by Hankey, 23 Jan. 1925, in Hankey to Lampson, 26 Jan. 1925, PRO/FO371/10727/C1218/459/18.
17. Cecil to Chamberlain, 17 Nov. 1924, cited in D. Johnson, 72.
18. Von Schubert to Sthamer, 29 March 1925, K2090/K566977–79, cited in E.C.M. Breuning: *Germany's Foreign Policy between East and West*, 'East versus West: the Opening Moves', p. 62, unpublished DPhil thesis, University of Oxford, 1965. The pages of this thesis are not numbered consecutively throughout. Therefore the chapter title as well as the page number will be given in all subsequent references.
19. *An Ambassador of Peace*, III, 28.
20. Memorandum by von Schubert, 5 Feb. 1924, German Foreign Ministry (GFM) 2368/E490734–37.
21. Memorandum on Security and the League of Nations, by von Schubert, 11 Feb. 1924, GFM 2368/E490752–57.
22. Sthamer to von Schubert, 5 Dec. 1924, GFM 9518/H282551–52, cited in Stambrook, 243.
23. Memorandum by von Schubert, 29 Dec. 1924, GFM 4509/E124822–23.
24. Memorandum by von Schubert, 14 Jan. 1925, GFM 4509/E124805–9.
25. Memorandum by von Schubert, 5 Feb. 1924, GFM 2368/490734–37.
26. H.L. Bretton: *Stresemann and the Revision of Versailles; a Fight for Reason* (Stanford: Stanford University Press, 1953), 86–7.
27. Jacobson, 5–6, 41.
28. Memorandum by Stresemann, 9 Feb. 1925, cited in E. Sutton (ed.): *Gustav Stresemann, his Diaries, Letters and Papers*, II (New York: Macmillan, 1935–1940), 59–60.
29. Statement issued by Stresemann to the German Press, 7 March 1925, cited in Sutton, 63–4.

30. Speech by Stresemann to the Foreign Affairs Commission of the Reichsrat on 3 Jan. 1925, GFM 4504/E121873–90.
31. Statement issued by Stresemann to the German Press, 7 March 1925, cited in Sutton, 66–7.
32. Statement by Stresemann in the Reichstag, 18 May 1925, cited in Sutton, 82–3.
33. Note by Stresemann on a conversation with D'Abernon, 3 Aug. 1925, cited in Sutton, 151–3.
34. D. Johnson, 1961, 79; Stambrook, 238–9, 245.
35. D'Abernon to Curzon, 6 Dec. 1923, British Library Additional Manuscripts (BL Add MSS) 48927, D'Abernon Papers.
36. 'Memorandum respecting the Balance of Power in Europe and its effect on the Problem of Security', communicated in D'Abernon to Chamberlain, 7 Jan. 1925, PRO/FO371/10726/C459/459/18.
37. *An Ambassador of Peace*, III, 2 May 1925 (London: Hodder and Stoughton, 1931), 158–60.
38. D'Abernon's suspicion proved to be well founded. The Treaty of Berlin was signed between the Soviet Union and Germany in April 1926.
39. *An Ambassador of Peace*, III, 7 Feb. 1925, 238–9.
40. F.S. Northedge: *The Troubled Giant. Britain among the Great Powers, 1916–1939* (London: Bell, 1966), 255.
41. D'Abernon to Chamberlain, 1 March 1925, BL Add MSS 48928, D'Abernon Papers.
42. *An Ambassador of Peace*, III, 21. When this volume of diary was published, Chamberlain acknowledged that D'Abernon's assessment of British policy at this time had been correct. He wrote: 'I hoped eventually (but I must admit only eventually) to turn [it] into a reciprocal agreement with Germany.' Chamberlain to D'Abernon, 11 Sept. 1930, AC 39/2/35, Chamberlain Papers.
43. *An Ambassador of Peace*, III, 23.
44. Kaiser, *Lord D'Abernon und die englische Deutschlandpolitik, 1920–1926*, 371, 629.
45. 'Record of Conversation between the German Ambassador and Mr Lampson, 30 June 1925', communicated in Chamberlain to D'Abernon, 30 June 1925, PRO/FO371/10735/C8805/459/18.
46. Chamberlain to D'Abernon, 2 April 1925, AC 52/266, Chamberlain Papers.
47. E. Stern-Rubarth: *Three Men Tried… Austen Chamberlain, Stresemann, Briand, and their Fight for a New Europe* (London: Duckworth, 1939), 36.
48. *An Ambassador of Peace*, III, 10–20; Viscount D'Abernon: *Foreign Relations* (Oxford: Oxford University Press, 1930).
49. Lord D'Abernon: 'Stresemann', *Foreign Affairs*, 1930, 209–10.
50. Kaiser, 'Lord D'Abernon und die Entstehungsgeschichte der Locarno-Verträge', 95.
51. Stresemann to Brockdorff-Rantzau, 19 March 1925, GFM 4562/E155068–90.
52. Stresemann to von Hoesch, 15 Jan. 1925, GFM 3123/642046/51.
53. Extract from an article by Stresemann in the *Hamburger Fremdenblatt*, 14 Sept. 1925, cited in Sutton, 158–9.
54. M.-O. Maxelon: *Stresemann und Frankreich: deutsche Politik der Ost-West-Balance* (Düsseldorf, 1972), 283.

55. Viscount D'Abernon, 'Stresemann', 211.
56. Bretton, 90.
57. G. Post: *The Civil-Military Fabric of Weimar Foreign Policy* (Princeton: Princeton University Press, 1973), 47–50.
58. Chamberlain to D'Abernon, 12 Jan. 1925, AC 52/253, Chamberlain Papers.
59. Chamberlain to Crewe, 16 Feb. 1925, AC 52/189, Chamberlain Papers.
60. D'Abernon to Chamberlain, 16 Jan. 1925, AC 52/254, Chamberlain Papers.
61. Chamberlain to D'Abernon, 30 Jan. 1925, PRO/FO371/10727/C1454/459/18.
62. *An Ambassador of Peace*, III, 3 Feb. 1925, 136–7.
63. Stambrook; Kaiser: 'Lord D'Abernon und die Entstehungsgeschichte der Locarno-Verträge'.
64. *An Ambassador of Peace*, III, 20 July 1925, 177–8. Kaiser sees this as evidence of D'Abernon's pro-German sympathies, but overlooks his subsequent comments. Kaiser: *Lord D'Abernon und die englische Deutschlandpolitik, 1920–1926*, 322, 325, 331. According to Stambrook, by the end of 1924, D'Abernon had been persuaded to abandon the idea because the French would fear that the 'curtain' could be used as a screen to hide a new German war machine for use against France (p. 125). D'Abernon's later diary entries and dispatches suggest that he did not believe this to be so.
65. *An Ambassador of Peace*, III, 24 July 1925, 178–9.
66. *An Ambassador of Peace*, III, 20 July 1925, 177.
67. Chamberlain to Crewe, 16 Feb. 1925, PRO/FO371/10727/C2450/459/18.
68. E. Goldstein: 'The Evolution of British Diplomatic Strategy for the Locarno Pact, 1924–1925', in M. Dockrill and B. McKercher (eds): *Diplomacy and World Power. Studies in British Foreign Policy, 1890–1950* (Cambridge: Cambridge University Press, 1996), 130–1.
69. Cf. A. Sharp: 'James Headlam-Morley: Creating International History', *Diplomacy and Statecraft*, 9(1), 1998.
70. Memorandum by von Schubert, 14 Jan. 1925, German Foreign Ministry (GFM) 4509/E124805–9.
71. *An Ambassador of Peace*, III, 3 Feb. 1925, 135–6.
72. Memorandum by von Schubert, 20 Jan. 1925, GFM 4509/E122770–9.
73. Stambrook tentatively suggests that it is 'difficult to escape the conclusion D'Abernon was being deliberately mendacious' in his dealings with von Schubert (256).
74. Von Schubert to Dufour, 25 Jan. 1925, GFM 4567/E165308–11; von Schubert to Sthamer, 27 Jan. 1925, GFM 3123/E642125–26.
75. Memorandum by von Schubert, 20 Jan. 1925, GFM 4509/E122770–9. D'Abernon communicated the substance of the conversation to Chamberlain on the same day, PRO/FO371/10726/C946/459/18.
76. Memorandum by von Schubert, 20 Jan. 1925, GFM 4509/E124770–72.
77. Von Schubert to Sthamer, 19 Jan. 1925, GFM K2096/K56948–54, cited in Stambrook, 258.
78. Memorandum by von Schubert, 13 Jan. 1925, GFM 4504/E122307–9; Von Schubert to von Hoesch, 21 Jan. 1925, GFM 4509/E124765–9.
79. Stambrook, 259. The text is communicated in D'Abernon to Chamberlain, 20 Jan. 1925, *Documents on British Foreign Policy*, First Series, XXVII, 282–4.
80. D'Abernon to Chamberlain, 21 Feb. 1925, AC 52/262, Chamberlain Papers.
81. D'Abernon to Chamberlain, 3 May 1925, AC 52/267, Chamberlain Papers.

82. Chamberlain to D'Abernon, 2 April 1925, cited in C. Petrie: *The Life and Times of the Right Hon. Sir Austen Chamberlain*, II (London: Lovat Dickson, 1940), 271–4.
83. *An Ambassador of Peace*, III, 2 April 1925, 157–8.
84. Von Schubert to D'Abernon, 14 Jan. 1925, communicated in D'Abernon to Lampson, 14 Jan. 1925, PRO/FO371/10720/C777/124/18.
85. Memorandum by von Schubert, 5 April 1925, GFM 3123/E642993–3001.
86. Memorandum by von Schubert, 1 May 1925, GFM 4509/E126115–18.
87. Memorandum by von Schubert, 11 May 1925, GFM 4509/E126187–94.
88. A formal statement on the latter was made on 6 June 1925.
89. D'Abernon to Chamberlain, 26 May 1925, PRO/FO371/10732/C7142/459/18.
90. D'Abernon to Chamberlain, 28 June 1925, PRO/FO371/10735/C8770/459/18.
91. Memorandum by von Schubert, 28 July 1925, GFM 4509/E127442–47.
92. Memorandum by von Schubert, 3 July 1925, GFM 4509/E126988–7006.
93. *An Ambassador of Peace*, III, 3 July 1925, 153.
94. Von Schubert to von Hoesch, 11 July 1925, GFM 4509/E127112–19.
95. D'Abernon to Chamberlain, 24 July 1925, PRO/FO371/10737/C9857/459/18. In a memorandum written four days later the strength of von Schubert's views is evident. He complained that the Allies intended to 'fling down a draft treaty before [the German government] and thus present [Germany] with an "either-or"'. Memorandum by von Schubert, 28 July 1925, GFM 4509/E127442–47.
96. Von Schubert to Brockdorff-Rantzau, 16 Aug. 1925, K308/K106492–95, cited in Breuning, *'East versus West: Failure and Success'*, 163–4.
97. Memorandum by von Schubert, 24 July 1925, GFM 4509/E127412–14.
98. See also Memorandum by von Schubert, 28 Aug. 1925, GFM 4509/E127855–58.
99. Chamberlain to D'Abernon, 10 July 1925, cited in Petrie, 280.
100. Sthamer to von Schubert, 28 July 1925, GFM 3123/644118, cited in Breuning, *'East Versus West: Failure and Success'*,165.
101. Memorandum by von Schubert, 29 July 1925, GFM 4509/E127450–52.
102. Memorandum by von Schubert, 31 July 1925, GFM 4509/E127458–62.
103. Memorandum by von Schubert, 1 July 1925, GFM 4509/E127458–62. Von Schubert's emphasis.
104. D'Abernon to Chamberlain, 3 May 1925, *Documents on British Foreign Policy*, First Series, XXVII, 476–7.
105. D'Abernon to Chamberlain, 29 June 1925, PRO/FO371/10735/C8770/459/18. The full text of D'Abernon's meeting with Stresemann can be found in GFM 3123/D643748–54.
106. Note by Stresemann on a conversation with D'Abernon, 3 Aug. 1925, cited in Sutton, 151–3.
107. Chamberlain to D'Abernon, 30 June 1925, PRO/FO371/10735/C8770/459/18.
108. Ibid.
109. Chamberlain to D'Abernon, 17 July 1925, *Documents on British Foreign Policy*, First Series, XXVII, 683–5.

110. Chamberlain to D'Abernon, 28 July 1925, *Documents on British Foreign Policy*, First Series, XXVII, 701–4.
111. Ibid.
112. Chamberlain to D'Abernon, 30 July 1925, *Documents on British Foreign Policy*, First Series, XXVII, 707–8.
113. *An Ambassador of Peace*, III, 29 July 1925, 179–80.
114. Chamberlain to D'Abernon, 30 July 1925, *Documents on British Foreign Policy*, First Series, XXVII, 707–8.
115. Chamberlain to D'Abernon, 11 Aug. 1925, cited in Petrie, 281–3.
116. Chamberlain to D'Abernon, 11 Aug. 1925, *Documents on British Foreign Policy*, First Series, XXVII, 723–5.
117. Chamberlain to D'Abernon, 28 Aug. 1925, *Documents on British Foreign Policy*, First Series, XXVII, 746–7.
118. Chamberlain to D'Abernon, 22 Sept. 1925, cited in *Documents on British Foreign Policy*, First Series, XXVII, 784.
119. Chamberlain to D'Abernon, 24 Sept. 1925, PRO/FO371/10740/C12110/459/18.
120. Chamberlain to D'Abernon, 30 Sept. 1925, AC 52/297, Chamberlain Papers.
121. *An Ambassador of Peace*, III, 25 Sept. 1925, 189.
122. *An Ambassador of Peace*, III, 179–80.
123. Memorandum by von Schubert, 10 Aug. 1925, GFM 4562/E155733.
124. Von Schubert to von Hoesch, 20 Jan. 1926, GFM 4562/E156469–78.
125. Sthamer to von Schubert, 23 Jan. 1926, GFM 4562/E156500–02.
126. D'Abernon to Chamberlain, 25 Feb. 1925, PRO/FO371/10717/C2881/109/18.
127. *Akten zur deutschen Auswärtigen Politik*, Serie B IIi, No. 99.
128. Memorandum by von Schubert, 6 April 1926, GFM 2860/557026–36, cited in Breuning, 'Scylla and Charybdis', 166–7.
129. Memorandum by von Schubert, 6 April 1926, GFM 2860/557026–36, cited in Breuning, 'Scylla and Charybdis', 166–7.
130. Memorandum by von Schubert, 9 April 1926, GFM 2860/557077–84, cited in Breuning, 'Scylla and Charybdis', 183–5. Compare *An Ambassador of Peace*, III, 23 April 1926, 249–50, 252.
131. Memorandum by von Schubert, 9 April 1926, GFM 4562/E15692-22.
132. Breuning, 'East versus West: the Opening Moves', 10.
133. An account of the conclusion of the Treaty of Berlin can be found in Morgan, 268–71.
134. D'Abernon to Chamberlain, 8 Nov. 1924, PRO/FO371/9804/C17265/737/18.
135. *An Ambassador of Peace*, III, 31 Jan. 1924, 42.
136. *An Ambassador of Peace*, III, 5 March 1925, 145–6.
137. *An Ambassador of Peace*, III, 15 Nov. 1925, 198.
138. *An Ambassador of Peace*, III, 22 March 1926, 239.
139. *An Ambassador of Peace*, III, 5 April 1926, 247.
140. D'Abernon to Chamberlain, 25 April 1926, *Documents on British Foreign Policy*, Series Ia, I, 667.
141. *An Ambassador of Peace*, III, 30 March 1926, 244.

142. D'Abernon to Chamberlain, 9 April 1926, *Documents on British Foreign Policy*, Series Ia, I, 587–8.
143. *An Ambassador of Peace*, III, 29 April 1926, 252–3.
144. D'Abernon to Chamberlain, 19 Oct. 1925, AC 52/300, Chamberlain Papers.
145. Chamberlain, *Down the Years*, 152–3, 166.
146. D. Carlton: 'Great Britain and the League Council Crisis', *Historical Journal*, 11(2), 1968.

7 The Admission of Germany to the League of Nations, 1922–26

1. R. Henig: *The British Government and the League of Nations, 1919–1926*, unpublished PhD thesis, University of Lancaster, 1978. See also R. Henig (ed.): *The League of Nations* (London: Oliver and Boyd, 1973), 1–18.
2. F.S. Northedge: *The League of Nations. Its Life and Times, 1920–1946*, Third Edition (Leicester: Leicester University Press, 1988).
3. J. Spenz: *Die diplomatische Vorgeschichte des Beitritts Deutschlands zum Völkerbund, 1924–1926; ein Beitrag zur Aussenpolitik der Weimarer Republik* (Göttingen, 1966); C.M. Kimmich: *Germany and the League of Nations* (Chicago: Chicago University Press, 1976).
4. Tufton to Lampson, 28 April 1922, PRO/FO371/7568/C6347/6347/18.
5. Minute by Fisher to Chamberlain, 9 May 1922, PRO/FO371/7568/C6916/6347/18.
6. Memorandum by Sir Eric Drummond: 'German Admission to the League at the Next Assembly', 12 June 1922, PRO/FO371/7568/C8574/6347/18.
7. 'Maurice Hankey's Notes on a Conversation Held at 10, Downing Street on Wednesday, June 21 1922', PRO/FO371/7568/C9024/6347/18.
8. Ibid.
9. *An Ambassador of Peace*, II, 13 July 1922 (London: Hodder and Stoughton, 1930) 58; 14 July 1922, 62.
10. Wirth to D'Abernon, 25 July 1922, communicated in D'Abernon to Hankey, 26 July 1922, HLRO, F/54/2/33, Lloyd George Papers.
11. The main terms of this letter are also cited in Kimmich, 41–2.
12. Balfour to D'Abernon, 24 July 1922, *Documents on British Foreign Policy*, First Series, XX, 510–11.
13. Hankey to Lloyd George, 1 Aug. 1922, HLRO, F/54/2/33, Lloyd George Papers.
14. 'Memorandum respecting British Policy and the Admission of Germany to the League of Nations', 1 Aug. 1922, PRO/FO371/9820/C2072/2072/18.
15. Kimmich, 44–8.
16. 'Memorandum respecting the Admission of Germany to the League of Nations', 6 Feb. 1924, PRO/FO371/9820/C2072/2072/18.
17. Kimmich, 52.
18. D'Abernon to MacDonald, 12 June 1924, BL Add MSS 48926A, D'Abernon Papers.
19. Chamberlain to Salisbury, 2 Jan. 1925, cited in D. Johnson: 'Austen Chamberlain and the Locarno Agreements', *University of Birmingham Historical Journal*, 8, 1961.

20. 'Memorandum by Mr Nicolson on British Policy considered in relation to the European Situation; prepared in pursuance of directions from the Secretary of State', 20 Feb. 1925, PRO/FO371/10727/C2201/459/18.
21. Chamberlain to Crowe, 7 March 1925, PRO/FO371/10728/C3368/459/18.
22. Chamberlain to D'Abernon, 18 March 1925, PRO/FO371/10729/C4171/459/18.
23. London (Geneva) to Crowe, 15 March 1925, PRO/FO371/10728/C3725/459/18.
24. Chamberlain to D'Abernon, 2 April 1925, PRO/FO800/127.
25. *An Ambassador of Peace*, III, 2 April 1925 (London: Hodder and Stoughton, 1931), 17.
26. Chamberlain to D'Abernon, 1 Feb. 1926, PRO/FO371/11297/C1302/446/18.
27. Chamberlain to D'Abernon, 2 Feb. 1926, PRO/FO800/259.
28. J. Barros: *Office without Power* (Oxford: Oxford University Press, 1979), 149–50.
29. The plebiscite took place under the terms of the Treaty of Versailles.
30. D'Abernon to Curzon, 7 May 1922, PRO/FO371/7568/C6932/6347/18.
31. Speech by Stresemann in the Reichstag, 18 March 1926, cited in E. Sutton (ed.): *Gustav Stresemann, His Diaries, Letters and Papers*, II (New York: Macmillan, 1935), 522.
32. 'The New Year' by Dr Stresemann, published in *Die Zeit*, 1 Jan. 1925, communicated in D'Abernon to Chamberlain, 3 Jan. 1925, PRO/FO371/10712/C262/35/18.
33. C.M. Kimmich: *The Free City of Danzig and German Foreign Policy, 1919–1934* (New Haven, CT: Yale University Press, 1968), 73–4.
34. Memoranda by von Schubert, 19 Feb. 1925, 10 March 1925, 4509/E124954, E125472–83, cited in Kimmich, *Germany and the League of Nations*, 64–5.
35. Stresemann to the ex-Crown Prince, 7 Sept. 1925, cited in Sutton, 504.
36. *An Ambassador of Peace*, III, 15 March 1925, 149.
37. See D'Abernon's account of Hindenburg's activities, *An Ambassador of Peace*, III, 11 June 1925, 167–9.
38. Memorandum by Stresemann, 13 June 1925, 2860/555257–67, cited in E.C.M. Breuning: *Germany's Foreign Policy between East and West*, unpublished DPhil thesis, University of Oxford, 1965, 'East Versus West: the Precarious Balance', 106–8.
39. Chamberlain to Tyrrell, 8 Oct. 1925, PRO/FO840/1/5.
40. This is the argument put forward in Henig, unpublished thesis.
41. The text can be found in R. Henig (ed.): *League of Nations* (London, 1973), 184–5.
42. Breuning, 'East Versus West: the Opening Moves', 57–8.
43. Ibid.
44. Cited in 'Memorandum on Soviet Influence on Germany in connection with the question of Germany's entry into the League and of a Western Security Pact', 6 April 1925, PRO/ FO371/10730/C4844/459/18.
45. Memorandum by von Schubert communicated in von Schubert to Brockdorff-Rantzau, 26 Feb. 1925, 4562/E154993–5003, cited in Breuning, 'East versus West: the Opening Moves', 44–6.
46. Cited in 'Memorandum on Soviet Influence on Germany...'
47. Drummond to D'Abernon, 5 March 1925, BL Add MSS 51110, Cecil Papers.

48. Statement by Stresemann to the German Press, 7 March 1925, cited in Sutton, 69–70.
49. *An Ambassador of Peace*, III, 10 March 1925, 147. See also Barros, 167–9. Barros states that D'Abernon's warning was issued to Stresemann rather than to Luther.
50. Sutton, 72–3. It stated that no power entering the League could be exempt from all or part of Article 16 of the Covenant. It rejected the idea that Germany's disarmed state gave grounds from exemption from the military aspect of this Article. If Germany was admitted to the League, she would be expected to contribute to any military operations that League members became involved with but that the extent of that involvement would take full account of Germany's present military position. The extent of involvement in any economic sanctions imposed by the League would again be determined by the relative strength of the individual powers. The note concluded that the adoption of any other stance by Germany or any other power would be incompatible with League membership.
51. Note by Stresemann, 16 March 1925, cited in Sutton, 73–4.
52. Sthamer to von Schubert, 11 April 1925, German Foreign Ministry (GFM) 4562/E155195–202.
53. Note by Stresemann, 18 June 1925, cited in Sutton, 89–90.
54. Extract from Stresemann's diary, 13 Oct. 1925, cited in Sutton, 182.
55. Von Schubert to von Hoesch, 20 Jan. 1926, GFM 4562/E156469–78.
56. Memorandum by von Schubert, 31 March 1926, GFM 4562/E156751–9; D'Abernon to Chamberlain, 1 April 1926, *Documents on British Foreign Policy*, Series Ia, I, 566–8.
57. Memorandum to the Cabinet by Chamberlain, 9 March 1925, PRO/FO371/10748/C3538/471/18.
58. The British perspective on Article 16 is discussed in Henig, unpublished PhD thesis, 182–204.
59. Memorandum to the Cabinet by Chamberlain, 9 March 1925, PRO/FO371/10748/C3538/471/18.
60. Chamberlain to D'Abernon, 30 Jan. 1925, PRO/FO371/10727/C1454/459/18.
61. D'Abernon to Chamberlain, 25 Feb. 1925, PRO/FO371/10717/C2881/109/18.
62. London (Geneva) to Crowe, 9 March 1925, PRO/FO371/10728/C3375/459/18.
63. Chamberlain to Tyrrell, 8 Oct. 1925, PRO/FO840/1/5.
64. 'Memorandum by Sir A. Chamberlain respecting Poland and the Council of the League', 1 Feb. 1926, *Documents on British Foreign Policy*, Series Ia, I, 383–4.
65. Henig, unpublished PhD thesis, 122.
66. Meeting between Spicer and Selby, 4 Feb. 1926, PRO/FO800/259.
67. Cecil to Chamberlain, ? Feb. 1926, University of Birmingham Library, Austen Chamberlain Papers, cited in D. Carlton: 'Great Britain and the League Council Crisis', *Historical Journal*, 11(2), 1968, 354–64.
68. 'Memorandum by Viscount Cecil on the composition of the Council of the League of Nations', 8 Feb. 1926, PRO/FO800/259.
69. Chamberlain to D'Abernon, 7 Feb. 1926, PRO/FO371/11263/C2017/71/18.

70. See also Chamberlain to Max Muller, 8 Feb. 1926, *Documents on British Foreign Policy*, Series Ia, I, 405–6.
71. D'Abernon to Chamberlain, 15 Feb. 1926, PRO/FO371/11263/C1998/71/18.
72. D'Abernon to Chamberlain, 17 Feb. 1926, PRO/FO371/11263/C2087/71/18.
73. Chamberlain to D'Abernon, 18 Feb. 1926, PRO/FO371/11263/C2087/71/18.
74. *The Times*, 18 Feb. 1926, 20.
75. Chamberlain to D'Abernon, 19 Feb. 1926, *Documents on British Foreign Policy*, Series Ia, I, 454.
76. Ibid.
77. *An Ambassador of Peace*, 22 Feb. 1926, III, 225–7.
78. Ibid.
79. Chamberlain to D'Abernon, 19 Feb. 1926, BL Add MSS 48929, D'Abernon Papers.
80. *An Ambassador of Peace*, II, 6 March 1926, 229.
81. Minutes of a Cabinet Meeting, 3 March 1926, CAB 23/52.
82. Tyrrell to Chamberlain, 11 March 1926, PRO/FO800/259.
83. *An Ambassador of Peace*, III, 6 March 1926, 228–9; 12 March 1926, 233–4; 19 March 1926, 236.
84. Chamberlain to D'Abernon, 29 March 1926, Austen Chamberlain Papers, cited in Carlton, 60.
85. *An Ambassador of Peace*, III, 16 March 1926, 234–5.
86. Cecil to Chamberlain, 16 March 1926, BL Add Mss 51078, Cecil Papers.
87. *An Ambassador of Peace*, III, 23 April 1926, 249.
88. Tyrrell to D'Abernon, 1 April 1926, *Documents on British Foreign Policy*, Series Ia, I, 570.
89. *An Ambassador of Peace*, III, 13 Aug. 1926, 256.
90. Viscount Cecil: *All the Way* (London: Jonathan Cape, 1949), 178.
91. D'Abernon to the King, 17 Aug. 1926, BL Add MSS 48922A, D'Abernon Papers.
92. *An Ambassador of Peace*, III, 9 Sept. 1926, 260.
93. G. Stresemann: *Vermächtnis*, II, 558, cited in Breuning, 'Between Moscow and Geneva', 83.
94. Ibid., 562.
95. See for example, D'Abernon to Chamberlain, 15 Feb. 1926, PRO/FO371/11263/C1998/71/18; Chamberlain to D'Abernon, 18 Feb. 1926, PRO/FO371/11263/C2087/71/18.
96. D'Abernon to Chamberlain, 17 Feb. 1926, PRO/FO371/11263/C2087/71/18.
97. D'Abernon to Chamberlain, 18 Feb. 1926, PRO/FO371/11263/C2116/71/18.
98. D'Abernon to Chamberlain, 19 Feb. 1926, PRO/FO371/11263/C2147/71/18.
99. Stresemann to Brockdorff-Rantzau, 25 Feb. 1926, 2860/556815–6, cited in Breuning, 'Between Moscow and Geneva', 80–1.
100. *An Ambassador of Peace*, III, 12 March 1926, 234.
101. *An Ambassador of Peace*, III, 19 March 1926, 236.

102. *An Ambassador of Peace*, III, 22 March 1926, 240. Sthamer had sent an account of the attitude of the British government to Berlin, *Akten zur deutschen Auswärtigen Politik*, Serie B Ii, No. 193.
103. Ibid., 241.
104. D'Abernon to Chamberlain, 22 March 1926, PRO/FO371/11268/C3755/71/18.
105. D'Abernon to Chamberlain, 30 March 1926, PRO/FO371/11279/C4185/234/18.
106. Extract from *Deutsche Allgemeine Zeitung*, 19 April 1926, commenting on a speech made by Stresemann in Stuttgart on 18 April 1926, communicated in D'Abernon to Chamberlain, 23 April 1926, *Documents on British Foreign Policy*, Series Ia, I, 643.
107. D'Abernon to Chamberlain, 25 April 1926, PRO/FO371/11269/C4991/71/18.
108. Note by Stresemann, 11 Aug. 1926, cited in Sutton, 529–31.
109. Paraphrased in Note by Stresemann, 11 Aug. 1926, cited in Sutton, 529–31.
110. *Akten zur deutschen Auswärtigen Politik*, Serie B Iii, No. 35; No. 50.
111. D'Abernon to the King, 17 Aug. 1926, BL Add MSS 48922A, D'Abernon Papers; *An Ambassador of Peace*, III, 18 Aug. 1926, 257; *Akten zur deutschen Auswärtigen Politik*, Serie B Iii, No. 35.
112. *An Ambassador of Peace*, III, 20 Aug. 1926, 257.
113. D. Dutton: *Austen Chamberlain: Gentleman in Politics* (Bolton: Ross Anderson, 1985).
114. *An Ambassador of Peace*, III, 24 Aug. 1926, 258–9.

Conclusion

1. E.Y. O'Riordan: *Britain and the Ruhr Crisis* (London, Palgrave – now Palgrave Macmillan, 2001).
2. Chamberlain to D'Abernon, 11 Sept. 1930, AC 39/2/35, University of Birmingham Library, Austen Chamberlain Papers.
3. R.S. Grayson: *Austen Chamberlain and the Commitment to Europe. British Foreign Policy 1924–1929* (London: Frank Cass, 1997).

Bibliography

Unpublished primary sources

Great Britain

Public Record Office

Cabinet

International Conferences 1921–1924 CAB 29
Hankey Papers CAB 63
'Captured' papers from the *Politisches Archiv des Auswärtiges Amt*, 1920–1926:
Büro des Reichsministers

Subject	Serial number
England	2368
Frage der Aufgabe des passiven Widerstandes	3116
Verhandlungen mit der Allierten über einen Sicherheitspakt: Locarno	3123
Völkerbund	3147
Spa Konferenz	3243
Reparationsfragen	3243
Brüssel Konferenz	3375
Paris Konferenz	3375
Reparationen (Geheime)	3375
Londoner Konferenz	3398
Sanktionen	3398
Maßnahmen der Entente bei Nichterfüllung der Reparationen	3398
Cannes Konferenz	3398
Internationale Geschäftsleute-konferenz	3398
Londoner Konferenz	3398
Büro des Staatssekretärs	
Deutsche-englischer Handelsvertrag	4481
Vorbereitung ihr Londoner Konferenz	4492
Die Räumung der ersten Zone	4504
Sicherheitsfrage	4509
MICUM Vertrag	4521
Rückwirkungen der Garantie-paktverhandlungen auf die deutsche-russische Beziehungen	4562
Privatbriefe	4567
Politische Abteilung III	
Politische Beziehungen Englands zu Deutschland	K 1976

Foreign Office

Press	FO 358
Consular	FO 369
Political Correspondence	FO 371
Treaty	FO 372
News	FO 395
Private Office, 'Individual Files'	FO 794/11
Private Papers	FO 800
Proceedings of the Spa Conference	FO 840/2

Prime Minister's Office

Correspondence	PREM 1

Treasury

Financial Section	T 160
Establishment Section	T 162
Chancellor of the Exchequer's Office	T 172
Records of the British Delegation to the Reparation Commission	T 194
Financial Enquiries Branch	T 208

Private Collections of Papers

Birmingham University Library
Austen Chamberlain Papers

Cambridge University Library
Baldwin Papers
Crewe Papers
Hardinge Papers

Cambridge, Churchill College
Cadogan Papers
Hankey Papers
Kennedy Papers
Phipps Papers

Kew, Public Record Office
MacDonald Papers

London, British Library
Cecil Papers
D'Abernon Papers

London, House of Lords Library
Bonar Law Papers
Lloyd George Papers

London, India Office Library
Curzon Papers

Published primary sources

Germany

Akten das Auswärtiges Amt

Akten zur Deutschen Auswärtigen Politik 1918–1945: Serie A 1925–1933, *Bände* i–vi (1918–1925): *November 1918–September 1920* (Göttingen: Vandenhoeck und Ruprecht, 1982).

Akten zur Deutschen Auswärtigen Politik 1918–1945: Serie B 1925–1933, *Bände* Ii–IIii (*Dezember 1925–Juli 1926*) (Göttingen: Vandenhoeck und Ruprecht, 1966–68).

Akten der Reichskanzlei

Abramowski, G. (ed.): *Die Kabinette Marx I und II, 30 November 1923 bis 3 Juni 1924, 3 Juni 1924 bis 15 Januar 1925*, Bände I und II (Boppard am Rhein: Harald Boldt, 1973).

Erdmann, K.-D. and Vogt, M. (eds): *Die Kabinette Stresemann I und II, 13 August 1923 bis 6 Oktober bis 30 November 1923*, Bände I und II (Boppard am Rhein: Harald Boldt, 1978).

Harbeck, K.-H. (ed.): *Das Kabinett Cuno, 22 November 1922 bis 12 August 1923* (Boppard am Rhein: Harald Boldt, 1968).

Minuth, K.-H. (ed.): *Die Kabinette Luther I und II, 15 Januar 1925 bis 20 Januar 1926, 20 Januar1926 bis 17 Mai 1926* (Boppard am Rhein: Harald Boldt, 1977).

Schulze-Bidlingmaier, I. (ed.): *Die Kabinette Wirth I und II, 10 Mai 1921 bis 26 Oktober 1921, 26 Oktober 1921 bis 22 November 1922*, Bände I und II (Boppard am Rhein: Harald Boldt, 1973).

Vogt, M. (ed.): *Das Kabinett Müller I, 27 März 1920 bis 21 Juni 1920* (Boppard am Rhein: Harald Boldt, 1971).

Wulf, P. (ed.): *Das Kabinett Fehrenbach, 25 Juni 1920 bis 4 Mai 1921* (Boppard am Rhein: Harald Boldt, 1972).

Great Britain

British Institute of International Affairs: *Survey of International Affairs, 1920–1924* (Oxford: Oxford University Press, 1925–28).

Cmd. 2435: *Papers Respecting the Proposals for a Pact of Security made by the German Government on February 9 1925*, (London: HMSO, 1925).

Cmd. 2468: *Reply of the German Government to the Note handed to Herr Stresemann by the French Ambassador at Berlin on June 16 1925, respecting the Proposals for a Pact of Security* (London: HMSO, 1925).

Documents on British Foreign Policy 1919–1939, First Series, Vols II–XXVII (London: HMSO, 1967–84).

Documents on British Foreign Policy 1919–1939, Series Ia, Vols I–II (London: HMSO, 1967–70).

Debates of the House of Commons, Fifth Series.

Debates of the House of Lords, Fifth Series.

R.C. Self (ed.): *The Austen Chamberlain Diary Letters* (London: Cambridge University Press, 1995).

The Treaty of Peace between the Allied and Associated Powers and Germany (London: HMSO, 1919).
J. Vincent (ed.): *The Crawford Papers. The Journals of David Lindsay Twenty-Seventh Earl of Crawford and Tenth Earl of Balcarres, 1871–1940, during the Years 1892–1940* (Manchester: Manchester University Press, 1984).

The Soviet Union

Degras, J. (ed.): *Soviet Documents on Foreign Policy*, Vol I, 1917–1924 (Oxford: Oxford University Press, 1951).
——: *Soviet Documents on Foreign Policy*, Vol II, 1925–1932 (Oxford: Oxford University Press, 1951).

Newspapers

Economist
New Statesman
The Times

Secondary sources

Memoirs and biographies

Auffray, B.: *Pierre de Margerie (1861–1942) et la vie diplomatique de son temps* (Paris: Charles Klincksieck, 1976).
Bergmann, C.: *The History of Reparations* (London: Ernest Benn, 1927).
Busch, C.: *Hardinge of Penshurst: a Study in the Old Diplomacy* (Hamden, CT: Archon, 1980).
Cecil of Chelwood, Viscount: *All the Way* (London: Jonathan Cape, 1949).
——: *The Great Experiment* (London: Jonathan Cape, 1941).
Chamberlain, A.: *Down the Years* (London: Cassell, 1935).
——: *Peace in Our Time; Addresses on Europe and the Empire* (London: Cassell, 1928).
Crowe, S. and Corp, E.: *Our Ablest Public Servant. Sir Eyre Crowe, GCB, GCMG, KCB, KCMG,1864–1925* (Braunton: Merlin Books, 1993).
Curzon, Marchioness: *Reminscences* (London: Hutchinson, 1955).
D'Abernon, Viscount: *An Ambassador of Peace*, 3 Vols. (London: Hodder and Stoughton, 1929–1931).
——: *Eighteenth Decisive Battle of the World* (London: Hodder and Stoughton, 1931).
——: *Portraits and Appreciations* (London: Hodder and Stoughton, 1931).
D'Abernon, Viscountess: *Red Cross and Berlin Embassy 1915–1926* (London: John Murray, 1946).
Dutton, D.: *Austen Chamberlain: Gentleman in Politics* (Bolton: Ross Anderson, 1985).
Egremont, M.: *Balfour: a Life of Arthur James Balfour* (London: Pimlico, 1980).
Gilbert, M.: *Sir Horace Rumbold: Portrait of a Diplomat* (London: Heinemann, 1973).
Gilmour, D.: *Curzon* (London: John Murray, 1994).
Grigg, J.: *Lloyd George: from Peace to War 1912–1916* (London: Methuen, 1997).

Hankey, M.: *Diplomacy by Conference* (London: Ernest Benn, 1946).
Hardinge of Penshurst, Lord: *Old Diplomacy* (London: John Murray, 1947).
Hirsch, F.: *Stresemann: ein Lebensbild* (Göttingen, 1978).
Lloyd George, D.: *The Truth about Reparations and War Debts* (London: Heinemann, 1932).
——: *The Truth about the Peace Treaties* (London: Heinemann, 1938).
Marquand, D.: *Ramsay MacDonald* (London: Jonathan Cape, 1977).
Middlemass, K. and Barnes, J.: *Baldwin: a Biography* (London: Weidenfeld and Nicolson, 1969).
Mosley, L.: *Curzon: the End of an Epoch* (London: Longman, 1960).
Nicolson, H.: *Curzon: the Last Phase* (London: Constable, 1934).
Petrie, C.: *The Life and Times of the Right Hon. Sir Austen Chamberlain*, 2 Vols. (London: Lovat Dickson, 1939–1940).
Pogge von Strandmann, H.: *Walther Rathenau, Industrialist, Banker, Intellectual and Politician* (Oxford: Oxford University Press, 1985).
Pope Hennessy, J.: *Lord Crewe* (London: Constable, 1955).
Ronaldshay, Earl of: *The Life of Lord Curzon*, Vol III (London: Ernest Benn, 1928).
Roskill, S.: *Hankey, Man of Secrets*, Vol II (London: Collins, 1972).
Rowland, P.: *David Lloyd George: a Biography* (London: Barrie and Jenkins, 1975).
Saint-Aulaire, Comte de: *Confession d'un vieux diplomate* (Paris: Flammarion, 1953).
Salter, Sir J.A.: *Memoirs of a Public Servant* (London: Faber, 1961).
Siebert, F.: *Aristide Briand, 1867–1932: Ein Staatsmann zwischen Frankreich und Europa* (Stuttgart: Eugen Rentsch, 1973).
Soulié, M.: *La vie politique d'Edouard Herriot* (Paris: Colin, 1962).
Stresemann, G.: *Vermächtnis: der Nachlass in drei Bände* (Berlin, 1932–1933).
Sutton, E. (ed.): *Gustav Stresemann, his Diaries, Letters and Papers*, 3 Vols (New York: Macmillan, 1935–1940).
Sylvester, A.J.: *The Real Lloyd George* (London: Cassell, 1947).
Thimme, A.: *Gustav Stresemann: eine politische Biographie zur Geschichte der Weimarer Republik* (Hanover, 1957).
Vansittart, R.: *The Mist Procession* (London: Hutchinson, 1958).
Wickham Steed, H.: *Through Thirty Years*, Vols I and II (London, 1929).

Other surveys

Adamthwaite, A.: *Grandeur and Misery: France's Bid for Power in Europe 1914–1940* (London: Edward Arnold, 1995).
Anderle, A.: *Die deutsche Rapallo-Politik: deutsche-sowjetische Beziehungen, 1922–1929* (Berlin: Rütten and Loening, 1962).
Angell, J.W.: *The Recovery of Germany* (New York: Yale University Press, 1929).
Balderston, T.: *The Origins and Course of the German Economic Crisis, 1923–1932* (Berlin: Hauda und Spener, 1993).
Bariéty, J.: *Les Relations Franco-Allemandes après la Première Guerre Mondiale* (Paris: Éditions Pedone, 1977).
Barnett, C.: *The Collapse of British Power* (London: Eyre Methuen, 1984).
Bartlett, C.J.: *British Foreign Policy in the Twentieth Century* (Basingstoke: Macmillan, 1989).
Barros, J.: *Office without Power* (Oxford: Oxford University Press, 1979).

Bennett, G.H.: *British Foreign Policy during the Curzon Period, 1919–1924* (London: Macmillan, 1995).
Bidwell, P.W. (ed.): *Germany's Contribution to European Economic Life* (Paris: M. Rivière, 1949).
Birn, D.S.: *The League of Nations Union, 1918–1945* (Oxford: Oxford University Press, 1981).
Boadle, D.G.: *Winston Churchill and the German Question in British Foreign Policy 1918–1922* (The Hague: Martinus Nijhoff, 1973).
Bretton, H.L.: *Stresemann and the Revision of Versailles; a Fight for Reason* (Stanford: Stanford University Press, 1953).
Bullen, R. (ed.): *The Foreign Office, 1782–1982* (New York: University of America Press, 1984).
Carr, E.H.: *German-Soviet Relations between the Two World Wars, 1919–1939* (Baltimore: Johns Hopkins University Press, 1951).
Carsten, F.L.: *Britain and theWeimar Republic* (London: Batsford, 1984).
Connell, J.: *The 'Office'; a Study of British Foreign Policy and its Makers, 1919–1951* (London: Allan Wingate, 1958).
Craig, G. and Gilbert, F. (eds): *The Diplomats* (Princeton: Princeton University Press, 1953).
D'Abernon, Viscount: *Foreign Relations* (Oxford: Oxford University Press, 1930).
Davis, N.: *White Eagle. Red Star. The Polish–Soviet War 1919–1920* (London: Orbis, 1983).
DeConde, A.: *A History of American Foreign Policy*, Third Edition, II (New York: Scribner, 1978).
Dilkes, D. (ed.): *Retreat from Power: Studies in Britain's Foreign Policy of the Twentieth Century*, Vol. I, 1906–1939 (London: Macmillan, 1981).
Dockrill, M.L. and Goold, J.D.: *Peace without Promise: Britain and the Peace Conferences, 1919–1923* (London: Archon, 1981).
Dockrill, M.L. and McKercher, B.: *Diplomacy and World Power. Studies in British Foreign Policy, 1890–1950* (Cambridge: Cambridge University Press, 1996).
Dohrmann, B.: *Die englische Europapolitik in der Witschaftkrise, 1921–23* (Munich, 1980).
Doß, K.: *Das deutsche Auswärtige Amt im Übergang vom Kaiserreich zur Weimarer Republik* (Düsseldorf: Droste, 1977).
Feldman, G. and Holtfrerich, C.-L. et al. (eds): *The German Inflation Reconsidered: a Preliminary Balance* (Berlin: de Gruyter, 1982).
Felix, D.: *Walther Rathenau and the Weimar Republic. The Politics of Reparations* (Baltimore: Johns Hopkins University Press, 1971).
Fink, C.: *The Genoa Conference: European Diplomacy 1921–22* (Chapel Hill: University of North Carolina Press, 1984).
—— et al. (eds): *Genoa, Rapallo, and European Reconstruction in 1922* (Cambridge: Cambridge University Press, 1991).
Foot, M.R.D. (ed.): *War and Society* (London: Elek, 1973).
Freund, G.: *Unholy Alliance: Russian-German Relations from the Treaty of Brest-Litovsk to the Treaty of Berlin* (London: Chatto and Windus, 1957).
Gilbert, M.: *The Roots of Appeasement* (London: Weidenfeld and Nicolson, 1966).
Goldstein, E.: *Winning the Peace: British Diplomatic Strategy, Peace Planning and the Paris Peace Conference, 1916–1919* (Oxford: Oxford University Press, 1991).

Gottwald, R.: *Die deutsche-amerikanischen Beziehungen in der Ära Stresemann* (Berlin, 1965).
Grathwol, R.: *Stresemann and the DNVP, Reconciliation or Revenge in German Foreign Policy, 1924–1928* (Lawrence: Regents Press of Kansas, 1980).
Grayson, R.S.: *Austen Chamberlain and the Commitment to Europe. British Foreign Policy 1924–1929* (London: Frank Cass, 1997).
Haigh, R.H. and Morris, D.S. (eds): *German-Soviet Relations in the Weimar Era: Friendship from Necessity* (Aldershot: Gower, 1985).
Hazlehurst, C.: *Politicians at War* (London: Jonathan Cape, 1971).
Henig, R. (ed.): *The League of Nations* (London: Oliver and Boyd, 1973).
Holtfrerich, C.L.: *Die deutsche Inflation 1914–1923: Ursachen und Folgen in internationaler Perspektiv* (Berlin: de Gruyter, 1980).
Jacobson, J.: *Locarno Diplomacy. Germany and the West 1925–1929* (Princeton: Princeton University Press, 1972).
Jordan, W.M.: *Great Britain, France and the German Problem, 1919–1939* (London: Oxford University Press, 1943).
Kaiser, A.: *Lord D'Abernon und die englische Deutschlandpolitik, 1920–1926* (Frankfurt: Peter Lang, 1989).
Kennedy, A.L.: *Old Diplomacy and New* (London: John Murray, 1922).
Kent, B.: *The Spoils of War: the Politics, Economics and Diplomacy of Reparation, 1918–1932* (Oxford: Oxford University Press, 1991).
Keynes, J.M.: *The Economic Consequences of The Peace* (London: Macmillan, 1920).
Kimmich, C.M.: *The Free City of Danzig and German Foreign Policy 1919–1934* (New Haven, CT: Yale University Press, 1968).
——: *Germany and the League of Nations* (Chicago: University of Chicago Press, 1976).
Lauren, P.G.: *Diplomats and Bureaucrats: the First Institutional Responses to Twentieth Century Diplomacy in France and Germany* (Stanford: Stanford University Press, 1976).
Lentin, A.: *Lloyd George, Woodrow Wilson and the Guilt of Germany: an Essay in the Prehistory of Appeasement* (Leicester: University of Leicester Press, 1984).
Link, W.: *Die amerikanische Stabilisierungspolitik in Deutschland 1921–1932* (Düsseldorf: Droste, 1970).
Lowe, C.J. and Dockrill, M.L.: *The Mirage of Power: British Foreign Policy 1914–1922*, Vol. II (London: Routledge, 1972).
Maier, C.S.: *Recasting Bourgeois Europe: Stabilisation in France, Germany and Italy after World War I* (Princeton: Princeton University Press, 1975).
Maisel, E.: *The Foreign Office and Foreign Policy, 1919–1926* (Brighton: University of Sussex Press, 1994).
Maxelon, M.-O.: *Stresemann und Frankreich: deutsche Politik der Ost-West- Balance* (Düsseldorf, 1972).
McDougall, W.A.: *France's Rhineland Diplomacy 1914–1924: the Last Bid for a Balance of Power in Europe* (Princeton: Princeton University Press, 1978).
McKercher, B.J.C.: *The Second Baldwin Government and the United States, 1924–1929: Attitudes and Diplomacy* (Cambridge: Cambridge University Press, 1984).
McKercher, B.J.C. and Moss, D.J. (eds): *Shadow and Substance in British Foreign Policy, 1895–1939. Memorial Essays Honouring C.J. Lowe* (Edmonton: University of Alberta Press, 1984).

Michalka, W. and Lee, L.L.: *German Foreign Policy 1917–1933. Continuity or Break?* (Leamington Spa: Berg, 1987).

——: (eds): *Gustav Stresemann* (Darmstadt: Wissenschaftliche Buchgesellschaft, 1982).

Moore, S.: *Peace without Victory for the Allies, 1918–1932* (Providence, RI: Berg, 1994).

Morgan, K.O.: *Consensus and Disunity: the Lloyd George Coalition Government 1918–1922* (Oxford: Oxford University Press, 1979).

Northedge, F.S.: *The League of Nations. Its Life and Times, 1920–1946* (Leicester: Leicester University Press, 1988).

——: *The Troubled Giant. Britain among the Great Powers 1916–1939* (London: Bell, 1966).

Orde, A.: *British Policy and European Reconstruction after the First World War* (Cambridge: Cambridge University Press, 1990).

——: *Great Britain and International Security 1920–1926* (London: Royal Historical Society, 1978).

O'Riordan, E.Y.: *Britain and the Ruhr Crisis* (London: Palgrave – now Palgrave Macmillan, 2001).

Peden, G.C.: *Keynes, the Treasury and British Economic Policy* (London: Macmillan, 1988).

Rose, I.: *Conservatism and Foreign Policy during the Lloyd George Coalition, 1918–1922* (London: Frank Cass, 1999).

Rupieper, H.J.: *The Cuno Government and Reparations 1922–1923: Politics and Economics* (The Hague: Martinus Nijhoff, 1979).

Schuker, S.: *The End of French Predominance in Europe. The Financial Crisis of 1924 and the Adoption of the Dawes Plan* (Chapel Hill: University of North Carolina Press, 1976).

Spenz, J.: *Die diplomatische Vorgeschichte des Beitritts Deutschlands zum Völkerbund, 1924–1926; ein Beitrag zur Aussenpolitik der Weimarer Republik* (Göttingen, 1966).

Stamm, C.: *Lloyd George zwischen Innen- und Aussenpolitik: die britsche Deutschlandpolitik, 1921–1922* (Cologne: Verlag Wissenschaft und Politik, 1977).

Steiner, Z.S.: *The Foreign Office and Foreign Policy 1898–1914* (Cambridge: Cambridge University Press, 1969).

Stern-Rubarth, E.: *Three Men Tried... Austen Chamberlain, Stresemann, Briand, and their Fight for a New Europe* (London: Duckworth, 1939).

Tomes, J.: *Balfour and Foreign Policy, the International Thought of a Conservative Statesman* (Cambridge: Cambridge University Press, 1997).

Trachtenberg, M.: *Reparations in World Politics; France and European Economic Diplomacy 1916–1923* (New York: Columbia University Press, 1980).

Walsdorff, M.: *Westorientierung und Ostpolitik: Stresemanns Russlandpolitik in der Locarno-Ära* (Bremen, 1971).

Watt, D.C.: *Personalities and Policies: Studies in the Formation of British Foreign Policy in the Twentieth Century* (London: Longman, 1965).

Weidenfeld, W.: *Die Englandpolitik Gustav Stresemanns: theoretische und praktische Aspekte der Aussenpolitik* (Mainz, 1972).

Willson, B.: *America's Ambassadors to England, 1785–1928* (London: Macmillan, 1928).

Wolfers, A.: *Britain and France between Two Wars. Conflicting Strategies of Peace since Versailles* (New York: Harcourt, 1940).
Zimmerman, L.: *Deutsche Aussenpolitik in der Ära der Weimarer Republik* (Göttingen: Musterschmidit Verlag, 1958).

Articles

Artaud, D.: 'À propos de l'occupation de la Ruhr', *Revue d'Histoire Moderne et Contemporaine*, 17(2), 1970.
Bennett, G.H.: 'Britain's Relations with France after Versailles: the Problem of Tangier, 1919–1923', *European History Quarterly*, 24(1), 1994.
Bryant, F.R.: 'Lord D'Abernon, the Anglo-French Mission, and the Battle of Warsaw, 1920', *Jahrbücher für Geschichte Osteuropas*, 38(3), 1990.
Burk, K.: 'Economic Diplomacy between the Wars', *Historical Journal*, 24(2), 1981.
Carlton, D.: 'Great Britain and the League Council Crisis', *Historical Journal*, 11(2), 1968.
Cassels, A.: 'Repairing the *Entente Cordiale* and the New Diplomacy', *Historical Journal*, 23(3), 1980.
Chossudovsky, E.M.: 'The Beginning of Soviet Foreign Policy and Diplomacy', *Millennium*, 3(3), 1974.
——: 'Genoa Revisited: Russia and Coexistence', *Foreign Affairs*, 50(6), 1972.
Cornebise, A.E.: 'Gustav Stresemann and the Ruhr Occupation: the Making of a Statesman', *European Studies Review*, 2(3), 1972.
Costigliola, F.C.: 'The United States and the Reconstruction of Germany in the 1920s', *Business History Review*, 50(4), 1976.
Craig, G.: 'The Professional Diplomat and his Problems, 1919–1939', *World Politics*, 3(3), 1951–52.
Crowe, S.E.: 'Sir Eyre Crowe and the Locarno Pact', *English Historical Review*, 87(2), 1972.
D'Abernon, Viscount: 'German Currency: its Collapse and Recovery 1920–1926', *Journal of the Royal Statistical Society*, 80(1), 1927.
——: 'Stresemann', *Foreign Affairs*, 8(1), 1930.
Enssle, M.J.: 'Stresemann's Diplomacy Fifty Years after Locarno: Some Recent Perspectives', *Historical Journal*, 20(4), 1977.
Felix, D.: 'Reparations Reconsidered with a Vengeance', *Central European History* 4(2), 1971.
Fergusson, N.: 'Constraints and Room for Manoeuvre in the German Inflation of the Early 1920s', *Economic History Review*, 49(4), 1996.
Ferris, J.: 'The Greatest Power on Earth: Great Britain in the 1920s', *International History Review*, 13(4), 1991.
Gasiorowski, Z.: 'The Russian Overture to Germany of December 1924', *Journal of Modern History*, 29(2), 1958.
——: 'Stresemann and Poland after Locarno', *Journal of Central European Affairs*, 18(1), 1958.
——: 'Stresemann and Poland before Locarno', *Journal of Central European Affairs*, 18(3), 1958.
Gatzke, H.W.: 'Von Rapallo nach Berlin: Stresemann und die deutsche Russlandpolitik', *Vierteljahrshefte für Zeitgeschichte*, 4(4), 1956.
——: 'Stresemann: a Bibliographical Article', *Journal of Modern History*, 36(1), 1964.

Gatzke, H.W.: 'The Stresemann Papers', *Journal of Modern History*, 26(2), 1954.
Grathwol, R.: 'Gustav Stresemann: Reflections on his Foreign Policy', *Journal of Contemporary History*, 45(1), 1973.
——: 'Stresemann Revisited', *European Studies Review*, 7(2), 1977.
Grün, G.: 'Locarno: Idea and Reality', *International Affairs*, 31(1), 1955.
Jacobson, J.: 'Is there a New International History of the 1920s?', *American Historical Review*, 88(3), 1983.
——: 'Strategies of French Foreign Policy after World War I', *Journal of Modern History*, 55(1), 1983.
Jeanney, J.-N.: 'De la spéculation financière comme arme diplomatique. À propos de la première "bataille du franc" (Novembre 1923–Mars 1924)', *Relations Internationales*, 5(1), 1978.
Johnson, D.: 'Austen Chamberlain and the Locarno Agreements', *University of Birmingham Historical Journal*, 8, 1961.
Johnson, G.: 'Curzon, Lloyd George and the Control of British Foreign Policy, 1919–1922: a Reassessment', *Diplomacy and Statecraft*, 11(3), 2000.
——: '"Das Kind" Revisited: Lord D'Abernon and German Security Policy, 1922–1925', *Contemporary European History*, 9(2), 2000.
——: 'Lord D'Abernon, Sir Austen Chamberlain and the Origin of the Treaty of Locarno', *Electronic Journal of International History*, 1(1), 2000.
Kaiser, A.: 'Lord D'Abernon und die Entstehungsgeschichte der Locarno-Verträge', *Vierteljahrshefte für Zeitgeschichte*, 34(2), 1986.
Larner, C.: 'The Amalgamation of the Diplomatic Service with the Foreign Office', *Journal of Contemporary History*, 7(1), 1972.
Marks, S.: 'Reparations Reconsidered; a Rejoinder', *Central European History*, 5(2), 1972.
——: 'Reparations Reconsidered; a Reminder', *Central European History*, 2(1), 1969.
Morgan, K.O.: 'Lloyd George's Premiership: a Study in "Prime Ministerial Government"', *Historical Journal*, 13(1), 1970.
Morgan, R.P.: 'The Political Significance of German-Soviet Trade Negotiations, 1922–5', *Historical Journal*, 6(2), 1963.
O'Halpin, E.: 'Sir Warren Fisher and the Coalition, 1919–1922', *Historical Journal*, 24(3), 1981.
Sharp, A,J.: 'James Headlam-Morley: Creating International History', *Diplomacy and Statecraft*, 9(1), 1998.
——: 'Lord Curzon and British Policy towards the Franco-Belgian Occupation of the Ruhr in 1923', *Diplomacy and Statecraft*, 8(1), 1997.
——: 'The Foreign Office in Eclipse, 1919–1922', *History*, 61(2), 1976.
Soutou, G.: 'Die deutschen Reparationen und das Seydoux-Projekt, 1920–1921', *Vierteljahrshefte für Zeitgeschichte*, 23(2), 1975.
Stambrook, F.G.: '"Das Kind" – Lord D'Abernon and the Origins of the Locarno Pact', *Central European History*, 1(2), 1968.
Steiner, Z. and Dockrill, M.L.: 'The Foreign Office Reforms 1919–1921', *Historical Journal*, 17(1), 1974.
Turner, H.A.: 'Continuity in German Foreign Policy? The Case of Stresemann', *International History Review*, 1(2), 1979.
Turner, J.: 'State Purchase of the Liquor Trade in the First World War', *Historical Journal*, 23(2), 1980.

Vagts, A.: 'Lord D'Abernon', *Europäische Gespräche*, 1(2), 1930.
Vallentin, A. von: 'Lord D'Abernons Anteil an Deutscher Geschichte', *Europäische Revue*, 1(5), 1927.
Warman, R.M.: 'The Erosion of Foreign Office Influence in the Making of Foreign Policy, 1916–1918', *Historical Journal*, 15(1), 1972.
Williamson, D.G.: 'Walther Rathenau: Realist, Pedagogue and Prophet, November 1918–May 1921', *European Studies Review*, 6(3), 1976.
Wright, J.: 'Stresemann and Locarno', *Contemporary European History*, 4(1), 1995.
Yates, D.: 'The Manor House, Stoke D'Abernon', *Surrey County Journal*, 3(2), 1952.

Unpublished theses

Breuning, E.C.M.: 'Germany's Foreign Policy between East and West', DPhil, University of Oxford, 1965.
Henig, R.: 'The British Government and the League of Nations, 1919–1926', PhD, University of Lancaster, 1978.
Ryan, M.J.: 'Lord D'Abernon and Britain's Policy towards Germany 1920–26', Dissertation, Catholic University of America, 1975.

Index